The McDonaldization
of Social Work

DONNA DUSTIN
London Metropolitan University, UK

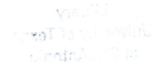

ASHGATE

Published by
Ashgate Publishing Limited
Gower House
Croft Road
Aldershot
Hampshire GU11 3HR
England

Ashgate Publishing Company
Suite 420
101 Cherry Street
Burlington, VT 05401-4405
USA

Ashgate website: http://www.ashgate.com

British Library Cataloguing in Publication Data
Dustin, Donna
   The McDonaldization of social work
   1. Social work administration - Great Britain 2. Social
   case work - Great Britain
   I. Title
   361.3'068

Library of Congress Cataloging-in-Publication Data
Dustin, Donna.
   The McDonaldization of social work / by Donna Dustin.
      p. cm.
   Includes bibliographical references and index.
   ISBN-13: 978-0-7546-4639-6
   1. Social service--Great Britain. 2. Human services--Great Britain. 3. Social case work--Great Britain. 4. Social work administration--Great Britain. I. Title.

HV245.D87 2008
361.30941--dc22

2007034435

ISBN 978 0 7546 4639 6

Printed and bound in Great Britain by TJ International Ltd, Padstow, Cornwall.

Contents

Acknowledgements

I would like to thank those who contributed to my early thinking about social work, especially Edith Close, my first social work supervisor and Alfred Kahn, Professor of Social Work at Columbia University. Norman Ginsburg and Georgie Parry Crooke, my PhD dissertation supervisors, provided invaluable support in shaping my policy and research perspectives. Stephen Fox and John Gabriel were sympathetic in negotiating the demands of my social work education role with my writing efforts. In addition, I would like to thank Sue Lawrence, Karen Lyons, Sam Whimster, Jean Thomas and the members of the Writing Group at the Department of Applied Social Sciences at London Metropolitan University for their discussions about care management and comments on drafts. I would also like to thank students in my Critical Perspectives on Diversity module for stimulating discussions about postmodernity and its relevance to social work practice. However, I take full responsibility for the ideas presented here. Any errors of fact or interpretation are mine alone.

Glossary of Terms

Assessment 'Assessment is a central feature of care management. It is a process in which a person's circumstances are fully analysed and her/his needs identified. A further feature of care management is that assessment is a self-contained process, carried out independently of the allocation of services' (Orme and Glastonbury 1993, 187).

Block Contracts An arrangement wherein 'purchase is made *en bloc* by the local authority and the case [care] manager simply negotiates for a "space"' (Stainton 1998, 140). 'With block contracts, the local authority agrees with providers to receive a specified level of services covering a number of clients. This enables a provider to set up a service, secure in the knowledge that a certain number of clients are going to be referred to justify the setting up costs' (Payne 1995, 204).

Calculability 'an emphasis on the quantitative aspects of products (cost) ... and service offered (the time it takes to get the product)' (Ritzer 1996, 9).

Care 'Feel concern, interest, or emotion' (Thompson 1996, 142). Care by a person or organization that has a personal interest in the welfare of the person being looked after, an interest based on 'shared identity' (Barnes 1999, 73) that flows from either family or community ties 'in a locality within which people interact in their daily lives' (Barnes 1999, 77).

Care Management/Care Manager (UK model) The label given to the model of organizing and overseeing the provision of a care package for a client who has been assessed, and whose needs are considered of sufficient priority to warrant the allocation of services. The member of agency staff whose job (wholly or partly) is care management is a care manager. This person is likely to be a social worker, but may be a different agency employee (such as a home care organizer or a nurse) or in certain circumstances could be a competent client managing her/his own care package (Orme and Glastonbury 1993, 187).

Case Management/Case Manager (US model) Three basic models include the broker model, the service management model and the managed-care model. The broker model involves the case manager advocating with agencies for requested services as they have no financial resources to spend on behalf of their clients. The service management model allows case managers to develop care plans knowing that they have access to funds available to pay for the plans. Managed care is based on prospective financing and makes case managers the most financially accountable. Other terms used are service coordination, care coordination, and resource coordination (Austin 1992, 62).

Choice 'Choice over goods and services can be established in markets through the act of buying, however, where these are distributed through administrative and professional means, the question of clients exercising choice can challenge received wisdoms about accepted welfare arrangements. It is difficult to increase choice for everyone, since the choices of some may restrict the choices of others' (Manning 1999, 84).

Commodification 'The process of commodification is one in which an increasing proportion of social objects are brought within the ambit of exchange relationships, so that they are bought and sold for money in a market' (Crooke and Pakulski 1994, 7). See Packages of Care.

Communicative Rationality Habermas's concept of reason as constituted through creating conditions for consensus out of the 'infinite diversity of subjective and conflicting meanings' (Lorenz 2004, 150).

Consumer 'Several labels are used to describe those who receive services. Traditionally in the personal social services they have been called clients, while the health services have referred to patients. In recent years the terms user and consumer have come into wider use, partly to reflect a growing interest in consumerist issues, and partly to reflect the language of commerce' (Orme and Glastonbury 1993, 188).

Contractualism/Contract Mode of Governance Legitimation of interactions and relationships established through agreed contracts rather than through hierarchical relationships (Gray and Jenkins 1999, 216).

Control (over Workers) '... the threat to use ... technology to replace human workers' (Ritzer 2004, 15), for example, in care management, the increasing use of computer programmes to assess need.

Deskilling In the context of Frederick Taylor's three principles of scientific management deskilling of workers is accomplished by: (1) managers gathering practice knowledge and formulating rules, formulae, that is, procedures based on practice knowledge, (2) removing 'brain work' from the shop and centralizing it in planning departments, (3) describing in detail the task which the worker is to accomplish as well as the means to be used in doing the work and instructing the worker accordingly (Braverman 1998 [1974], 77–83). '... the breaking down of skills into component parts and reducing skills to a series of simple repetitive operations' (Brown and Lauder 2001, 29).

Direct Payments '... direct cash payments to individuals in lieu of the support services they have been assessed as needing' (Petch 2002, 233).

Discourse 'A discourse is a set of ideas, practices and beliefs which coalesce to produce an over-arching picture of reality' (Symonds and Kelly 1998, 8). '... practices which systematically form the objects of which they speak' (Sarap 1993, 4).

Efficiency '... the optimum method for getting from one point to another' (Ritzer 1996, 9).

Empowerment 'Empowerment involves helping people to gain greater control over their lives and their circumstances' (Thompson 2002, 90). 'Generally set within the context of consumerism, empowerment refers the process by which clients (users, consumers) begin to take, or are helped to take, greater responsibility for their own lives and services' (Orme and Glastonbury 1993, 189). 'Recent developments in welfare debate have acknowledged that under the original 1948 arrangements, many clients of the welfare state were expected to be passive and grateful recipients of state handouts. There has now been a common criticism of this assumption on all sides in favour of clients having more power, dignity, respect, and autonomy through a process of empowerment' (Manning 1999, 85).

Enabling 'At its simplest level this is offering people support or making it easier for them to make and carry through their own decisions about their lives. However, within social work, the notion of enabling is part of the debate about the appropriate balance of "providing services" and "helping people to help themselves" (that is, enabling people)' (Orme and Glastonbury 1993, 190).

End of Expertise The 'end of expertise' is a postmodern criticism of absolute knowledge and the position that claims to expertise/knowledge is simply an exercise in power (Bartens 1995, 7). It is also related to the New Right preference for market mechanisms rather than professional knowledge and professional discretion in the distribution of scarce resources (Jessop 1994). Therefore the 'end of expertise' is related both to the rise of commodification and to the marketization of society and to the declining influence of autonomous professions within the New Right political discourse.

End of Progress The 'end of progress' is a criticism of the idea that knowledge would lead to social progress. This belief allowed the intervention of government in society and led ultimately to the welfare state. However, the belief that society could be improved by the application of rationality has been criticized by postmodernists who criticize rationality and New Right politicians who distrust anything but the market (Rosenau 1992, 7).

Fordism Fordism describes the use of modern rationality, or scientific management, to create efficient organizations that could mass-produce tangible goods. Fordist organizations have been identified with standardized and undiversified products, mass consumption, vertical hierarchical management, centralized bureaucracies, professional demarcation with clear differences in the activities and role expectations among workers and collective philosophies (Symonds and Kelly 1998, 34).

Globalization 'In its market sense, the tendency for the world to become one market, in which goods will be produced where costs are lowest and sold where costs are highest' (Baldock 1999, 108).

Grand Narrative 'A term in post-modernist writing applied to wide-ranging and comprehensive schemes such as communism or fascism, designed to perfect human society' (Manning 1999, 85). See Metanarratives.

Hermeneutics   Truth in context or context dependent truth. '... a philosophical and methodological alternative to positivism' (Lovelock and Powell 2004, 185). 'A term from the Greek word "to interpret" ... refers to theories of understanding and interpretation, emphasizing the importance of interpreting meaning ...' (Harrington 2005, 321). '... now that transcendent truth seems forever out of reach, hermeneutics must replace our former aspirations to objectivity' (Bartens 1995, 11).

High Modernity   '... a set of circumstances in which dispersal is dialectically connected to profound tendencies toward global integration' (Giddens 1990, 150).

Hyperreal   'The generation of models of a real without origin or reality' (Baudrillard 1983, 2). 'Hyper-reality is a new condition in which the old tension between reality and illusion, between reality as it is and reality as it should be, has been dissipated' (Sarap 1993, 165).

Instrumental Power   Professional power based on knowledge of procedures and resources (Toren 1972).

Instrumental Rationality/Reason   Habermas's view of reason as associated with systems that are 'guided by principles and criteria of efficiency, necessary for the structural integration and material reproduction of society, by impersonal mechanisms best exemplified by the working of the market' (Lorenz 2004, 150).

Keynesian/Beveridge Welfare State   '... government policies which redistribute income over a typical working-class life-cycle, and from the better-off to poorer groups in the population, to meet a defined range of needs' (Taylor-Gooby 1999, 560).

Late Capitalism   '... a *purer* stage of capitalism than any of the moments that preceded it' (italics in the original) (Jameson 1984b, 55). '... the prodigious expansion of capital into hitherto uncommodified areas' (Jameson 1984b, 78).

Lifeworlds   '... aspects and processes in which people experience themselves as communicating actors capable of expressing intentions and giving meaning to their worlds' (Lorenz 2004, 146–7).

McDonaldization   'The process by which the principles of the fast-food restaurant are coming to dominate more and more sectors of American society as well as of the rest of the world' (Ritzer 1996, 1).

Managerialism   '... the introduction of business-oriented principles and personnel into the running of the public services' (Miller 1999, 33). As an aspect of New Public Management, 'a shift toward managerial forms of organizational coordination' (Clarke, Gerwirtz and McLaughlin 2001, 6).

Meals-on-wheels   A service wherein meals are delivered daily to older or infirmed service users who cannot cook for themselves. This service is by provided by local authority social services departments (SSDs) and is intended to help people remain in their own homes and prevent admission to a residential facility.

Metanarratives '… global world views, master codes. Metanarratives are modern and assume the validity of their own truth claims, however, mini-narratives, local narratives, traditional narratives are just stories that make no truth claims and are therefore more acceptable to postmodernists' (Rosenau 1992, xii). See Grand narrative.

Modernity An era and a world view marked by the growth of scientific enquiry and a valorisation of rationality as the organizing principle for social life which began in the 1700s with the Age of Enlightenment (Rosenau 1992, 5, Taylor-Gooby 1989, 389, Howe 1994, 513), the main features of which are a belief that history has a direction and purpose or teleology, an attempt to develop universal categories of experience, representation and explanation through theory or metanarratives, and a belief that the nation state has a role to play in improving society (Parton 1994, 27).

Need Need can be interpreted as absolute need, comparative need, expressed need, felt need, intermediate need or normative needs (Liddiard 1999, 129).

New Public Management (NPM) Managerialism, that is, 'continuous increases in efficiency, the use of ever-more-sophisticated technologies, a labour force disciplined in productivity, clear implementation of the professional management role, managers being given the right to manage' (Walsh 1995, xiii).

Normative Power Normative power is exercised through establishing a professional relationship with a service user and using that relationship to shape their behaviour in a socially acceptable manner. Normative power is related to the 'use of self' in a casework relationship (Toren 1972).

Other The 'other' is the collective of those excluded from privileges (women, people of color, non-heterosexuals, children, unemployed) by the liberal humanist subject (white, male, heterosexual, adult, rational, employed) who accords privilege to itself (Bartens 1995, 8).

Packages of Care/Care Packages 'Once a person's assessment is completed, there is a process of identifying whether that person's needs warrant service provision (matters like statutory responsibility and the availability of resources come in here) and if a high enough priority is agreed then appropriate services are sought. Within care management, services should be carefully planned, identified and established to meet the assessed needs of the client. Services set up in this way form the care package' (Orme and Glastonbury 1993, 187). See commodification.

Performativity Judgement based on outcomes. 'Modern criteria by which judgement is made on the basis of pragmatic performance or outcome. Postmodernists argue that performativity discourages diversity and autonomy, flexibility and openness' (Rosenau 1992, xiii). Social workers work with intangibles to produce tangible outcomes. Intangibles include people's emotional states, their personal histories, their self-images, their goals, their values, their religious beliefs or lack of them. They work with these intangibles to produce tangible outcomes upon which their performance is judged.

Post-Fordism   Post-Fordist organizations imply more customized and specialized products, shorter production runs, that is, smaller and more productive systems and the decline of huge factories, new technologies which make flexible production profitable and computerized equipment which can be easily re-programmed. These factors require more flexible forms of management. Workers must be more productive and have more diverse skills in order to handle new, more demanding and sophisticated technologies. They must be able to handle more responsibility and operate with greater autonomy, and more differentiated work patterns (Ritzer 1996, 151).

Postmodernism   'The rejection of "grand narratives" in theory and the replacement of a search for truth with a celebration of the multiplicity of (equally valid) perspectives' (Burr 1995, 185). 'Term referring to the contemporary movement of thought which rejects totalities, universal values, grand historical narratives, solid foundations to human existence and the possibility of objective knowledge. Postmodernism is sceptical of truth, unity and progress, opposes what it sees as elitism in culture, tends toward cultural relativism and celebrates pluralism, discontinuity and heterogeneity' (Eagleton 2003, 13 in Harrington 2005, 326).

Postmodernity   The term postmodernity describes as a world that has not yet come to terms with what 'is', and is still struggling with what has just now ceased to be (Toulmins 1985) or as a social order 'which has not yet fully emerged' (O'Brien and Penna 1998, 193). 'A condition – a set of changes, transitions and processes perceived to be taking place at the social, political, economic and cultural level' (Williams 1992, 204–5). '… the general feeling that we are living through a period of marked disparity from the past', the idea that 'nothing can be known with any certainty', that '"history" is devoid of teleology and consequently no version of "progress" can plausibly be defended', and that 'a new social and political agenda has come into being' (Giddens 1990, 46). 'The … development of a higher stage of capitalism marked by a greater degree of capital penetration and homogenization across the globe' (Best and Kellner 1991, 3).

Predictability   '… the assurance that products and services will be the same across time and locales' (Ritzer 1996, 10).

Professions   'Occupational groups distinguished by their specialist knowledge and expertise, their position (or autonomy) in relation to clients and employing organizations and ethos (that is, the values which vocation demands are to be promoted for the benefit of the profession and its clients)' (Gray and Jenkins 1999, 216).

Purchaser/Provider   'Traditionally within the personal social services the agency which purchases services for its clients (that is provides the budgetary resources) also directly provides the necessary services. At a subsidiary level only there has been some separation of the purchasing and providing roles, as in the way a statutory agency contracts with and funds a voluntary organization to carry out certain tasks. Within the framework of new community care services (and indeed within the National Health Services) the argument has been made that greater efficiency will follow from a wider separation of the roles of *purchaser* and *provider*, even where both are part of the same employing agency' (Orme and Glastonbury 1993, 191).

Quasi-markets 'Markets in social services, such as schools and healthcare, set up administratively to encourage different providers to compete with each other in the hope that this will motivate them to increase quality, or at least cut costs, and that consumers will get greater choice as a result' (Manning 1999, 87). 'Where internal markets or contracting out are limited by regulations that mean the arrangements are not fully exposed to market competition' (Baldock 1999, 109). Quasi-markets are different from ordinary markets because: 'the competing suppliers of services … are not necessarily privately owned or concerned with the maximization of profits; and in the areas such as community care and health care the consumers are represented in the market, not by themselves, but by agents (for example, a care manager in a local authority social services department or a fund-holding GP). Such developments are also "quasi" markets because the purchasing power of consumers under these new arrangements is not expressed in terms of cash, but in the form of an ear-marked sum which can only be used for the purchase of a particular service' (Butcher 1995, 116).

Reflective Practice '… the ability to be aware of the "theory" or assumptions involved in professional practice, in order to close the gap between what is espoused and what is enacted, in an effort to improve both' (Fook 2004, 18).

Reflexive Practice/Reflexivity 'The reflexivity of modern life consists in the fact that social practices are constantly examined and re-formed in the light of incoming information about those very practices, thus constitutively altering their character' (Giddens 1990, 38). Information produced changes the environment from that which the information was gathered and this has led to a sense of uncertainty. 'Modernity is constituted in and through reflexively applied knowledge, but the equation of knowledge with certitude has turned out to be misconceived' (Giddens 1990, 39). '… the ability to recognize that all aspects of ourselves and our contexts influence the way we … create knowledge' (Fook 2004, 18).

Regulation Approach A policy paradigm that conceptualizes welfare in conjunction with the need for government to create a national economy that is strong enough to compete internationally (Jessop 1994).

Residual/Selective Benefits 'Commonly used to describe "means tested" benefits, those only provided to those whose incomes and resources fall below a prescribed level' (Baldock et al., 1999, 14).

Role of Social Workers Instrumental, normative, legislative (Toren 1972); care management, community social work and counselling social work (Payne 1995, 2); reflexive-therapeutic, socialist-collectivist, individualistic-reformist (Payne 2005, 8–9); managerial technicist (Harlow 2003).

Schumpeterian Workfare State 'Term used … to describe development of system to replace the Keynes/Beveridge welfare state, in which the political emphasis is on the creation of highly competitive, low-waged, flexible labour force rather than redistribution to guarantee reasonable working-class living standards. The system is seen as better adapted to cope with the demands of a globalized economic system' (Taylor-Gooby 1999, 560).

Scientific Management   See Fordism.

Service User   For the purposes of this study, a service user is an individual who receives the services of a care manager. See User.

Simulacra   '... substituting signs of the real for the real itself' (Baudrillard 1983, 4). 'The culture of the simulacrum comes to life in a society where exchange-value has been generalized to the point at which the very memory of the use-value is effaced' (Jameson 1984b, 66). 'Term in postmodernist theory ... denoting copies that cannot be distinguished from the original things that they copy, thus collapsing all distinction between originals and non-originals, or between the "real" and the "fake"'(Harrington 2005, 328).

Social Construction/Social Constructionism   This paradigm includes the following key elements: a critical stance towards taken-for-granted knowledge, historical and cultural specificity, a belief that knowledge is sustained by social processes, and a belief that knowledge and social action go together (Burr 1995, 2–5). 'By "social constructionism", we mean that beliefs about the world create the reality of that world, as opposed to the position that the world reveals what is really there' (Kessler 1998, 133 n1). 'Term referring broadly to any theories that regard reality as socially constructed or "constituted" by individuals in contexts of interaction, as an outcome of interpretive "definitions of the situation"' (Harrington 2005, 328).

Social Theory   A term which suggests '... a broad, interdisciplinary approach to the study of society, of which sociology is a part' (Best 1994, 48n1). Social theory can be used to study ways in which broad patterns of social change have actively altered our everyday experiences of everyday life (Miles 2001, 2). Social theory is focused on current change in social life that is 'based in grounded contexts ... that can help us look at our own lives in new and insightful ways' (Miles 2001, 2).

Social Work   '... a profession whose area of activity has been located at the interface between the individual and society, between the citizen and the state, between the solidarity process of society and the processes of marginalization' (Washington and Paylor 1998, 336).

Spot Purchasing/Spot Contracts   'Spot contracts are specific arrangements for an individual client, made where there are many alternative providers and care managers can be given the budget to make an arrangement, or where there is a specific need (for example, meals-on-wheels [see definition above] cannot be delivered, so a local café is asked to deliver a meal to a specific client) or where a highly specialized service has to be negotiated. ... This provides flexibility, but an increase the cost of each case because the provider must take the financial risk of few cases being referred' (Payne 1995, 204).

Systems   The economic and state administration networks '... which ensure the material reproduction of society via the media of power and money' (Lorenz 2004, 147).

Universal Benefits   '... welfare benefits provided to all who fall into certain contingencies ... regardless of their income or wealth' (Baldock et al., 1999, 14).

User An individual who is 'genuinely receiving service in a position where they are or should be participating in the development and management of the services' is sometimes referred to as a 'user' (Payne 1995, xv). This term has not been used in this study because the term 'user' can also describe a drug addict or a person who manipulates others for their own gain. See Service User.

Use of Self See normative power (Toren 1972).

Introduction

The purpose of this book is to explore and evaluate the impact of care/case management, on social work practice and professional status in the UK using social theory as a lens through which to understand the advent of care management. In this introduction, I discuss 'starting points', first in terms of my interest in the changes to service delivery systems in the recent past and secondly, how I began the research into the impact of care management, the findings of which are presented in Part II. I also discuss the possible audiences for this book and present an outline of subsequent chapters.

Personal and Professional Starting Points

Rationality and objectivity are the goals of modern research, but research always comes from a point of view or a perspective. Our personal biographies shape our perception of the world and it is very difficult to separate ourselves from our personal history (Witkin and Saleebey 2007, 44). Researchers need to strive for transparency and tell the reader 'where they are coming from' so that the reader can put findings in context. It is therefore appropriate to declare my cultural starting points so the reader can interpret the findings of research presented in this book. It is important to outline how my personal/professional experiences have firstly, shaped my views on care management as a feature of social work in Western capitalist societies and secondly, how they shaped my research into care management.

I grew up in the 1950s in Midwest America. Going back a long way, before I knew what a Poor House was (also called a workhouse in England), I remember sometimes hearing my grandmother talk about 'ending up in the Poor House' when she was worried about 'making ends meet'. The English Poor Laws enacted in 1834 shaped my grandmother's concept of poverty, even though both her parents emigrated from Sweden to the United States in their teens and she was born in the US in 1886. This seems to me to represent an example of the international spread of ideas about poverty and of the means of dealing with poverty even before our current concept of globalization. Of course, my grandmother raised three children as a widow in the 1930s Great Depression, so she knew a thing or two about coping with poverty.

My sister contracted polio just at the time when the polio vaccine was introduced. She spent nine months in hospital in an 'iron lung'. The hospital bill was $10,000, which was a great deal of money then and completely beyond the means of my family to pay. My mother still talks about the nun chasing her down the hospital corridor demanding that the bill be paid. My parents faced bankruptcy and loss of everything they had struggled to achieve. In the end, philanthropy came to the rescue. My mother wrote to Eleanor Roosevelt, wife of ex-President Franklin D. Roosevelt, and asked for her help. Amazingly, Mrs. Roosevelt wrote back to say that the hospital bill had been paid, probably through her contacts with a charity called The March of Dimes. This experience made me aware of financial vulnerability for health and other reasons that are beyond the individual's control.

After qualifying as a social worker in 1969, I worked as a psychiatric social worker in a large state mental hospital, which represented institutionalization at its height. My role was to re-locate elderly mentally ill (EMI) patients in community facilities. I distinctly remember practically dragging an 80-year-old woman off her ward, myself on one side and a nurse on the other side, her heels dug into the linoleum, as part of the transfer of EMI patients to community-based nursing homes, perhaps an unenlightened example of multidisciplinary work. This elderly woman had been hospitalized for 60 years. The hospital was her home and she did not appreciate this progressive approach to her care. Looking back, I think I should have tried to delay these moves. The patients did not have a choice about moving, but I should have demanded time from management to prepare them for the changes they were experiencing, and worked with them through the process of change to facilitate whatever choice was possible. I should have at least tried to test the limits of my power as a professional in a large state bureaucracy. This was in the very early stages of planning toward the closure of large institutions in the US. Institutions are dehumanizing, but I learned that once an individual has been institutionalized, great care needs to be taken to re-orient that person to life in the community. This care was not always apparent in the closure of large mental hospitals in the United States.

I also worked at the other end of this process when, as an employee of state government, I worked with voluntary agencies that were applying for funds to provide services for learning disabled people living in the community after the closure of large asylums. I reviewed the care that residents received in these facilities, some of which were progressive, but some of which were miniature asylums that replicated the problems of larger facilities unless threatened with withdrawal of funding. At least as a representative of the state with control of funding, I was in a position to monitor whether these facilities were providing the stimulation and care they were contracted to provide and had some leverage to ensure that they fulfilled their commitments to vulnerable people.

Closure of mental hospitals in the US was a key shift toward 'care in the community'. In 1967 Governor Ronald Reagan signed the Lanterman-Petris-Short Act which led to the closure of California's mental hospitals (Bambauer 2005) as a cost cutting measure. 'Case management arose in the USA as a solution to the difficulties of providing community care to people with severe mental disorders' (Marshall et al., 1995, 409). However, in the early stages of the closure of mental hospitals, people were not given the support they needed (Macarov 1995, 140). My experience was that during this time mentally ill people were put on the street with very little preparation or support.

I again witnessed the early effects of care in the community while living in New York in the 1970s studying at Columbia University. Floridly mentally ill people were walking the streets of New York as a result of 'care in the community' initiatives similar to those instituted in California by Ronald Reagan: the man propped against a wall masturbating at 113th and Broadway, the woman with several flower pots tied to her head with a scarf who screamed all night in the apartment building next to mine. When I went to the laundromat, I had to avert my eyes from a woman with one set of clothes standing naked in the corner while her clothes washed. It soon became apparent to policy makers that newly discharged psychiatric patients needed support to cope with their new-found freedom outside hospital walls. They would need systematic coordinated attention to their needs in the community, whether it was called case management or care management.

In 1978–1979 I lived in London while completing a Master's degree at the London School of Economics. I worked as a hospital social worker part-time at the Royal Free Hospital. I then worked as an Assistant Professor of Social Work in Canada in the early 1980s, where the traditional approaches to care seemed largely unchanged and casework was the norm. In 1983 I moved back to London where I took a post as a social worker in a local authority 'patch' in North West London working within a community development model of service delivery. This was the post-Barclay Report (1982) era of community-based social work practice in local government areas called local authority Social Services Departments (SSDs), established since 1970. Care in the community policies had been to gradually close large psychiatric hospitals since the 1950s, but they still existed. It is somewhat ironic that it was called community-based work when many people were missing from the community because they were still incarcerated in large institutions, that is, people with mental health problems in mental hospitals, people with learning disabilities in various institutions and elderly people in residential and nursing homes. However, the goal for 'patch' social workers was to know their local communities, develop services and contribute to community networks of support. An example of this approach was when I worked with a community nurse to set up cooking classes for local residents who had diabetes. I brought in a local woman with diabetes to teach the classes.

During my time in this 'patch' I worked with one couple who had two young children. The mother had epilepsy which was difficult to control and her husband was recovering from a drug addiction. They were devoted parents struggling with a myriad of problems. Under Section 1 of the Children and Young Persons Act of 1963 governing work with children and families, social workers could provide financial support to prevent family break-up and could give families small amounts of money without management approval. Social workers often used 'Section 1 money' liberally to help struggling families even if the reasons were not, strictly speaking, 'to prevent family break-up'. When the couple came in at the end of a week with no money, I gave them enough to purchase disposable nappies although there was not an imminent danger of the family breaking up. As the amount I gave was under the figure which required line manager approval, I used my professional discretion to help this family. I felt like a modern-day Robin Hood, taking money from the rich, albeit through taxation, and giving it to the poor. The use of such minor professional discretion was to be curtailed by the introduction of Care Management.

In 1989 the Berlin Wall fell, which I regarded as symbolic of wider changes. Growing up during the Cold War, I was convinced that Communists were going to attack the US. The fall of the Berlin Wall was an iconic event for me. It was widely regarded as an end to the Cold War and by some as the triumph of capitalism over communism. I am not alone in this perception. 'Neo-liberalism was strengthened with the collapse of the socialist countries in 1991 and the end of the most obvious alternative to capitalism' (Harlow 2003, 30). The fall of the Berlin wall symbolized the end of communism as a political system, but it also meant that efforts at collective action were simultaneously discredited. Mishra (1998, 481) refers to it as 'the collapse of the socialist alternative'. To me, the fall of the Berlin Wall meant that free market capitalism had won the day and that efforts at collectivism were tainted by Communism and its failure. Individualism ruled. Poor people would be seen as responsible for their own poverty. The importance of structural issues was subsumed to an individualistic ethos where individuals were responsible for their own fate.

After working as a Hospital Team manager and a Mental Health Team manager in England, I joined London Metropolitan University in 1992 as a Senior Lecturer. One of my roles was to visit social work students on placement. It was in visiting social work agencies that I became aware of changes in social work practice in England. On one visit, the student discussed a piece of work which involved a woman who needed to be re-housed. There were a number of family problems underlying the woman's request for re-housing. The student demonstrated how she had dealt with the woman's housing needs. As I usually did, I asked the student about how she had established a professional working relationship with the woman. The practice teacher stopped me and said that the identified need had been addressed and that there was no need for a professional relationship. I was taken aback. My norm was casework. All my casework instincts were that the student needed to help this woman deal with the reasons behind her request to move house. The woman had serious family problems, which could only get worse without some action or intervention. But the student was not allowed to help beyond the identified need. It was clear that the role of the social worker had changed.

This incident was part of my growing awareness of the changes to the role of social workers in local authority Social Services Departments, indeed changes to the entire service delivery system in the UK. One of the reasons for undertaking the research presented in this book was to try to make sense of these changes over time and across different settings. I had come to Britain with a great appreciation of its post-World War II social democratic welfare state, a kind of quasi-socialism that stood in stark contrast to the raw capitalism I experienced growing up in the United States. It seemed that this welfare state was being dismantled under Prime Minister Margaret Thatcher, friend of President Ronald Reagan who was directly responsible for the precipitous closure of mental hospitals in the US. The welfare state, which involved a degree of social democratic collectivism, was being rejected in favour of market-led principles, as part of the globalisation, or the Americanisation (Jameson 1984b, 57), of the world economy.

Research Starting Points

I started to think about the implications of care management following the passage of the National Health Service and Community Care Act (NHSCCA) in 1990. This legislation was implemented between 1990 and 1993. It was significant because it introduced the 'purchaser/provider split'. Purchasers were people who assessed service user need in order to purchase services. Providers were people who met needs by providing services. It was clear that there were significant changes ahead for the role of social workers. At a very tangible level, SSDs were being completely reorganized and social workers had to apply for their own jobs. Numbers of posts in teams were cut back and the workers knew that only some of them would get their jobs back. Targets were set and performance reviews measured whether workers had met their targets. This sat awkwardly with the caring role for which social workers had been trained. When I embarked on this study in 1997, I was fortunate to have been able to formulate a research design that captured social workers' reaction to these changes shortly after they were implemented. There were still social workers working as care managers who had worked as social workers before the changes were introduced. They were in a unique position to have experienced two different models of service delivery.

I did not begin this research trying to fit care management into the McDonaldization thesis. My research, which began to take shape in 1997, was intended to explore the implications for the role of social workers working in a service delivery system in transition from a supposedly collectivist ethos to an ethos which emphasized cost containment and cost reduction. I began interviewing care managers and their team managers in 1998. I had a sense that things were changing, but could not put a name to the overarching changes that seemed to be taking place. I used open-ended questions to explore what social workers thought about the changes, trying to be receptive to what it meant to them, which is one of the advantages of qualitative research.

When I read *The McDonaldization of Society* by George Ritzer (1996), it became apparent to me that social work was being McDonaldized in much the same way that other public sector services were. McDonaldization had relevance to and 'made sense of' social workers' disquiet about care management. I therefore have reported what social workers said in response to my question and analysed the responses in terms of McDonaldization's requirements for calculability, predictability, control and surveillance. The McDonaldization thesis is set in wider concepts related to social theory, of which it is a part.

The aim of the research was to explore the impact of care management, implemented in 1993 in the UK, on the practice and status of social work in Local Authority Social Services Departments (SSDs). In carrying out this research, I used qualitative research methods, including in-depth interviews with individual managers and focus groups with teams of care managers. Qualitative methods were used in this research because these methods are concerned with understanding the meaning of events from the perspective of actors in their own situation (Oakley 1999, 156) and allowing a range of perspectives to emerge (Ritchie and Spencer 1994, 188). Qualitative methods enabled a deliberate exploratory approach with a tolerance for ambiguity and contradiction (Mason 1996, 4) that reflected the social reality I was investigating.

Care Management and Work with Children

This research focused on the generic impact of care management, rather than care management to any one client group. The analysis of the impact of care management on work with children is integrated in the wider analysis of the impact of care management on the role of social workers. Care managers are managers of the services that other professionals provide. This is true of care management in work with both children and adults. Both children's teams and adult teams were interviewed as a part of this research. Care managers in children's teams interviewed for this research did not provide 'direct' services to children. These care managers assessed children's needs and then referred the children on to teams that worked with children on a longer term, analogous to the work of care managers with adults. Therefore, the comments of care managers who worked with children are integrated in the wider discussion of the impact of care management on social work practice. The features of care management in work with children as well as adults are the deskilling of the social work role, highly prescriptive procedures, dependence on technology and cost containment. Cost containment has affected social work with children as well as work with adults (Jones 2001, 558).

Managerialism and checklist approaches apply to work with children in the same way that they apply to work with adults (Garrett, 2003, Munro and Calder 2005, Green 2006, 251). The current focus of systems devised to work with children in the UK has shifted from children in need of protection, to the broader definition of 'children in need'. The Framework for the Assessment of Children in Need and their Families (Department of Health et al., 2000) makes assessment the key to work with children in the same way that assessment is the focus of care management with adults.

The 'child development' approach has taken the place of the 'risk' approach. Elaborate assessment protocols have been developed to assess needs of children. (Department for Education and Skills, accessed 26 June 2007). Computerized systems are now designed to pick up a cause/effect relationship between factors entered into assessment databases. The intention of the systems in place is that when relevant information is 'fed into' electronic databases, predictions concerning need will emerge. New systems have necessitated a restructuring of work with children, including multi-agency work with children and the demise of specialist work, consistent with the deskilling of social workers. Preventive work is located with health services, education services and the voluntary sector. Protection is constructed as one of a possible range of needs. In the process of an assessment, if a social worker becomes aware of the need for protection of a child, then a further procedure is invoked.

The three critical points in this system are the ContactPoint, the Common Assessment Framework and the Integrated Children's System (Department for Education and Skills, accessed 27 June 2007). The ContactPoint is a national online directory, available to authorized staff who need it to do their jobs. The database includes information from a range of people with different professional perspectives and levels of training in work with children. The Common Assessment Framework (CAF) is the next stage if concerns are raised at the Contact Point. The CAF is a generic assessment for children with additional needs, which can be used by practitioners across all children's services in all local areas in England. It aims to help early identification of need, promote coordinated service provision and reduce the number of assessments that some children and young people go through. Information is collected by 'tick box' and no special training is needed to complete this assessment. The third stage of the assessment framework is the Integrated Children's System (ICS). This has several levels, going from least problematic to most intensive levels of work, that is, the initial assessment, the core assessment, the Section 47 (investigating abuse), the child protection conference, and the Looked After Child Review carried out with children who are in the care of the local authority Social Services Department (SSD).

Tools developed in 2000 for the Assessment Framework became the cornerstone for the implementation of policies adopted in Every Child Matters. The intention of Every Child Matters: Change for Children, published in the UK in November 2004, was to prevent child abuse through multi-agency working and information sharing with common assessment frameworks used across relevant organizations. Key elements of the Every Child Matters agenda include multi agency working, active partnership with parents and the use of key workers in co-coordinated services to provide family support. Commissioning of services in the community and the importance of care managers acting as links between these services and the needs of children are paramount in meeting the needs of vulnerable children.

Restructuring of children's services has moved the emphasis from child protection to family support (Campbell 1997, 245). These two perspectives should not be mutually exclusive (Davies 2007, forthcoming). However, an emphasis on family support can miss evidence of need for protection as the entry point to the services is staffed by people who are not trained in child protection. Child protection is a specialized activity in which only a small minority of social workers are trained. Child protection practitioners feel that their expertise and abilities are not valued and are cynical about the effectiveness of the systems set up to help children (Spicer in Campbell 1997, 245).

Care management has similar features in work with all clients groups. The themes that run through care-managed work with children as well as adults is the dependence on technology in the form of computerized programmes to access risk and the parallel loss of discretion associated with a deskilled social work role.

Audiences for this Book

Social workers

The purpose of this book is to introduce social work audiences to social theory and apply social theory to a better understanding of care management. Social workers work at all levels of service provision, from unqualified care workers to academics who teach social work and social work researchers. This book is intended mainly for social work academics and postgraduate social work students because the purpose is to apply social theory to the practice and to understand the status of social work within the care management model of service delivery. In Part I, social theory is applied to an exploration of the impact of care management on social work. Part II can be read as a 'stand alone' section by practitioners who are interested in what their colleagues think about care management at the level of practice. Social work practitioners can use examples of dilemmas presented by practitioners to reflect on the systems and structures they work in and the way they work within these systems. Implications for the social work practice are drawn in the last part of the book.

Managers

Managers of social care will read this from a management perspective. Hopefully, managers can use this book to take a reflexive approach to their work (Giddens 1990, 38). For managers, this would mean continually analysing the current service delivery reality in terms of incoming information. This could contribute to the creation of organizations and systems that are both efficient and responsive to human need. Efficiency should not be the only or the highest goal as it does not carry with it an intrinsic ethic of ameliorating human need. Efficiency is not always effective (Hoyle and Wallace 2005, 35). Managers need to think about efficiency in terms of its purpose and should not consider saving money through efficiency as their only purpose in management. They need to think about the purpose to which efficiency is put, even if it is related to Utilitarian ideas about the greatest good for the greatest number or Kantian ideas about choice (Valesquez et al., 2006).

Social theorists

Finally, those with a social theory perspective may be interested in the application of social theory to care management social work. It needs to be recognized that all of us have been or will be service users of some description at some time in our lives, whether it is as a user of health, education or social services. The issue of how we organize services and the ethos of these services will affect us all. This application of theory to the understanding of social work practice aims to contribute to the debate about the usefulness of social theory in reflecting on current social developments. Although complex, a multiperspectivist approach advocated by Kellner (1999, 186) is taken here. Ritzer has focused on one theoretical perspective to great effect in his consideration of McDonaldization. However, he himself has advocated a multiperspectivist approach to McDonaldization. '... the issues of concern in McDonaldization would lend themselves nicely to more academic treatises looking at the phenomena under consideration simultaneously using a number of different perspectives' (Ritzer 1999, 237). Through a multiperspectivist analysis, I hope to increase our understanding of the issues of McDonaldization as adopted in the delivery of social services. It is hoped that the reader, whether they are academics, policy makers, providers or recipients of social services, will use the findings and analysis discussed here to reflect on the wider social forces that affect the provision of social services in the current climate of late capitalism.

Outline of Chapters

Because this book may be of interest to different audiences, a glossary has been included at the beginning of the book with key terms from both social theory and social work. Relevant terms from social theory are defined for social workers who may not be familiar with these terms and social work terms used in the book are included for non-social workers. I take as my model the glossary provided by Rosenau (1992), which I found very helpful. Definitions signal how terms in this discussion will be used. From a social theory perspective, the concepts within social theory are perhaps too complex for simple dictionary definitions. However, the purpose of the glossary is to provide signposts to readers in unfamiliar territory. Academics may find definition of social work terms useful. Conversely, social work readers may find definitions of social theory terms useful. Providing a glossary on this topic is more a heuristic device meant to provoke thought than a 'last word' definitive list of terms. The definitions provided are tentative, but at least provide a starting point from which concepts can be considered and argued.

Part I, including Chapters 1 and 2, is an introduction to the theoretical and policy issues preceding and surrounding the implementation of care management. In Chapter 1, I discuss concepts from social theory that are relevant to an understanding of the introduction of care management policies. I then discuss characteristics of modern and postmodern discourses. The political manifestations of postmodernity are investigated and linked to care management as a feature of the post-Fordist welfare state. Working conditions for social workers within the post-Fordist welfare state, including issues of managerialism and professionalism are addressed.

Chapter 2 introduces issues in the delivery of social services that are core to most industrially developed societies, but which are especially relevant in the English-speaking world. Early social work practices and perspectives were established in England and spread through England's colonial expansion. A brief history of social service provision in the United Kingdom is presented to establish the climate which fostered the introduction of care management in the UK. The role of social workers in the UK is largely tied to their employment in local organizations. Politically inspired legislation has changed its role in different social and political eras. Social workers have been constructed as caseworkers in the Seebohm Report (1968), community workers in the Barclay Report (1982) and purchasers and enablers in the Griffiths Report (Griffiths 1988). The argument is made that the introduction of care management in local authority Social Services Departments (SSDs) has had a significant impact on social work practice and professional standing.

Part II, beginning with Chapter 3, presents social workers' perceptions of the impact of care management on their practice. Managerialism, required to operate a care management model of service delivery, is a direct challenge to the use of professional discretion and has been deskilling from a casework perspective. Issues associated with the introduction of care management are the restructuring of SSDs, increased procedural requirements, whether services are actually needs-led, increased surveillance of social workers, decreased discretion of social workers and a decline in their ability to form a professional (casework) relationship with service users.

Chapter 4 addresses care managers' perception of policy attempts to construct service users as consumers of services and as customers with consumer rights. The issue discussed is whether the consumerist approach inherent in New Public Management (NPM) can change the status of clients to that of consumers with rights and whether the provision of social care can empower service users as citizens. The claim that care management offers more choice to service users is examined.

Chapter 5 addresses the professional status of social workers in the context of the deprofessionalizing effects of care management and the enhanced professional status offered by professional registration. The issue of whether or not social workers will migrate from SSD purchaser work to private/voluntary provider work is explored. Advantages and disadvantages of registration are examined. Taken together with the professional registration of social workers, care management offers opportunities for professional recognition and employment in the 'mixed economy' of care.

In Part III, a summary and analysis of issues raised in Parts I and II is undertaken. Chapter 6 addresses the issue of whether and to what degree care management can be considered social work. It is argued that care management has McDonaldized social care and thus social work. Social work has been subject to an application of Fordist management techniques to achieve efficiency, predictability, calculability; surveillance by managers is very much a part of this exercise. The rationale behind the introduction of care management has been that it will enhance post-Fordist consumer choice. However, it is argued that the appearance of choice has been created, but not the reality of choice. In spite of the changes brought about by the care management model of service delivery, care management retains elements of casework and may be viewed as a specialist response to conditions of late capitalism.

In Chapter 7, the focus is on 'how social workers should go on' considering the conflicts and complexities inherent in care management work. Social workers need to take a critical reflexive stance, based on professional ethics, social justice and human rights, to ensure that the needs of service users and carers remain at the forefront of practice and to avoid being overwhelmed by narrowly conceived bureaucratic measures instituted to ensure efficiency and cost containment. The ongoing debate about whether social work is (mechanistic) 'science' or (creative) 'art' is revisited in terms of McDonaldized measures to make social workers more rational, efficient, predictable and calculable. The relevance of social theory for social work is interrogated in this chapter. Some of the ironies of the application of McDonaldization to the design of social services are discussed. The most obvious negative aspect of McDonaldization is the 'irrationality of rationality', introduced through a highly managerialized approach to social service delivery. Measures are considered to resist the negative aspects of McDonaldization.

Donna Dustin
London, 2007

PART I
THE MACRO PERSPECTIVE

Understanding the Introduction of Care Management – Theory and Context

Introduction to Part I – Chapters 1 and 2

A social theory 'macro' perspective is adopted in Part I to examine the phenomenon of 'care management', as it is referred to in Britain, or what is called 'case management' in the US. Chapter 1 presents a social theory/social policy framework for understanding the social and political changes associated with the introduction of care management. Globalization implies that we live in a diverse, postmodern world. Yet measures such as care management are modern, rational ways to measure input and output in service delivery systems and contain cost. Management itself is analysed in terms of perspectives within management theory because management has become central to the operation of care management.

An analysis of care management using social theory is part of an effort to develop a 'synthetic analysis of contemporary social developments' (Seidman 1992, 72) by employing a number of theoretical frameworks to examine the large scale social trends that have led to their development. This perspective takes into account the way in which history, culture, social policy, monetarist economics, neo-liberal politics and NMP principles intersected, leading to the imposition of care management on social work practice in Social Services Departments (SSDs) in England, initially in work with adults, but increasingly in work with children. This 'macro' analysis is balanced against the results of 'micro' qualitative research, discussed in Part II, which was carried out to assess the day to day impact on social workers who practice as care managers.

In Chapter 2, care management is placed in an international perspective. Care management originated in the Unites States and has been introduced in a range of English-speaking countries. The implications of the care management model of service delivery for social workers in the UK are considered. Its introduction in the national structures of UK local government social services systems has had far reaching implications.

Chapter 1

Theorizing Social Change

Introduction

In this chapter, theoretical perspectives on the broad social changes that have led to care management are explored. The influence of wider social changes on the organizations that deliver social welfare services both in the UK and elsewhere begins with a discussion of social theory *per se*. These changes, including the rise of New Right politics, the quasi-market state and New Public Management (NPM) have contributed to the creation of the care-management role, which has had a direct impact on social work practice in local government organizations, which are called local authority Social Services Departments (SSDs) in the UK. It is argued that with the escalation of capitalist pressures and the globalization of culture (Kellner 2007), the introduction of care management to social work practice will spread and its influence on social work practice will extend beyond the US and the UK (George 1998, 28).

Consistent with this definition of social theory, a 'multiperspectivist' approach (Kellner 1999, 186) is employed to analyse how care management as social policy and a model of welfare provision emerged, how it came to take the forms it has and the relationships between policies and programmes in the UK (O'Brien and Penna 1998, 6). The perspectives employed to study the implementation and the practice of care management include the history of social welfare provision and aspects of social policy, social theory and management theory. Social policy refers to 'principles and practices of state activity … relating to redistribution in pursuit of welfare' (Miller 1999, 14). Social theory studies the way that social change affects our everyday lives (Miles 2001, 2) so it is an active process, a means to an end, and a way of theorizing what is happening around us (Miles 2001, 163). Like Miles (2001, 2), I do not consider myself a social theorist. However, I believe that concepts from social theory can illuminate social work issues. Social theory should inform social work and social work should inform social theory (Lovelock et al., 2004, 16). Social theory contributes to the analysis of care management, and conversely, a study of the application of care management to social work practice offers insights for social theory.

The relevance of social theory to social work is discussed first. The characteristics of modern and postmodern discourses are explored. The concept of a discourse, defined as 'a set of ideas, practices and beliefs which coalesce to produce an over-arching picture of reality' (Symonds and Kelly 1998, 8) is useful because it conveys the idea that social reality can be constructed in different ways at different historical points in time. It is argued that there is a relationship between postmodernity as late capitalism and New Right politics. The relationship between managerialism inherent in care-management models of service delivery and professionalism is discussed. At the level of the organization, the parallel concepts of Fordism/post-Fordism will be applied to SSD organizations. Two contrasting management theories, Theory X and Theory Y, will be defined and explored in relation to understanding the management of care managers. It will be argued that the concept of McDonaldization contributes to an understanding of the changes in SSDs because it postulates that modern Fordist management methods developed in the industrial sector have been applied to non-industrial sectors to enhance efficiency, predictability, calculability and control of service provision (Ritzer 1996).

The Relevance of Social Theory to Social Work

The value of social theory, from a social work perspective, is that it is applied. Social work is an applied activity which draws on sociology. However, some find classical sociological theories difficult to apply to social work practice. These theories seem 'distant from everyday reality and appear to exist on an abstract and remote plane where the ability to theorize appears to be more important than the relevance of the theory itself' and where 'theorists appear to belong to a club from which the rest of us mere mortals are barred' (Miles 2001, 2). Social theory is concerned with issues such as globalization and postmodernity, which were not, by definition, concerns of classical sociological theorists such as Durkheim, Marx, Parsons and Weber. Social theory is current, grounded and relevant and can therefore make a contribution to understanding the context of their work current changes.

Social theory refers to the use of complex theoretical frameworks to analyse macro social structures. It is interdisciplinary and can include economics, history and philosophy. It examines and interprets the meaning of large scale trends. It focuses on social forces in society. Social theory is therefore relevant to an analysis of care management because the introduction of care management as a model of social services delivery has arisen out a complex combination of historical influences, globalization and political thinking. Social theory is linked to the concept of the sociological imagination that interprets the meaning of social facts (Mills 1959). Current social theorists such as Jameson and Ritzer draw upon and apply insights from classical sociologists such as Marx and Weber to make current social developments understandable to those not trained in classical sociology.

Ritzer (1996) has applied Weber's theory regarding the 'iron cage' of bureaucracy to an analysis of service industries, introducing the term 'McDonaldization' to describe the growing tendency to apply rational bureaucratic measures to businesses that provide tangible services in the areas of food, health, leisure and travel. The 'McDonaldization' concept will be applied to an analysis of the rise of care management as an intensification of Weber's bureaucratic principles applied to organizations that provide social care services.

Ritzer's thesis is used in this book to analyse the impact of care management as a model of service delivery on social work practice with further implications for the profession itself. The relationship between current social work practice and McDonaldization has been observed by social work authors (James 2004, Parton 2004,

36–37). The McDonaldization thesis will be applied to an analysis of care management as 'part of a historical tradition in which social theory is used to critique society and thereby provide the base for its betterment' (Ritzer 1993, xiii in Kellner 1999, 203).

Issues of ethics and social justice are an accepted part of social theory, in contrast to classical sociology, which is intended to be 'scientific' and 'rational'. Sociologists can never be completely objective because they are part of the social phenomenon they are studying, unlike physicists or geologists. Social theorists accept bias, but are aware of its effects, which is more realistic than a claim to objectivity. The application of social theory, as exemplified by Ritzer with his McDonaldization thesis, allows the non-sociologists to apply social theory.

The benefit of social theory lies in its potential for shedding light upon circumstances that are often taken for granted (Miles 2001, 163). It makes insights drawn from classical sociology immediately useful to those experiencing social change. It is hoped that the application of social theory to an analysis of care management will provoke debate about issues that otherwise might be taken for granted and thus contribute to reflective practice among practitioners in social care settings and managers of these services.

Modernity and Postmodernity

Although the terms 'modern' and 'postmodern' are now commonplace in contemporary social science, the meaning of these concepts is contested (O'Brien and Penna 1998, 186). Most writers link the emergence of modernity to the rejection of magic, traditional or religion as forms of social authority characteristic of pre-modern or traditional societies (Katz 1996). Modernity was marked by the growth of scientific enquiry and a valorization of rationality as the organizing principle for social life in the 1700s with the Age of Enlightenment (Rosenau 1992, 5; Taylor-Gooby 1989, 389; Howe 1994, 513). The main features of modernity are a belief that history has a direction and purpose or teleology, an attempt to develop universal categories of experience, representation and explanation through theory or metanarratives, a valuing of reason as the basis of all activity, and a belief that the nation state has a role to play in improving society (Parton 1994, 27).

Modernity has been characterized by a search for truth, that is, universally valid foundations for human knowledge and action based on rationality and science, referred to as positivism or empiricism. A contrasting postmodern position is that truth and meaning are context-dependent and predictable from a particular horizon or point of view, referred to as interpretivism. The belief that knowledge can be applied to achieve social progress is central to modernity (Sheppard 2006, 61). The problem with modernity is that it has not been able to deliver on its promise to improve society or make the world a better place. 'The modern project has not so much been abandoned or forsaken by the tide of history … as substantially devalued and discredited by the very development of modernity itself. The erosion of confidence, of trust and faith, in its core assumptions and objectives has been a direct consequence of modern practices and their uneven effects' (Smart 2000, 457). The 'postmodern' is associated with the perspective that modernity has not brought the progress it promised. The myth that knowledge would bring emancipation is no longer believed (Lyotard 1984; xxiv in Seidman 1992, 345). Instead modernity has brought with it the efficiency of the killing in the Holocaust (Bauman 1989, 13), the degradation of the environment.

The postmodern can be divided into the intellectual postmodern and the material postmodern (Wilson 1998). The intellectual postmodern is referred to as 'postmodernism' and refers to changes in ways of thinking about or understanding the world. Postmodernism is 'a particular shift in theory and analysis, which is itself part of the condition' (Williams 1992, 204–5), most importantly, a challenge to the possibility of absolute knowledge in the area of the social 'sciences'. Social work has drawn upon the social sciences and therefore postmodernism is relevant to social work knowledge. In the modern era, social work knowledge was drawn eclectically from a range of metanarratives, both sociological and psychological or psychiatric, all of which are now subject to challenge. In care-management practice, issues of theory and 'knowing' have been challenged by the practical necessity to purchase services at the lowest price within the quasi-markets of care.

The material postmodern is referred to as postmodernity and encompasses current conditions and changes that are taking place such as globalization, the information technology revolution and the triumph of market capitalism, fragmentation and superficiality. It is synonymous with Jamison's (1984) 'culture of late capitalism'. The term postmodernity refers to the political and economic condition in which social work is currently practised (Fawcett and Featherstone 1998, 68; Penna and O'Brien 1996; O'Brien and Penna 1998, 136; Ginsburg 1998, 26).

Material postmodernity, that is, 'a condition – a set of changes, transitions and processes perceived to be taking place at the social, political, economic and cultural level' (Williams 1992, 204–5) is the most relevant concept to use when analysing care management because it encompasses the material changes that have occurred at the level of the organization of social welfare services. Some reference will be made to elements of postmodernism because postmodernism, which implies different ways of thinking, has contributed to changes in the material circumstances of service delivery.

Material postmodernity refers to the increasing tendency in society to commodify previously intangible services. The process of commodification entails the construction of previously intangible services, for example 'care', as tangible measurable commodities that can be bought and sold through contracts in commercial exchanges. This is directly relevant to the introduction of care management, making 'care' a commodity to be bought and sold. Thus in the postmodern era, professionals have been exposed to market principles and their 'knowledge' subjected to measurement in terms of economic efficiency. The 'expert' is increasingly valued in terms of how much they can do, that is, calculable output, rather than for the intrinsic value of their knowledge. The metanarrative of the professional is exposed to market forces. Within this discourse, users of services become constructed as customers or consumers.

The shift from a modern to a postmodern discourse has been described as a transition from standardization, uniformity and universalism to heterogeneity, fragmentation, diversity and difference (Williams 1992). Modernity sought universality, homogeneity, monotony and clarity, and fought the enemy of 'ambivalence, indeterminacy and undecidability' (Bauman 1997, xvi). In addition, the transition from modernity to postmodernity is characterized by 'the idea that "truth" has gone out of fashion' (Carter 1998, 7). From a postmodern perspective, knowledge in the social sciences is now regarded as socially constructed (Burr 1995) rather than an absolute reflection of tangible reality.

While modernists portray social knowledge in absolute terms known as metanarratives, intellectual postmodernists regard social knowledge as constructed, situational, conditional and open to question. Modern certainty has been replaced by postmodern doubt (Sheppard 2006, 4). They cast knowledge as relative and constructed by those who have the power to define social reality. From the perspective of the intellectual postmodern, changes in ways of thinking about truth and knowledge have led to a questioning of modern certainties. If these postmodern constructions of knowledge are accepted, then everything is relative, knowledge is de-centred and politics are central to everyday life. Postmodernity replaces reason with relativity and politics (Parton 1994). This perspective contributes to an understanding of the way in which political quasi-market solutions to social problems have superseded the application of professional social knowledge. It also constitutes a challenge for social workers whose claims to knowledge within the modern era were already tenuous.

A potential problem that social workers can have with intellectual postmodernism is that some of its strands of thought are completely relativistic and nihilistic. These theorists argue that there is no truth and no reality. Rosenau (1992) calls these thinkers 'sceptical postmodernists'. This is not a helpful position for social workers who must deal with the material tangible realities of people's lives, as well as the less tangible social/psychological elements. People who need social work services have real, tangible problems that need to be resolved both for their benefit and for the benefit of society. In Rosenau's terms, social workers are more likely to be 'affirmative postmodernists', if they use these terms at all, because for affirmative postmodernists, 'post-modern theory ... is unsystematic, heterological, de-centred, ever changing, and local ... it is personal in character and community-specific in focus' and 'is valuable for its own sake and does not claim special authority for itself' (Rosenau 1992, 83). This perspective on social work theory is interesting because it relates directly to social workers' eclectic use of theory and to the idea of a hermeneutic 'person in context' understanding of truth in social workers' work with service users. These issues are revisited in Chapter 7.

The issue as to whether modernity and postmodernity are distinct phenomena or whether they overlap is contentious (Rosenau 1992, 5n4). There are continuities and discontinuities between modernity and postmodernity. 'In many ways it is helpful to see postmodernism as a critique of certain tendencies within modern thought, but not as the proclamation of an entirely new kind of society' (Harrington 2005, 274). One view is that postmodernity is a further development of modernity (Giddens 1990, 46; Miles 2001, 164). Giddens (1990, 150) uses the term 'radical modernity' or 'high modernity' to describe postmodernity as an exaggeration of modern tendencies in society. Giddens's position is consistent with Frederick Jameson's (1984b) version of postmodernity as 'late capitalism'. While 'there has certainly been a sea change in the surface appearance of capitalism since 1973, the underlying logic of capitalist accumulation and its crisis tendencies remain the same' (Harvey 1989, 189).

Bartens also uses the term 'high' modernity (Bartens 1995, 246), but does not object to the term 'postmodernity' as long as we acknowledge the important continuities with the earlier stages of modernity (Bartens 1995, 247). However postmodernity is defined, it depends for its existence upon economic and technological conditions that were a product of modernity, specifically, modern science and technology. Within social work, Walker (2001) argues for the perspective that there is continuity between modernist and postmodernist epistemologies. Postle also argues that social work is operating between modern and postmodern epistemologies (Postle 1999). The most logical position would seem to be that we are between the modern and the postmodern in a borderline space between the two paradigms (Best and Kellner 1997).

For purposes of this analysis, postmodernity will be defined as an exaggeration of modernity or as a further development of modernity, rather than being qualitatively different from modernity or a 'break' with modernity, consistent with the terms 'high modernity' and 'late capitalism'. Postmodernity is not something different from modernity. It is more of the same at a higher, more advanced level of capitalism, based on increased reference to instrumental rationality. Further, the perspective is taken that social work is between modernity and postmodernity in a particular sense. Modern Fordist management techniques, represented by NPM and managerialism, have been imposed upon social workers to achieve a postmodern outcome, that of the commodification of services and consumer choice.

The idea that we live in a postmodern age is contested. However, issues associated with the concept of postmodernity are discussed widely in the literature, including social work literature (Parton 1994, Walker 2001; James 2004; Sheppard 2006). Nigel Parton has written prolifically on issues of postmodernity in relation to social work (1994, 1996, 2004). For example, he has provided an insight as to why Evidence Based Practice (EBP), which is a very modern concept, has come to the fore in a postmodern era characterized by rapid change and uncertainty (Parton 2004, 35). EBP is based on modern, narrow scientific ideas and related to managerialism and care management, but the current era is marked by diversity and relativity. Parton observes that this paradox can be reconciled by understanding that EBP and managerialism were introduced to bring certainty to an uncertain postmodern environment. This is a crucial point in understanding the introduction of 'modern' care-management policies in a 'postmodern' era.

McDonaldization can be regarded as both modern and postmodern. At its heart, McDonaldization is a modern phenomenon based on rational instrumentality. It is the hyperreality of McDonaldization that can be regarded as postmodern (Baudrillard 1983). Giddens (1990) argues that while some regard postmodernity as a break from the past, it should be regarded as an intensification of modernity, a higher order of what has gone before, as 'high modernity' or 'late capitalism'. 'High' modernity implies an exaggeration of modern principles, such as the rapidly expanding work of science seen in the internet and the escalating significance of consumer capitalism in Western societies. From this perspective, postmodernity is not different from modernity; it is modernity taken to its extreme. McDonaldization is based on modern principles but it functions as an example of the exaggeration, or a higher level, of capitalist principles. The use of modern principles in what is regarded as a postmodern era could be seen as an attempt to impose some modern certainty on an increasingly uncertain postmodern era (Parton 2004, 35).

New Right Economics, the 'Commodification of Everything' and the Post-Fordist Welfare State

In the UK, the retreat from the post-War Keynesian welfare state is consistent with elements of both postmodernity and the rise of New Right politics. Both postmodernists and new right politicians are antagonistic to centralized government intervention in the life of the individual. This involves an antagonism to public expenditure, increasing emphasis on self-help and family support, the centrality of individual responsibility and the extension of commodification (Parton 1994, 9). Both New Right politicians and postmodernists value production and consumption of tangible goods and, by implication, the market. Both distrust the power of 'experts'. Further areas of agreement include the following: firstly, pluralism (changing groups of citizens that form and reform alliances across various issues) as an alternative to 'socialist' central planning, anti-stateism and anti-bureaucracy; secondly, minimal government and the dismantling of the welfare state; and thirdly, individualism, increasing individual freedom of choice and deregulation (Rosenau 1992, 165). New Right politicians disapprove of big government, campaign to 'get government off people's backs' and favour market solutions to social problems. The Conservative approval of local solutions to local problems and disapproval of centrally planned solutions is consistent with postmodern rejection of metanarratives in favour of 'small' narratives (Sarup 1993, 146). In fact, Sarup goes so far as to say, 'Politically, it is clear that thinkers like Lyotard and Foucault are neo-conservatives. They take away the dynamic upon which liberal social thought has traditionally relied. They offer us no theoretical reason to move in one social direction rather than another' (Sarup 1993, 155). Habermas also thought that postmodernism was a form of neo-conservatism (Best 1994, 45). The market seems to have filled the vacuum left by an abandonment of modern metanarratives.

State-sponsored welfare programmes and the concept of social work emerged during the modern era, which was characterized by respect for knowledge and the development of metanarratives that were expected to contribute to social progress. Postmodernity suggests a questioning of modern social knowledge and those who claimed to 'know', characterized by the 'end of expertise' (Rosenau 1992, 7). Postmodernity relates to the abandonment of the belief that social improvement could be achieved through the efforts of the welfare state (Clarke 1998, 171). Both concepts are directly relevant to social workers working in SSDs. The efficacy of social work knowledge has been questioned. The imposition of care management upon social workers represents a challenge to social work knowledge claims. The increasingly market orientation of care management represents a retreat from the belief that knowledge could be applied to achieve social progress with a preference for market mechanism to distribute scarce resources (Jessop 1994).

If no version of 'progress' based on the application of knowledge can plausibly be defended (Giddens 1990, 46), then a vacuum seems to have been created, which may explain the rise of consumer capitalism (Bartens 1995, 59, Sarup 1993, 181). Material postmodernity replicates and reinforces the logic of consumer capitalism (Jameson 1984b). These concepts are relevant to care management where services are constructed as commodities to be bought and sold. Service users are to be considered 'customers' in a 'market of care'.

Because of the spread of information technology and economic globalization, the nation state no longer holds the power over its internal affairs that it once did, giving rise to the 'end of the nation state'. The state is being 'hollowed out' from above by international agencies such as the United Nations and regional bodies such as the European Union, from below by devolution and subsidiarity, and sideways by the creation of agencies such as NGOs and quasi-market authorities (Rhodes 1997). The 'hollowed out' nation state responds to economic globalization by 'subordinating social policy to the push for economic innovation and competitiveness, negotiating agreements on trade and technology and political economy aimed not at the national economy, but at the latter's insertion into the fragmented demand structure of the international economic system' (O'Brien and Penna 1998, 153).

New Right politicians seem to have turned to the quasi-market to fill the vacuum left by intellectual uncertainty. Market solutions are consistent with commodification, a salient feature of late capitalism. The 'commodification of everything' is a term attributed to Baudrillard (Sarup 1993, 161). It is argued that within SSDs an effort has been made to commodify formerly intangible care as represented in the term 'packages of care' and to 're-imagine' clients as consumers (Harris 2003, 130). Commodification is consistent with capital accumulation discussed below in relation to the Regulation Approach.

Contemporary welfare arrangements have been identified as postmodern or post-Fordist. The mid-1970s has been identified as the crisis point that marked the transition from a Fordist regime of accumulation to a post-Fordist regime of accumulation with the accompanying reorganization of capital, labour, production and the market (Bartens 1995, 183) and the transition from a Fordist welfare state system to a post-Fordist approach to welfare provision (Carter and Rayner 1996, 348). The contemporary welfare state in Britain can be regarded as post-Fordist because of the fragmentation of the welfare state itself, the movement away from collectivist social provision toward an individualist or consumerist model of provision, a decline in forms of authority with the distrust of and challenge to the forms of professional authority institutionalized in the welfare state, and the abandonment of the concept of progress or social improvement through the welfare state (Clarke 1998, 171–2). Economic globalization is also relevant to the consideration of the post-Fordist welfare state and is consistent with the influence of neo-liberalism globally regarding capital accumulation. It is therefore closely related to the concept of postmodernity as late modernity, 'high modernity' and the intensification of capitalist influences on national policies, including welfare policies.

The influence of economic globalization on welfare states has been cited by Jessop who uses a Regulation Approach framework to discuss the transition from the Keynesian Welfare State to the Schumpeterian Workfare State (Jessop 1994). Nation states have been 'hollowed out'. Internal social policy decisions must now be made with regard to how such decisions will affects a country's international economic competitiveness. Thus New Right welfare policies, including the introduction of care management, were part of the effort to make Britain more economically competitive in the international economic system by containing the cost of the welfare state.

The Regulation Approach framework conceptualizes welfare in conjunction with the need for government to create a national economy that is strong enough to compete internationally. The two main concepts central to the Regulation Approach, the accumulation regime and the social mode of economic regulation, have been used to analyse the rapid changes in social security policy since the 1980s, using workfare as an example (Grover and Stewart 1999, 74). The accumulation regime highlights the need for policies to increase capitalist production and consumption. The social mode of economic regulation refers to the need for 'norms, institutions, organisational forms, social networks and patterns of contact to sustain capital accumulation' (Jessop 1994, 14). The introduction of community care policies, the targeting of service provision and the purchaser/provider split can be seen as social modes of economic regulation, policies which were intended to increase Britain's economic competitiveness. From this perspective, welfare policies must be designed to support economic competitiveness rather than being a drain on national spending. Grover and Stewart (1999) describe a discourse which suggested that 'the welfare system itself was a barrier to greater levels of employment and economic prosperity' echoing the findings of the Poor Law Commission of 1834 which found that the provisions for the relief of poverty were creating poverty (de Schweinitz 1975).

Absolute truth and hence 'the expert', central precepts of modernity, have been called into question by intellectual postmodernists who reject metanarratives (Rosenau 1992, 6). It is argued that this distrust of experts and metanarratives is linked to an intensification of another aspect of modernity, that is, capitalism, marketization and commodification, leading to material postmodernity. If it is accepted that there is no absolute truth, everything is relative and experts can no longer make truth claims or apply knowledge to social progress, then as observed earlier, the market would seem to be the best way to address social problems. Commodification, the move to the market, may be associated with and be a response to the loss of certainty and the end of absolute truth. Professional expertise can no longer dictate what is best for individuals or society. Professionals no longer have the authority to legislate; they can only interpret (Bauman 1987). More specifically for care managers, they can only interpret in terms of quasi-market realities.

From this perspective, the market becomes the most effective and efficient way of distributing goods and services. Professionals who were trusted to use their knowledge to contribute to social progress in the modern era no longer go unchallenged. Because 'trust in science, technology and experts – social workers – has been undermined, audit has increased' (Parton 1996, 112). Professionals have become subjects of increased surveillance. Professionals, especially those within the rational bureaucracies of the welfare state must deal with increasing scrutiny and quality control measures as trust in their knowledge has declined (O'Neil 2002).

These changes in the national government structure have implications for social workers as bureau-professionals whose role has involved the application of modern metanarratives to achieve social progress. Social workers accomplished this application of knowledge through their positions in bureaucratic structures created by national government. When government changes the structures through which social workers function, these changes will have significant impact on their roles and the knowledge needed to carry out their activities.

Fordism, Post-Fordism and Taylorism

Fordism and post-Fordism are the organizational manifestations of modernity and postmodernity. Fordist organizations are associated with modernity and post-Fordism organizations are associated with postmodernity. These concepts are of direct relevance to an analysis of social workers' practice because organizations are very important to social work practice; organizations both facilitate and restrict social workers' practice. The concepts of Fordism and post-Fordism will therefore be explored as they contribute to an understanding of organizational changes that have affected social workers in their role as care managers in SSDs.

Fordism describes the use of modern rationality, or scientific management, to create efficient organizations that can mass-produce tangible goods. Fordist organizations have been identified with standardized and undiversified products, mass consumption, vertical hierarchical management, centralized bureaucracies, professional demarcation with clear differences in the activities and role expectations among workers and collective philosophies (Symonds and Kelly 1998, 34). The characteristics of Fordist organizations are mass production of homogeneous goods, inflexible technologies, standardized work routines, otherwise known as Taylorism, increases in productivity resulting from economies of scale as well as the de-skilling, intensification and homogenization of labour and the growth of a market for mass-produced items or the homogenization of consumption patterns (Ritzer 1996, 150–51).

Post-Fordist organizations are, on the other hand, identified with diversified, specialized products, niche group consumption with horizontal management and decentralized organizations, professional skill-mix flexibility, and an individualized philosophy (Symonds and Kelly 1998, 34). Post-Fordist organizations imply more customized and specialized products, shorter production runs, that is, smaller and more productive systems and the decline of large factories, new technologies which make flexible production profitable and computerized equipment which can be easily re-programmed. Workers must be more productive and have more diverse skills in order to handle new, more demanding and sophisticated technologies. They must be able to handle more responsibility and operate with greater autonomy, and more differentiated or fragmented work patterns (Ritzer 1996, 151).

While Fordism is associated with the homogeneous consumption patterns and inflexible technologies of factory assembly lines, post-Fordism is associated with the diversified consumption patterns and flexible technologies that have been made possible by the advent of computerization of machinery (Ritzer 1996). Standardized work routines or Taylorist production techniques associated with Fordism have been replaced by more flexible work patterns, for example, part-time work and short-term contracts, leading to post-Fordist working conditions. Both employers and employees must now be prepared to change their work expectations quickly in response to market conditions, including changing jobs to respond to changing job markets.

Within Fordist production units, economies of scale involved 'piece work', or the fragmentation of whole jobs into separate parts, which deskills the work force (Rothschild 1973, 129 in Brown and Lauder 2001, 30). Whole jobs are broken down into component parts, reducing skill of a worker to a series of simple repetitive operations to improve efficiency. In social work, the casework role has been fragmented into the purchaser role and the provider role (Wilson 1993, Kirkpatrick et al., 1999). Care management 'split the social work role, which was central to social work identity' (Sheppard 2006, 64). When the jobs are reduced to component elements of the larger job, workers are deskilled in that they are only taking responsibility for a portion of the whole process of service provision (Ritzer 1996, 151). Managers gain power because they are the only ones with a perspective on the 'whole' process.

In social work, deskilling has been effected by fragmenting or breaking up the skills of those who work in welfare provision. Jobs are broken into component parts and skilled work is given to lower paid, contracted-out workers (Williams 1992, 201), for example, home care assistants who go into the homes of older people to assist them with activities of daily living. Intense surveillance of these workers is facilitated by technological advances, such as the use of mobile phone tracking (Dinsdale 2003, 136).

Deskilling of professional workers is happening in a number of areas. An example from the field of health illustrates the concept of deskilling. In a study by Ravetz (2000), it was found that when health managers were trying to make nursing practice more streamlined, efficient and cost effective, they observed that the senior nurse bathed patients on their admission to hospital. This seemed a misuse of her advanced skills so managers reorganized services, making it a junior nurse role to bathe patients on admission. What managers did not realize was that the senior nurse used the bathing of new patients to examine them and obtain their social histories. The managerial demotion of bathing to a task for unskilled staff deskilled the senior nurse and deprived the patient of the application and the use of her skills to screen patients on admission. This is an example of managers deskilling a professional with their emphasis on efficiency, which ultimately reduced the effectiveness of the service provided.

Post-Fordist organizations, which respond to niche markets, individualizing products and service provision, demand more intense effort from workers in order to tailor services to fit the individual needs of customers. This description of post-Fordist organizations has relevance for care managers. Needs-led services are intended to respond to consumer choice, but the purchaser role represents a narrowed focus of activity. Care managers do not provide services. Care managers only take responsibility for assessing, purchasing and reviewing and not for provision of services. Therefore, they both work harder and they are deskilled.

In the current climate, the commodification and marketization of welfare and the measurement of welfare effectiveness in terms of efficiency or 'value for money' has affected the relationship between managers, professionals and service users. Social workers in the statutory sector have been McDonaldized in that they have been subjected to an intensification of Fordist management techniques, originally used to produce tangible goods. These techniques, referred to as managerialism in the statutory social services context, have been applied to the production of intangible services, that is, 'care'. Managers have assumed greater power relative to professionals because economic efficiency is the priority and managers are responsible for promoting economic efficiency. Service users are constructed as consumers of services or customers who have choice. These current conditions, described as postmodern or post-Fordist, have had a direct impact upon social workers who practise as care managers in SSDs within the 'logic of late capitalism' and influence our 'attempt to think about our present time in history' (Jameson 1984b, 85).

Fordist/Post-Fordist Working Conditions and Care Management

Parton observes that the social context within which social work operates has changed, and he identifies this change in terms of a shift from modernity to postmodernity. In the modern discourse, social workers were part of the operation of 'governmentality' and 'welfarism', an exercise of power in which the population was governed 'at a distance' by promoting social responsibility and the mutuality of social risk (Parton 1994). 'The social' was a sphere between the family and the state where intervention was acceptable (Howe 1996, 81). This social construction or discourse allowed a compromise between the liberal notion of the free individual, on the one hand, and the socialist vision of an all-encompassing state that would have threatened the family.

With the Thatcher victory of 1979, a new discourse was introduced with implications for the practice of social work. New service boundaries were created (Parton 1994, 24). Key elements of social work practice were new forms of resource allocation, which depended on assessment as a means to regulate and review (Parton 1994, 25). According to Parton, social work has undergone a change of discourse in the way that it has been circumscribed and prioritized. It would seem that 'the social', defined by Payne as the space between the state and the family is being redefined by the state as the sphere between the individual and the market. The social worker role in SSDs, which was to mediate between the service user and the state, has been replaced by a role that emphasizes meditation between the service user and the market via their position within the state, as represented by their employment within SSDs. This is reflected in the change in role and title from social worker or caseworker to care manager.

The three paramount responsibilities for SSDs in this new discourse are now to take a comprehensive strategic view of all sources of care, recognize that the direct provision of services by social workers is only part of local patterns of care and accept that the major part of the social work function is promoting and supporting the participation of other and different sources of care, which is an instrumental rather than a normative role. The new discourse involves welfare pluralism, that is, plural provision, decentralization, contractual rather than hierarchical accountability, and consumer involvement in decision-making (Parton 1994, 25).

Jameson's (1984b) description of postmodernity (superficiality, fragmentation and new technologies which prescribe and 'flatten' interaction with service users) has relevance for the experience of care managers. Social workers still try to use theory to understand the underlying meaning of service users' behaviour, but these efforts are marginalized by managerialistic demands for performativity and tangible, purchasable outcomes. In this sense, social workers are between the modern and the postmodern (Postle 1999) in that they still try to apply their existing knowledge to achieve social progress even though the focus of management is on narrowly defined calculable and measurable outcomes. Prescribed standardized scripted (Harris 2003, 2) interactions with service users contribute to an element of superficiality for care managers. The purchaser/provider split has fragmented the continuity that was implicit in the casework model of social work practice. New technologies have affected social work practice, for example, in the use of computer programs to assess need and to monitor the activities of care managers. The use of technology to monitor care managers has facilitated greater surveillance of workers' activities (Dinsdale 2003, 136).

There is some irony in the observation that Fordist management techniques (Brynon 1984) have been applied to care managers in order to achieve post-Fordist outcomes for service user. The post-World War II Keynesian model of service delivery was Fordist, providing standardized services through large-scale, centralized, hierarchical, corporately managed bureaucracies (Stoker 1989, Roach 1992). From this perspective, casework was Fordist in that it was service led and oriented to categories of service use. Care managed services are intended to be needs-led (post-Fordist and consumer oriented) rather than service-led (Fordist and production oriented).

Social workers as care managers could now be said to be working in a McDonaldized context in that their work is increasingly directed by managers and they are expected be more consumer oriented or needs-led, in other words, to assess needs and tailor packages of care to meet individual need. The NHSCCA could be described as an attempt to move away from service-led (Fordist production orientation) to needs-led (post-Fordist consumer orientation). In order to achieve this post-Fordist needs-led outcome, Fordist management techniques have been applied to care managers to ensure their compliance. This is consistent with Ritzer's discussion of post-Fordism as an exaggeration of Fordist management practices applied to the service sector for the purpose of increasing consumer choice.

The McDonaldization thesis is therefore relevant to the analysis of social workers' roles as care managers. Fordism could be described as production oriented, summed up in Ford's famous dictum that 'people could have any colour car they liked as long as it was black'. The focus was on production, or in the area of social care, on the provision of standardized services dispensed and overseen by 'expert' professionals. Post-Fordism would, on the other hand, be more oriented to what the customer wants. A post-Fordist organization would focus on diversifying and promoting consumer choice, that is, doing market research and assessing what the customer wants before production takes place, which is consistent with SSDs' responsibility to consult with service user groups about the provision of services to them. Care management could be regarded as post-Fordist and consumer oriented in that the emphasis is on identifying an individual's needs and tailoring service delivery to meet those needs.

The Fordist/post-Fordist conceptual framework can be applied to care management because new ways of working required re-designed or restructured welfare organizations. These restructured organizations were to be oriented to consumption of services by service users (the needs-led approach) rather than production of services by social workers (the service-led approach). Social workers working as care managers have been subjected to Fordist management techniques in order to facilitate a post-Fordist consumer choice for service users. For example, Fordist/McDonaldized organizations are characterized by hierarchy and rules where creativity is not valued (Ritzer 1996, 15). Discretion is part of creativity. The loss of discretion reported by care management is consistent with proceduralized managerialized activities that make creativity difficult.

For the purposes of this study, conditions within which SSD social workers now work will be defined as postmodern, or more specifically post-Fordist, although a paradox exists in that some aspects of social work have become more Fordist, specifically the increased levels of managerial control, in the post-Fordist emphasis on consumer choice. This paradox can be understood from the perspective that an exaggeration of Fordist bureaucracies and management techniques has been used in an attempt to create post-Fordist outcomes as represented by choice and needs-led services.

The McDonaldization of service delivery involves the application of factory management techniques to the delivery of intangible services, characterized by efforts to increase efficiency, predictability, calculability and control (Ritzer 1996). This process involves an exaggeration or a stretching of modern Fordist management procedures developed to produce tangible goods and applying these techniques to the provision of intangible services, resulting in what has been referred to as post-Fordism. The application of modern Fordist techniques to current late capitalist circumstances tends to support the conceptualization of current social conditions as 'high modernity' and late capitalism, implying a further development of modernity, rather than 'post' modernity, which implies something that comes 'after' modernity and is different from modernity. Thus the social conditions and the social organization experienced within the current era do not represent a sharp break with modernity, but rather an intensification of modernist tendencies. The current era, whether it is described as late capitalism, 'high modernity' or postmodernity, is characterized by economic globalization, commodification, fragmentation, superficiality, rapid change or centrifugality, all of which are based on an increasingly sophisticated use of modern technology.

Managerialism and Professionalism in the Post-Fordist Service Sector

Fordist management techniques have been applied to social workers acting as care managers in the statutory sector. These techniques have also been referred to as scientific management or 'Taylorism', discussed above, after F.W. Taylor (1947) who laid down the principles of time and motion studies. He studied the quickest, most efficient workers and then required all workers to emulate their work practices (Ritzer 1996, 150). These Fordist principles have been applied to social workers in the form of standards, competencies and routinized practices (Lymbery 1998, 863). One example is the routinization of assessment through prescriptive assessment schedules. (See Davies 1986, 274 for an example of a community care interviewing schedule.) The purchaser/provider split mimics the division of labour found in the factory labour processes. It fragments the process of service provision, it is an attempt to control the profession, and it contributes to de-professionalization (Dominelli 1996, Dominelli and Hoogvelt 1996, Sheppard 1995).

NPM is 'new contractualism' (Lane 2000, 14) wherein measurement of input and output is central. Managers have been considered key elements in the enforcement of contracts. The intensification of Fordist managerialistic practices in post-Fordist organizations creates stress for professionals working in these organizations. While this business-like approach may be appropriate in some sectors of government activity, it may not be appropriate to all sectors. '... the soft sector part of the public sector has certain special qualities that any coordination mechanism must take into account. Thus the supply of goods and services within ... social care involves (1) a strong dose of professionalism; (2) a considerable consideration of rights or entitlements; (3) a mixture of quantity and quality that often defies definition; and (4) an urgency in need. These characteristics do not make the application of NPM tools run smoothly in the organisations of the soft sector, one may predict' (Lane 2000, 158). Social Services are part of the 'soft sector' and these comments have a high degree of relevance for social workers working as care managers. Professionals have a distinct ethos and are responsible not only for service provision, but 'they are also watching over the implementation of universal values transcending the concerns of government' (Lane 2000, 14). Thus in the soft sectors, such as social care, where quality as well as quantity are at issue and professionals are protecting professional values that transcend the concerns of government, it may be expected that the relationship between managers and professionals will involve a degree of conflict.

Managerialism is important both to immediate effects of care management and to the longer-term issue of professional identity and status of social work (Exworthy and Halford 1999, Spratt 1999). The concepts of Fordism and post-Fordism contribute to an understanding of the way in which managers have gained power over professionals working in organizations, calling into question professional knowledge, consistent with the postmodern suspicion of the 'expert'.

Managerialism is central to the political commitment to introduce markets and a mixed economy of care (Clarke et al., 1995, Pollitt 1993) and is associated with maximization of efficiency and profit. Managerialism or 'the right to manage' has assumed growing influence in this new discourse of care management (Clarke et al., 1995). The Taylorist or managerialistic search for the greatest efficiency and the highest productivity with an emphasis on standards, competencies and routinized practices, has been imposed on social workers practising as care managers. Managers can be seen as the mediators between expert knowledge and the allocation of resources in the reconstruction of social workers as care managers (Parton 1994, 26).

Managerialism has been associated with the deskilling of social workers and the perception among social workers that the realm within which they can exercise professional discretion has been reduced. 'Professionals are sliding down the slope of deskilling, degradation and Taylorism' (Murphy 1990, 72). For example, computerized protocols have been used to standardize work and to standardize relations with service users in social work.

The splitting or fragmenting of the purchaser/provider roles has been described as analogous to the manufacturing industry where progress was achieved by dividing work into its component parts (Wilson 1993, 121) or what is referred to as 'piece work'. However, in the social services as in the manufacturing industry, workers find that the organization of work which results in a completed outcome more satisfactory than 'piece work'. Pollitt makes the link between Taylorism, Frederic Taylor's preoccupation with bureaucratic control procedures through the scientific measurement of working practices, and 'the recent epidemic of electronically-mediated public-service systems of performance indicators, individual performance reviews and merit pay' (Pollitt 1993, 16). Professionals resist these electronic systems because either they do not understand them, they think these systems will reduce their traditional freedoms, or they fear that they will be replaced by technology and lose their jobs. These fears can 'result in an oppositional culture whereby staff adopt strategies of resistance' to the 'privileged' status of performance indicators (Jacobs and Manzi 2000, 85).

Fordism, Managerialism, Theory X and Theory Y

Modernity, Fordism and managerialism are clearly related, although a direct link between them does not seem to have been made in management literature. Managerialistic practices could be viewed as being consistent with Theory X, from the literature on management (Sheldrake 1996, Coulshed and Mullender 2001). The basic assumption of Theory X is that workers do not want to work and that the role of the manager is to maximize efficiency and to structure the working environment to extract the maximum labour from workers (McGregor 1985, Sheldrake 1996; Coulshed and Mullender 2001, 39). A belief that workers resist work and that managers must be authoritarian in order to ensure that employers produce as much work as possible is consistent with Fordist managerialism and Theory X from management theory.

Fordist Theory X management techniques such as time and motion studies, performance targets and performance indicators, historically used in factory settings, are increasingly used to manage care managers. One of the elements of post-Fordist working arrangements is the need for workers to work harder and be more productive (Symonds and Kelly 1998). Applied to caring services, this management approach can result in a superficial approach to work. Superficiality (Jameson 1984b, 66) has been described by Jameson as being a feature of what he called late capitalism. The links between managerialism and Theory X seem relatively clear.

In contrast to Theory X, 'Theory Y' assumes that workers have an inherent desire for self-actualization through their work. Theory Y takes the view that the best way to motivate workers is to match the goals of the individual worker with the goals of the organization. The basic assumptions of a Theory Y approach to management are that work is central to a person's identity, people want to work and that work is part of self-actualization, related to Maslow's hierarchy of need, the pinnacle of which is self-actualization (McGregor 1985, Sheldrake 1996, Coulshed 2001, 39). From a Theory Y perspective, work is self-actualizing and contributes to personal worth. If the individual worker is striving for the same goals that the organization is striving for, then the manager does not have to impose artificial means of extracting the maximum labour from the worker.

The links between postmodernity, post-Fordism and a more 'person centred' Theory Y non-managerialistic approach are less clear. Paradoxically, the postmodern post-Fordist welfare state is marked by Fordist managerialistic Theory X management techniques rather than what should logically be postmodern Theory Y management techniques. Post-Fordist outcomes require an exaggeration of Theory X management rather than what should logically be Theory Y management. However, a Theory Y management approach would be difficult to maintain in the managerialistic culture of SSDs. The reason Theory Y management can be difficult to maintain in SSDs is that professional goals are sometimes divergent from organizational goals. It would therefore be difficult to exercise the Theory Y precept of linking the goals of the individual professional social worker with the goals of the SSD organization because the imposition of factory-oriented productivity is not consistent with professional values. The purchaser/provider split, which mimics the division of functions found in factory 'piece work' and values output, is at odds with professional emphasis on process and input. Therefore, Theory Y management would be difficult to maintain in the management of social workers working as care managers.

Care management has developed within increasingly Fordist bureaucratic systems with stricter lines of accountability and rational structures. '... Social work managerial ideas have been absorbed from the new managerialism of market economies. Current managerial practices have clear linear models of causation and use crude target setting as the basis of action. The focus is on key performance indicators, national standards and quality measures. The approach to achieving these various targets is usually based on ever more prescriptive procedures and guidelines' (Bilson and Ross 1999, 115). Social work, in the form of care management, has adapted to the current late capitalist context of practice.

An important feature of bureaucracies, modernity and new managerialism is the desire to exercise control over uncertainty. The procedures and policies that direct people within bureaucracies are well intentioned. They contribute to surveillance of workers. However, procedures can reduce discretion and creativity and make the people who enact the procedures feel that they are being directed by factors other than their knowledge and skills. Within modernity, predictability, certainty and minimization of risk are aspired to. One way to increase control and reduce uncertainty is to exercise increased surveillance over the activities of staff. Ritzer, drawing on the theories of Max Weber, identified control and predictability as being important attributes of bureaucracies. Ritzer has illustrated this phenomenon in the rise of McDonaldization, which is Fordism applied to the services sector. Managerialism brings control over uncertainty, but in doing so, it has a tendency to suppress creativity and the use of individual discretion. Weber's 'iron cage' of bureaucracy has become the 'velvet cage' of McDonaldization (Ritzer 1996, 177). The consequences of suppressing the creativity of factory workers can perhaps be justified, but suppressing the creativity of professionals could have negative consequences for the service user. Social workers need to be creative in their work with service users. The issue arises as to whether casework can be practised within managerialized care-management roles, or whether it is a 'secret occupation' within care management (Postle 2001).

Conclusion

Social theory has been discussed in order to lay the conceptual groundwork for an understanding of the broad features of contemporary society that have led to care management. Care management has been discussed in terms of material postmodernity and the tendency to commodify care. A discussion of modernity and postmodernity has put care management in the anomalous position of being 'modern', that is, rational, predictable, calculable, standardized, in a postmodern era characterized by fragmentation, diversity and difference. McDonaldization is discussed as a modern phenomenon based on rational instrumentality. New Right politics and the pre-eminence of the quasi-market in social care are linked to the rise of the post-Fordist welfare state. Fordism has been linked to the material postmodernity and a New Right discourse that has placed care managers as mediators between the service user and the market. The paradox of Fordist Theory X management techniques being set in post-Fordist bureaucracies to facilitate service user choice has been explored.

Chapter 2 continues the exploration of the factors that have led to the introduction of care management. It is argued that care management will spread with the late capitalist 'commodification of everything'. The changes to social work practice brought about by the introduction of care management in the UK are analysed.

The Context of Social Change: Globalization, McDonaldization and the Introduction of Care Management

Introduction

The purpose of this chapter is to argue that as a relatively new model of service delivery, care management is an adaptation to conditions of late capitalism. It is expected that social services organisations will increasingly adopt care management as the model of choice because of the globalizing market economy. There are implications for social work wherever this model is adopted. A brief history of social service provision in the United Kingdom is presented to establish the climate that fostered the introduction of care management in the UK.

Early ideas about social work were established in England and spread throughout the English-speaking world, for example to the United States and Australia, during England's colonial expansion (de Schweinitz 1975, 113). These ideas have swirled around the globe and come back to be adapted into England's social services delivery systems. For example, care (case) management originally developed in the United States and then was adopted in the UK in 1990. It is argued that English social workers' experience with care management has relevance for social workers in other national contexts. It is hoped that this in-depth exploration of care management in the UK will facilitate discussion about how care/case management may affect social workers in other national contexts.

Social work is a consistent feature of Western democratic capitalist societies. Social work identity is tied to activity rather than a specific knowledge base. It is about getting things done for and with people. Social work activities are constructed in response to social need in local contexts (Lawrence et al., 2003), but are increasingly influenced by international conditions and events. Social work often has close ties to the state so its professional practice is tied to political shifts. These factors mean that the concept of social work is fluid and precarious.

It is argued that the care-management model of service delivery, called either care management or case management, leads to the McDonaldization of social work practice. Social workers are increasingly working in models of service provision that cast them as enablers or brokers rather than providers of services, managing the care provided by other social care professionals. 'Management of care' refers to the increasing tendency to regard the delivery of social services as a business with services regarded as commodities, objects or packages to be bought and sold. The idea of social workers 'managing care' as opposed to 'providing care' has only arisen in the last few decades. Two contradictory orientations now exist in social work: a professional social work practice based on relationships between worker and service user versus a contrary model of social workers as administrative care managers mediating between potential consumers and resources available for purchase. Care management with its 'domination of practice by managerial dominance and budgetary consideration' (Lavalette and Ferguson 2007, 2) is spreading as the preferred model for delivery of social services in Western industrialized countries as they strive to modernize and contain public expenditure.

The introduction of care management in the UK is discussed in terms of the people most affected by care management. Implications can be drawn for social workers in other national contexts where care management is introduced. Any change in a model of services provision will affect the people who are part of that system, including managers, providers and recipients of service. It is clear that changes in service delivery systems introduced through care management are having an effect on social workers and the service users who are the customers or consumers in this new equation of services (Ritzer 1996, 130). The 'poacher turned gamekeeper' analogy is used to convey the effect of care management on the statutory social work role in the UK.

Care Management as a Feature of Western Neo-liberal Democracies

In Western advanced capitalist countries, social work has become a business to be based on commercial principles. Harris (2003) explores this theme in his book *The Social Work Business*. Davis and Leonard (2004) use the phrase 'Social Work in the Corporate Era' to discuss the issue. Care management is a manifestation of social work in the Corporate Era, which is discussed in Chapter 1 as the era of 'late capitalism' or 'high modernity'.

As capitalism and McDonaldization have expanded globally, so care management has been adopted in a number of countries of Western neo-liberal democracies. McDonaldization 'has shown every sign of being an inexorable process, sweeping through seemingly impervious institutions and regions of the world' (Ritzer 2004, 2). McDonald's is an example of the globalizing tendencies of free market principles. It is not surprising therefore that care/case management has been adopted in a number of countries. Just as McDonaldization has been evident worldwide, so care management and the managerialist underpinnings necessary to its functioning have 'risen to dominance ... in the most advanced liberal societies in the Western world, particularly North America, the United Kingdom and Australia' and to some extent Canada (Meagher and Parton 2004, 14).

This model of service delivery has been implemented in the US (McAuley and Safewright 1992, McAuley et al., 1999; Capitman 1985), the UK (Davies and Challis 1986), Canada (Davies and Leonard 2004), Australia (Meagher and Healy 2003), Italy (Bernabie et al., 1998), Hong Kong (Mackenzie et al., 1998) and the Nordic countries (Askheim 2003). The history, economy and political systems in each of these settings is different, therefore the introduction of care management will have impacted on social workers in different ways in these different contexts (Harris and McDonald 2000). Care management is often not a feature of Third World countries because their histories and cultures are different from Western industrialized countries. Either they do not have the infrastructure to support care management as a feature of their statutory social services systems, which are often in their infancy, or it may be a result of political issues as in southern European welfare states (Ferrera 1996, Ferrera 1998).

Social workers working in state-run bureaucracies have been subject to the McDonaldization of social services through New Public Management (NPM) applied to public sector workers. 'Central to implementing this process of reappraisal and reform is managerialism, or NPM, which, it has been argued, is a European (George 1998, 28–9) and a worldwide phenomenon (Hood 1991a in Harris 2003, 33). Managerialism involves the monitoring, assessing and regulating of both workers and organizations for the purpose of maximizing market forces (Harris 2003) and fitting social work into this current corporate model (Davies and Leonard 2004). Taken together, these developments have had a significant impact on the delivery of social work services through the introduction of care management.

Social workers are employed mainly in the social welfare bureaucracies of Western countries. The study of bureaucracies and rationalization of services is most closely associated with Max Weber (1864–1920). George Ritzer has extended Weber's principles by developing the concept of McDonaldization, which is based on modern bureaucratic principles, but is an exaggeration, intensification or refinement of these principles applied to service sector organizations. The McDonaldization thesis therefore contributes to an understanding of the changing social services bureaucracies within which social workers function.

A country's concept of need is a reflection of its historical and cultural 'interpretations of need' (Haney 2002, 7), and social work is a reflection of its historical, political, economic and cultural context (Lawrence et al., 2003). Care management is part of a trend toward individualism and the reduction of government commitment to public services, parallel trends in the delivery of social services developed during the Reagan/Thatcher era. Both political leaders were neo-conservatives who believed in a minimal role for the state. Case management developed in the US during the 1970s and 1980s, corresponding with Reagan's tenure as Governor of California from 1967 to 1975 and his Presidency between 1981 and 1989 (Austin 1992, 61). Care management developed under Thatcher in the UK in the late 1980s and early 1990s. Reagan and Thatcher were simultaneously influenced by the globalization of capital and contributed to the globalization of capital. Both the US and UK welfare systems reflected these trends.

It is interesting to compare the histories of the social services delivery systems in the US and the UK with regard to the impact of care management in these two countries. Although the US and UK are both English-speaking Western democracies, they of course have different histories. They have come to care management/managed care from different points. Traditionally, the US and UK welfare systems were both mainly residualized services until World War II, one exception being Roosevelt's New Deal during the 1930s depression in the US (Leuchtenburg 1963). After World War II, UK social policy diverged from US social policy when it introduced a higher level of universal benefits, most notably the National Health Service (NHS). In Britain, this period is referred to as the 'post-War Welfare State' or the Keynesian

Welfare State. It can be seen as an aberration from the historical Poor Law norm of means-tested, residualized, stigmatized service delivery. This stands in contrast to policies in the US, where there has never been a sustained commitment to universal social services. Government-provided services would have been contrary to the ethos of rugged individualism and survival of the fittest, or what could be called the Frank Sinatra 'I did it my way' approach to welfare.

The US and the UK have arrived at care management from different routes. This has made a difference in impact of care management in these two settings. In the UK, there was, at least officially, a fifty-year suspension of the Poor Laws. 'Homes fit for heroes' was a term used in the UK after World War I to characterize government responsibility for building low rent housing for returning soldiers and their families (Thane 1982, 145), but it also presaged the emerging central government policy of providing social security to citizens in the 1940s. The Beveridge Report (Beveridge 1942) set out to destroy the 'five giants', social problems related to unemployment, disease, squalor, ignorance, idleness and want. This typifies the idea that modern knowledge could be used to solve social problems. A factor that may have led to greater social provision for citizens in the UK than the US was the proximity of the Russian Revolution to England. The threat of the Russian Revolution was physically closer to the UK than it was to the United States, and the monarchs of the UK and Russia were related to each other. Therefore, the UK may have felt greater urgency about inoculating its citizens against the threat of communism or pre-empting the allure of communism by providing more social security than did their more distant US cousins.

Interestingly, Beveridge did not think that social workers would be needed in the UK after the introduction of the post-World War II Welfare State. This was similar to the view in communist countries, that is, that socialism would eliminate the need for social workers. However, it soon became apparent that the bureaucracy associated with the delivery of welfare services, even at this early stage of development, was so complicated that some people needed help to negotiate the systems set up to meet their needs. The election of Margaret Thatcher in 1979 marked a return to the norm of residualized social services policy in the UK similar to those in the US with her philosophy of individualism, referred to at the time as 'greed is good' and her 'no such thing as society' ethos (Thatcher 1987).

The voluntary sector in the UK and US were different prior to the introduction of care management. The introduction of care management was a bigger shock in the UK than in the US. The 'cradle to grave' security that was established as the norm for UK citizens who grew up in the post-World War II era of social policy was suddenly reduced. For example, older people who thought that they would be looked after for their whole lives suddenly found that they had to sell their homes to pay for their own residential care. The introduction of managed care or case management in the US would probably have seemed more an extension of existing principles than the unexpected reversal of policy experienced in the UK. The US has maintained its voluntary sector throughout its history because government-provided programmes never existed on the scale that they did in the UK. This is in contrast to the UK where the voluntary sector experienced a decline after World War II because the state took an increased role in the services. Because the voluntary sector was in decline prior to the introduction of care management in the early 1990s, the voluntary sector had to be encouraged, expanded, strengthened and reoriented to play a part in 'care in the community' policies and care managed services.

The Context of Changes Affecting Social Work in the UK

Care management was implemented in the UK by the passage of the NHS and Community Care Act (NHSCCA) (1990) and has brought 'radical changes' (Braye and Preston-Shoot 2003, 1) to social work practice. Care management is a process involving assessment of individual service-user need, purchase of services to meet identified need and review of the delivery of those services. Although care management can be undertaken by any individual (Cheetham 1993, 157, Sheppard 1995, 4), SSDs are the lead agencies in its implementation (Griffiths 1988, Sec. 1.3) and statutory social workers in SSDs have been given the main responsibility for care management. The intention of the care-management model of service delivery was to meet individual need, provide services in the community (more specifically, in a service user's own home and the surrounding community rather than in large permanent institutions), provide choice in a mixed economy of care and promote cost reduction through 'value for money' measures (Clarke et al., 2000, 260). Some feel that these changes brought about the virtual abandonment of the post-World War II Seebohm model of service delivery characterized by broadly based services available to the community and the introduction of a narrowed service model, with services available only to the most vulnerable and dependent members of society (Alaszewski 1995, 69). The generic casework model of intervention was fragmented with the introduction of the purchaser/provider split, which was intended to promote efficiency by developing a Fordist division of labour. The care manager became a purchaser, responsible for the assessment of need and the management of scarce resources, attempting to meet needs while keeping costs within available budgets.

The introduction of care management has been described as the greatest challenge to social work in the last twenty years (Sheppard 1995) and has created a number of tensions for social workers practising as care managers. An important element of these changes has been the closer involvement of team managers in the day-to-day activities of social workers. The level of professional discretion, which was acceptable during the pre-Griffiths SSD practice of social work, has been greatly reduced. A social worker's accountability has become more closely tied to the organization, which has created conflicts between the demands of the employer and good professional practice. While some regard bureaucratization and professionalization in the same way (Meagher and Parton 2004, 13), it is argued here that professionalization can counter the demands of bureaucratization. With the introduction of registration of social workers in the UK in April 2005, this accountability to the organization must now be balanced against accountability to the professional registering body. If a social worker is asked to do something that is contrary to the requirements of their professional association, they will have to weigh this against the requirement of their professional organization because if they do not, they could lose their professional registration, which would be the end of their professional career.

Care management is regarded by some social work practitioners as a deskilled version of social work (Carey 2007). Because anybody can act as a care manager, that is, friend, family neighbour, other professional, service user themselves or their carer, no professional training is required to be a care manager. Further, the opportunity to practise casework skills has been limited by the fragmented purchaser role. Social workers acting as care managers have skills that are not required within the care-management role. They are expected to assess need and purchase provision of services, but they are not intended to be involved in the provision of direct services. Therefore, one of the hallmarks of casework, an ongoing professional casework relationship with service users, is not possible for care managers. Without an ongoing professional relationship with service users, the care manager role is perceived as a superficial role by some social workers.

Cost has become paramount in the provision of services. This is part of a general trend toward commodification (Sarap 1993, 161, Harlow 2003, 30), which can be regarded as the increasing tendency to buy and sell services which were previously not within the ambit of the market. The consumption of these services has become increasingly important in society, contributing to a purer form of capitalism (Dickens and Fontana 1994, 4). Commodification is a characteristic of the current era, which can usefully be regarded as high modernity or late capitalism (Jameson 1984b).

For example, with regard to cost, a main aim of the NHSCCA was to eliminate the 'perverse' incentive created by state funding of nursing home care. The UK government at national level was saying 'that it wanted old people to stay at home for as long as possible because that was the most cost-effective and desirable thing to do, but at the same time it was pushing large sums of public money into expensive residential and nursing home care' (Lewis and Glennerster 1996, 5). In one giant policy initiative, government therefore withdrew state funding of nursing home care and privatized nursing home care. The privatization of caring services made them a purchasable or 'calculable' (Ritzer 1996, 9) commodity. However, the intensification of calculability and commodification as factors in the provision of care may have introduced another perverse incentive: the perverse incentive of profit-making in service provision. It is possible that profit is a perverse incentive in social care because profit can only be produced by maximizing income, that is, charging the highest possible prices, minimizing costs by paying low wages to care employees and keeping operating costs low, all of which tendencies could have a perverse effect on the quality of care provided.

An example of what was considered the 'perverse' effect of money on caring is the British policy of encouraging voluntary blood donations rather than paying donators for their blood (Titmuss 1971). Titmuss argued against the commodification, that is, the buying and selling, of blood. It was argued that if the health service paid for blood donations, it set up a dynamic which would encourage the poorest and most 'at risk' people to offer their blood in exchange for payment, that is, drug addicts and alcoholics. It was argued that where blood was offered as a 'gift' the quality of the blood would be better. The giving rather than selling of blood fostered social altruism; the fabric of society would be stronger because caring would not depend on a cash transaction.

Social workers may object to the commodification of caring services, however, it must be recognized that social work itself is a part of the commodification of caring. In a traditional pre-industrial society, caring is an unpaid activity carried out by the family or the church (Macarov 1995). In the modern era, marked by the industrial revolution, social work emerged as a secular commodification of caring in that individuals were paid to care for 'strangers' (Clarke 1993, 5). In this current era of late capitalism (Jameson 1984b), commodification of caring has been extended to include the sale and purchase of caring services. Social workers were not prepared for their role in this new more advanced level of the commodification of caring. The costing of services related to economic efficiency and the oversight of other professional inputs into the care of vulnerable service users were new experiences for social workers. Tensions have arisen between the empowerment of service users to live independently in the community and the new emphasis on cost containment.

Historically, the social work role has been ambiguous (Howe 1986, 160, Clarke 1993, 20), mediating between various configurations of power in society as these changed over time. The introduction of care management has contributed to the ambiguity of the social work role. Is care management social work, or is it not social work? If social workers do not regard care management as 'real' social work, will they avoid SSD care-management work and prefer to work in the provider sector where they can practise in a more traditional casework role? It is argued that care management has fundamentally altered social work as practised in SSDs through fragmentation of the generic casework role, the increasing commodification of services and increased managerial surveillance of social work activities.

Social work has only recently achieved the status of a registered profession in Britain. Its bureau-professional or semi-professional status was enhanced by the incorporation of social services into the bureaucracies of the welfare state after the report of the Seebohm Committee (1968). The registration of social workers was proposed in 1998 (Modernizing Social Services 1998, 89) and implemented in 2005. Registration has had the effect of establishing the title 'social worker' as a protected title and therefore is having an impact upon the identity of social workers and their employment opportunities within the new 'mixed economy of care'. With registration and a protected title, social workers' identity may increasingly come to be established by registration rather than by employment in a social work post.

The Main Actors in UK Care Management

Language and terminology are important because words represent and establish the existence and meaning of phenomenon (Bartens 1995, 7, Rosenau 1992, 92). Therefore terms used in the UK to describe these three groups will be defined. The three main groups of people directly affected by these changes in the UK have been service users, social workers and social work managers. The term 'service user' refers to individuals who are recipients of SSD services in this study; the term does not include informal carers, although informal carers have been affected by the introduction of care management. Terms used to describe recipients of care manager services tend to have ideological connotations. For example, the term 'client' traditionally used by social workers connotes a power relationship with service users in which the social worker is the expert in relation to vulnerable service users and the client is the 'object' of social work intervention (Payne 1995, xi). The term 'customer' has been introduced through quasi-market reforms in the context of NPM, which is the application of management techniques developed in industry to the public sector, focusing on efficiency and productivity, and the 'primacy of market-based coordination' (Walsh 1995, xiv). In this climate, service users are constructed as consumers in the mixed economy of care. However, the term 'customer' excludes those who cannot purchase, whether with their own money or through state-provided benefits, and is therefore a term that excludes rather than includes, consistent with the targeted and selective nature of care management. While there are some who argue that the term 'citizen' should be used (Adams 1996a) it is not commonly used in referring to recipients of care management services arguably because it connotes political rights which are not easily applicable in a market oriented and selective welfare model. Although partnership is advocated within community care policies, the term 'partner' is not generally used to refer to recipients of SSD services. Payne (1995, xv) refers to those who 'are genuinely receiving services' as 'users'. However, the term 'user' will not be employed in this study because it has connotations of taking from society without giving anything back and also because 'user' is sometimes used as a shortened term for 'drug user'. The term 'service user' will be employed in this study because it is the most neutral term available.

The terms to describe the social work role vary with the time and place where it is practised. Social work is shaped by the context within which it operates. 'Social work has no essential nature' and is therefore relative to the context in which it is practised (Howe 1986, 160). It is a social construction (Burr 1995, Payne 1997, 15). Social work practice is copied endlessly from one setting to another, each time changing slightly to fit its new context. It does not exist as an objective or tangible reality. Social work adapts itself to whatever situation it is applied to and its activities can be interpreted from a plurality of perspectives. It is therefore a complex phenomenon to represent or identify with a single term.

Social work, to use a postmodern term, is a 'simulacrum', a simulation or a copy of a copy for which the original has disappeared (Baudrillard 1983). Care management is a copy of social work, and social work is a copy of 'real' care, that is, care by a person or organization that has a personal interest in the welfare of the person being looked after. Care management is far removed from the feminist ethics of care which is based on the mother-child relationship which emphasizes sacrificing one's self for the good of the other and a concern for the whole person (McAuley et al., 1999, 6). Care management is an example of the 'real' no longer being a reflection of something else that was considered real; instead, it is a copy that 'feeds off itself till the point of emaciation' (Baudrillard 1983, 144). Care management could be regarded a simulacrum of care, an 'emaciated' or 'thin' form of caring without very much reference to 'real' care.

But a simulacrum is more than that. A simulacrum is a model that creates a reality, for which there is no 'real' original (Baudrillard 1983, 3). Care management could be considered a model of caring for which no original exists at all. Care management is a model of service that 'substitutes signs of the real for the real itself'

(Baudrillard 1983, 4). It is full of ironies, inconsistencies and unintended effects. Care management has been proposed as a way of caring for the most vulnerable. But whether it is real care or not is debatable as it bears little resemblance to care by families and communities with a shared identity. However, it is risky to criticize existing policies for not delivering 'real' care because whether care management is 'real' care or not, it is all we have; it would be difficult to replace. It would be almost impossible to return to anything resembling 'real' care as we think of it in traditional communities. 'It is dangerous to unmask images, since they dissimulate the fact that there is nothing behind them' (Baudrillard 1983, 9). There is nothing behind care management, in the same way that there is nothing behind much political rhetoric. However, whether impersonal, urban, industrialized Western societies could return to anything resembling 'real care' is debatable.

The common terms used to describe people who practise social work are 'social worker' and 'caseworker'. When the activities of social work change, should the name that it calls itself change? If social work in SSDs after the NHSCCA is called 'care management', what should social work before the NHSCCA be called? It would be possible to call social work in SSDs before the introduction of the NHSCCA 'casework', 'traditional social work', 'Seebohm social work' or 'pre-Griffiths' social work. For the sake of uniformity, social work in SSDs before the NHSCCA will be referred to as 'casework'. Social workers who practise care management in SSDs after the NHSCCA will be referred to as 'care managers'.

The role of the care manager is to assess a service user's need as defined by agency criteria, to recommend purchase of services and to review the provision of these services in assessment teams serving older adults, disabled adults and children. Care managers can only recommend purchases to their team manager for authorization, as they do not hold their own budgets. The services recommended for purchase are called 'packages of care' because services can be drawn from a range of sources in the public and private sector, referred to as the 'mixed economy' of care. Care managers are expected to reviews care packages periodically to determine whether the services being delivered to service users are meeting the needs that were initially identified. Services are subject to being withdrawn if the eligibility criteria is revised upward and the service user is no longer entitled to the service (Neate 1996).

The term 'team manager' is used to describe the direct line manager of a team of care managers. Team managers in this study had all worked previously as social workers, generally rising through the ranks of SSD bureaucracy to arrive at a management position. Therefore, they would have had experience both of social work practice in Seebohm SSDs and the implementation of care-management procedures. Team managers of assessment teams were responsible for ensuring that care managers followed prescribed procedures in the assessment of service user need. Team managers were responsible for budgets and had the authority to give or withhold approval of the purchase of services recommended by care managers.

The last twenty years have witnessed significant changes in the delivery of social services. The welfare service delivery model has been reorganized from a post-War redistributive model to a quasi-market model intended to conserve scarce resources, promote 'value for money' and thus to enhance Britain's ability to compete economically in the international marketplace. The focus of care provision has continued to move from large remote institutions to small local community-based initiatives. Changes in the welfare state and in community care policies have resulted in changed SSD social work practice. Changes in these three areas will therefore be addressed: firstly, the welfare state; secondly, community care policies, and thirdly, social work role and practice.

Changes in the UK Welfare State – Nation State to Quasi-market State

Changes in the role of social workers, from caseworker to care manager did not arise in a vacuum. These changes are linked to the changes in the wider service delivery system and indeed to broader issues such as the decline of the nation state (Rhodes 1997, Brown and Lauder 2001, 200) and the rise of the quasi-market state. The political and economic context of changes from the post-World War II Keynesian welfare state to the introduction of New Right quasi-markets of care will be reviewed with the implications for social workers and the delivery of social services.

The experience of World War II led to 'expectations of a better and more just society with welfare provision for all' (Adams and Shardlow 2000, 121). One of the effects of World War II was to create a sense of social solidarity marked by a willingness to accept collective state intervention (Thane 1982, 223) and a collectivization of responsibility for society's most vulnerable members (Adams and Shardlow 2000, 119). The report prepared by Beveridge (1942) proposed the creation of a collectivist state system of welfare based on social insurance (Adams and Shardlow 2000, 121). Social workers did not have a defined role in the early post-War welfare arrangements (Thane 1987, 14). It was assumed that people preferred programmes based on their contributions rather than those based on distinctions between the deserving and the undeserving poor (Adams 1996a, 4), which characterized previous systems of service delivery. A social welfare system based on contributory principles made social workers marginal to the operation of that system until the late 1960s with the report of the Seebohm Committee (1968) and the subsequent Local Authority Social Services Act (LASSA) (1970).

Beveridge's prediction that social workers would not be necessary after the introduction of his welfare measures was consistent with his view that the National Health Service would wither away once health needs were met. Clearly this did not happen. The numbers of social workers needed grew year after year. Richard Titmuss, the well-known British social policy guru observed in 1965 that whenever a social problem was identified there was a call for more social workers (Titmuss 1965, 85).

In post-War Britain, central government actively intervened in areas that were previously left to market forces. Keynesian economic policies were adopted to create full employment. These policies involved government in the management of the economy and were significant because they involved a 'Middle Way' between Capitalism and Socialism, or 'planned capitalism' which was intended to avoid the excesses of inflation and depression or 'boom and bust' economic cycles (Cutler and Waine 1994, 8). The policies of the then Labour party received cross party support, referred to as the 'welfare consensus' or 'Butskellism' (Adams and Shardlow 2000, 122). This consensus continued until the mid-1970s.

Policies such as full employment depended on the existence of a closed, bounded economy wherein the national government had control over economic factors. The state institutions were the chief complement to market forces in the post-War mixed economy (Jessop 1994). '… Professionally delivered forms of quasi-universal' services (Williams et al., 1999, 3) were accepted. A 'growth in citizenship' was associated with state intervention to provide social services as a right (Thane 1982, 290).

In the late 1960s and early 1970s, the British economic situation changed. The oil crisis of 1973 and 1979 brought a downturn in government revenue, making it increasingly difficult to fund public services (Ellison and Pierson 1998, 2). The economy was in such a crisis in the mid-1970s that the government was required to appeal for funds from the International Monetary Fund (IMF) to avoid bankruptcy (Harris and McDonald 2000, 56). The IMF granted Britain financial assistance, but imposed conditions, one of which was that Britain should reduce the size of its welfare state. This had implications for social workers who were just beginning to establish themselves in the bureaucracies of the welfare state after the passage of the Local Authority Social Services Act (LASSA) (1970).

The condition that Britain should reduce the size of its welfare state was significant because it is an example of the decline of the nation state (Rhodes 1997), economic globalization (Carter 1998, 8), and the nation's loss of absolute control over its internal affairs. Internal spending decisions became subordinate to 'the fragmented demand structure of the international economic system' (O'Brien and Penna 1998, 153). In contrast to the era of political consensus wherein economic policies were shaped by social policies, social policy became subordinated to economic policy.

Parallel with these events was the rise of the New Right and the end of the welfare consensus. New Right ideology promoted free market capitalism, privatization of previously government-provided services, minimal taxation, individualism and the minimal state (Green 1988). This has also been referred to as 'a welfare regime … tightly controlled by the centralized state, but organizationally dispersed through the creation of the three "Ms" – markets, managers and mixed economies' (Williams et al., 1999, 3). The decline of the nation state has been accompanied by the rise of quasi-market initiatives that would not have been acceptable during the post-War collectivist welfare state in which some services were available as a right based on citizenship (Walsh 1995, 59). Current trends are moving toward a situation wherein 'Unlike the nation state, the market state will not see itself as more than a minimal provider or redistributor; it will simply try to maximise the choices available to individuals' (Bobbitt 2003), an apt description of care management.

With the election of the Thatcher Conservative government in 1979, New Right ideologies began to inform government policy on social welfare. Thatcher's ideologies would be recognizable to Americans as the philosophy of rugged individualism and self reliance and a denial of the need for a degree of collective security or community cohesion. Residualized social services policies were reactivated, drawing the UK back to its Poor Law roots and bringing it in line with policies in the US. However, there was resistance to New Right policies in the UK (Cutler and Waine 1994, 24). It took six years, from its election in 1979 to 1985, for the government to produce proposals for reform (Johnson 1995, 35). Even then, 'The Thatcher government's proposals for reform in its 1985 White Paper were essentially in the modified Beveridge tradition' (Green 1988, 173). Rather than a completely free-market approach, which would have been difficult to implement because of support for the existing welfare arrangements, a 'mixed economy' approach was advocated to take advantage of private enterprise principles such as efficiency and competition (Sheppard 1995, 10) without abandoning altogether the collectivist principles and the involvement of government in the delivery of social services that marked the post-War welfare state.

New Right ideology promoted market-led processes to re-structure the public sector. It involved privatization and the imposition of commercial criteria in the residualized state sector. This role of the state was to regulate the activities of service providers in a mixed market of care, not to provide services.

British politicians introduced the NPM model of public administration with the emphasis on business contracts and efficiency (Lane 2000) and managerialism. The five main beliefs underpinning managerialism identified by Pollitt (1993, 2) are: that economically defined productivity will increase social progress; that productivity increases will come from ever-more sophisticated technologies; that the application of technologies can only be achieved with a disciplined labour force in accordance with the productivity ideal; that management is a separate and distinct organizational function and plays a crucial role in planning, implementing and measuring the necessary improvements to productivity; and that to perform this crucial role, managers must be granted reasonable room to manoeuvre, in other words, that managers must have the 'right to manage'.

NPM replaced post-War public administration with 'a new set of practices and values, based upon a new language of welfare delivery which emphasises efficiency and value for money, competition and markets, consumerism and customer care' (Butcher 1995, 161). NPM is also marked by the separation of purchaser and provider, contractual relationships, competition and 'attention to outputs and performance rather than inputs' (Clarke et al., 2000, 6). In this description of NPM, it can be seen that private sector market values have been applied to the management of the public sector. NPM has implications for the relationship between managers and professionals in public sector social services. Managers' criteria for successful management are measurable performance and outputs. Professionals have traditionally been oriented to inputs, that is, to the process of working with people guided by their knowledge claims and values. In this situation, conflict can be engendered between managers who value output and professionals who value input.

The welfare state has been considerably refigured with the New Right abandonment of the post-War collectivist ethos and the introduction of market forces into the provision of social services. A further element of New Right thinking that was consistent with this shift in policy was the hostility to 'producer groups' or professionals (Cutler and Waine 1994, 14). In the post-War collectivist welfare state, forms of authority were institutionalised. There was increasing use of social workers within the bureaucracy of the welfare state (Parry et al., 1979). In the 1960s and 1970s, every time a social problem was identified, there was a call for more social workers (Titmuss 1965, 85). In the provision of collectivized services, government depended upon professionals such as doctors, teachers and social workers to deliver the services, resulting in considerable power for these professionals. In order to curb this power and consistent with their preferred market model of effectiveness, efficiency and economy, the Thatcher government stressed the importance of performance and the role of managers in ensuring performance. Managers assumed a significant role in introducing market efficiency in service delivery and curbing the power of professionals.

In practice, the New Right welfare state involved the withdrawal of government from direct provision of services, value for money, a mixed economy of welfare and increasingly centralized regulation of service provision with the state as regulator of services rather than the provider of services. While the state has retained some responsibility for management of social services, non-state providers have been encouraged in a quasi-market of care. Care management is a prime example of this approach to the delivery of social care. The role of care managers in bringing together the disparate sources of care to meet individual need has been central to the implementation of quasi-market approaches to care.

Changes in the Location of Care in the UK – Institutional Care to Community Care

The three historic aims of Community Care in the UK were firstly, deinstitutionalization or the discharge of mentally ill people and people with learning difficulties from long stay hospitals and the avoidance of further admissions to such facilities; secondly, to promote a mixed economy of care and the rationalization of social services, social security and health care systems to avoid the perverse incentives of the 1980s, wherein there was an incentive for SSDs to pass the expense of residential care to central government; and thirdly, the creation of a form of care in which people needing long-term care could gain flexibility, independence and support while living in their own homes in the community (Payne 1995, 50).

The concept of community care had been widely accepted in the United Kingdom since the 1950s (Payne 1995, 32). The pattern of institutional care set up during the Poor Law was criticized as dehumanizing and costly. The Seebohm Report (1968) and the report of the Barclay Committee (1982) each represented efforts to enhance care provision in the community within their respective political and economic climates. However, finding a mechanism to fund services in the community was not straightforward (Johnson 1995, 26, Walsh 1995, 63, Baldwin 2000, 22).

With Seebohm, the intention was to provide services to all those who were living in the community (Harris 2003, 14), but if there were not facilities to meet an individual's needs in the community, then residential care, hospitalization or institutionalization were acceptable options. With Care in the Community policies, institutional options were narrowed. However, with larger numbers of people being cared for in the community, only the neediest could be served. There was a transition from Seebohm, a broadly based service available to the community, to Griffiths, a more targeted service available only to the most vulnerable and dependent members of society (Exworthy and Halford 1999).

The Thatcher government's Care in the Community policies were combined with reform of welfare service delivery to contain cost by closing large institutions, encouraging private provision of care and curbing the power of professionals. The Griffiths Report introduced the purchaser/provider split, separated the purchasing function from the provision of services, and introduced the care manager as the purchaser. The role of the Griffiths social worker was fragmented. The decision about what services were needed was separated from the provision of services. This role was marked by the specific intention to meet identified needs of individuals in community settings within specified budgets. Thus the management of scarce resources was central to this role.

In order for formerly institutionalized people to be cared for in community settings and to prevent further admissions to institutional care, community-based services had to be developed and put into place. SSDs were required to provide formal Community Care Plans to identify how they were meeting the needs of people in their communities (NHSCCA 1990, 55). It was important that a system of service delivery be designed that would meet needs in the community in a way that was consistent with the New Right market-led ideological imperatives.

Care in the community was expected to cost the government less than care in large institutions for three reasons: The people cared for would be more independent. The overhead expenses of large institutions would be removed. Non-paid personal help by family and friends could be utilized (Payne 1986, 13). One problem with this approach was that it meant placing the burden of care on the poorest and most oppressed, with 'the worst off helped by the only slightly better off' (Payne 1986, 17).

The Griffiths Report (1988) set the framework for the Conservative government's Care in the Community policies and was followed by the White Paper Caring for People (Department of Health 1989) and the NHSCCA (1990). The Griffiths Report represented the culmination of efforts to provide care in the community consistent with New Right market-led ideologies. Quasi-markets provided the mechanisms to fund provision of services in the community that had eluded earlier policy makers. Sir Roy Griffiths, in his Report to the Secretary of State for Social Services, recommended that 'Local social services authorities should, *within the resources available* (italics added) assess the community care needs of their locality ..., identify and assess individual needs, taking account of the personal preferences of users (and those of informal carers) and design packages of care best suited to enabling the consumer to live as normal a life as possible; arrange the delivery of packages of care to individuals ...; and act for these purposes as the designers, organisers and purchasers of non-health care service, and not primarily as direct providers, making the maximum possible use of voluntary private sector bodies to widen consumer choice, stimulate innovation and encourage efficiency' (Griffiths 1988, Sec. 1.3).

The question must be asked whether 'taking account of personal preferences' equates to a needs-led service. That aside, needs-led services, driven by service-user need rather than service-provider needs, were intended to both save money and respond to individual need, creating an on-going dilemma in the practice of care managers as to which element was emphasized, cost reduction or meeting need. Within the New Right pressures to reduce the cost and size of the welfare state, this tension is underscored by the phrase 'within available resources' (Griffiths 1988, Sec.

1.3). This phrase highlights the quasi-market orientation of care in the community policies. It signals the limited resources available to meet need and that need would not be met if resources were not available, a position reinforced by the Gloucester ruling in 1994 (Drakeford 1998, 225, Horder 2002, 116; Mandelstam 1999). The phrase 'packages of care' and the reference to service users as 'consumers' reinforced a commodified approach to service provision and the quasi-market orientation of the policies. The assessment process was to be carried out without regard to whether the needs could or would be met. The decision about the purchase of services to meet need was to be based on criteria of need as defined by SSD eligibility criteria and availability of funding. While assessment serves to sensitize the care manager to the wishes of the service user, the eligibility criteria are established by the SSD (Cowan 1999, 98) and are a mechanism used increasingly to ration resources (Neate, 1996). These factors place care managers in an ongoing conflict between identifying need and meeting need.

The White Paper *Caring for People* (Department of Health 1989) endorsed the recommendations for a market economy that would transform SSDs from monopoly providers of social care into purchasers of services (Adams 2002, 96). The NHSCCA embodied these principles. Care management can be seen to be part of New Right political strategy to contain costs and control social work professionals through managerialism and quasi-market contract compliance.

The mixed economy of care involved the 'large scale extension of independent provision of social care in addition to (and frequently as a replacement for) existing publicly provided social care' (Sheppard 1995, 8). The use of independent or private agencies involved using market forces to bring efficiency and lower cost. The requirement that service providers compete with one another in order to be approved by the SSD as a provider agency was a market mechanism intended to bring efficiency and cost reduction. SSDs still needed to develop, plan and devise a strategy for service provision because they were still responsible for overall provision. However, service providers would be exposed to market forces in that they would be required to bid for contracts to provide services. Theoretically, SSD in-house providers of service would be required to bid against external private, voluntary and not-for-profit agencies for contracts with their own SSD.

Adams and Shardlow (2000, 125) identify three ideas central to the drive to link the social and economic dimensions of welfare services: the production of welfare approach, the concept of managerialism, and the introduction of consumerism into the provision of social care. The production of welfare approach involves commodification of services through unit costing, and the quantification and measurement of inputs and outputs. The concept of managerialism involves rational planning, needs-led assessment based on eligibility criteria, targeting, separation of purchasing from provision of service, managerial rather than professional criteria determining priorities, new roles and skills such as commissioning, service contracts, care management, short term goals and performance indicators. Consumerism involves the commodification of care through the identification of tangible performance targets, the costing of inputs and outputs, increasingly prescribed and monitored professional activities and the imposition of a competence-based approach to national occupational standards for social workers. Market principles and a managerial emphasis on performance or 'performativity' (Rosenau 1992, xiii) have contributed to a curbing of professional discretion and hence professional power and have had a marked effect on the practice of social workers as care managers.

Changes in the UK Social Work Role – Casework to Care Management

The role of social workers in the UK is largely tied to their employment in local organizations. Politically inspired legislation has changed its role in different social and political eras. Social workers have been constructed as caseworkers in the Seebohm Report (1968), community workers in the Barclay Report (1982) and purchasers and enablers in the Griffiths Report (1988).

In order to understand the changing social work role, a perspective on the nature and history of social work is needed. A number of paradigms have been put forward to explain the general principles that underlie social work in all practice settings. Perhaps the most common is the 'care and control' dichotomy (Horner 2003, 26). Webb and Wistow suggest that much of social work can be seen to contribute to one or more of three basic functions: social control, the promotion of change and social maintenance (Webb and Wistow 1987, 18).

Payne has put forward two paradigms of social work. The first paradigm is specific to community care and describes the roles of social workers as: care management, community social work and counselling social work (Payne 1995, 2). The second paradigm takes a wider perspective of social work functions (Payne 1996) and identifies three types of social work. The first is 'reflexive-therapeutic' social work, which promotes individual growth, self-fulfilment and change. The second is 'socialist-collectivist' social work. From this perspective, social work seeks co-operation, mutual support and social change that will empower oppressed individuals. The third is 'individualistic-reformist' social work. This perspective sees social work as an aspect of welfare services to individuals in society and does not seek social change but rather seeks to accommodate a better fit between societies and individuals. Although Harlow has added a perspective that is specifically related to care-management practice, 'managerial technicist' social work (Harlow 2003, 33), care management is clearly situated in Payne's (2005, 9) individualistic-reformist model of social work practice.

Social work developed as an aspect of modernity that contributed to the effort 'to bring discipline and order, progress and improvement to the human condition' (Howe 1996, 81). In social workers' attempts to help individuals and contribute to the modern goal of social progress, elements of modern social sciences were incorporated in their training, but their work was defined more by its activities than its knowledge base (Philp 1979). From this perspective, social work is a 'moral/ practical' activity rather than a 'rational/technical' activity (Parton and O'Bryne 2000, 30) and is defined more by what it does than what it knows, a feature of social work that has been accentuated in the care manager role. Schon (1983) argues that professionalism is marked by 'reflection-in-action' rather than 'technical rationality'. Therefore, to the degree that care management is marked by technical rationality it is not a professional activity.

Philp's position is that the social work role emerged during the Industrial Revolution and developed four identifiable elements that continue to be relevant. These four elements are: firstly, mediation between those with power and those without power; secondly, the integration of marginal individuals into society; thirdly, representation, or 'speaking for', marginal individuals to those with the power to help them, which could include advocating for the individual; and lastly, surveillance or social control through 'the allocation, organisation and institutionalisation of rights' (Philp 1979, 102). Philp's model provides a useful context within which to consider the changes that have taken place in the imposition of the care manager role upon social workers in SSDs. Negotiating with service users, informal carers, public services and commercial suppliers over care for service users has become a significant role for social workers employed as care managers. Philp's model of the role of social work argues that negotiation and mediation have been a fundamental part of the social work role since its inception in the mid-1800s. From this perspective, negotiating with and for service users is not a new function for social work. It has simply been adapted to the practice of care management. Philp's model of social work is therefore useful in considering the changes that care management has introduced for social workers working within Payne's (1997, 4) individualistic-reformist welfare model of social work practice.

Social work as an identifiable modern entity arose in the England as a response to the Industrial Revolution, a period between the mid-1700s and the mid-1800s (Denny 1998, 10, Midwinter 1996, 43). The Industrial Revolution brought rapid social changes including the transition from a rural to an urban society, the breakdown of families and a growing gap between the wealthy and the poor. Social work's early role involved firstly, the re-moralizing of the poor and secondly, mediation between the rich and the poor. According to Walton (1975 in Parry et al., 1979, 24), 'The first sign of modern social work appeared during the 1850s with the introduction of paid welfare work activities associated with the church and directed mainly at the moral welfare of women and girls'. In the late 1800s, social work emerged in the social space between the rich and the poor and mediated between those with and without power, representing the poor and powerless as deserving of assistance from the rich and powerful (Philp 1979, 93).

The Society for Organizing Charitable Relief and Repressing Mendacity, also called the Charity Organization Society (COS), was founded in 1869. It represented an attempt to organize relief giving by applying the German 'casework' approach (Thane 1982, 22) to eliminate the indiscriminate administration of relief. One of the reasons for its formation was a suspicion that the poor were going to more than one charity for assistance (Parry et al., 1979). The COS established a centralized system of case files to prevent the duplication of assistance and was therefore based on surveillance of the poor.

The casework approach involved an examination of a prospective client's background. This scrutiny served the function of distinguishing the deserving from the undeserving poor and reflects a thread in social work history that constructs service users as 'generally unworthy and manipulative' (Jones 1996, 197). A moral judgement was made about service users (Payne 1999, 253). Caseworkers in this position had the power to grant services to those they considered deserving and deny services to those they felt were not deserving. The surveillance and gate-keeping role arose early in the history of social work. Once a client was accepted as deserving of assistance, the casework approach involved regular visitation and the professional normative 'use of self' (Toren 1972) in an ongoing relationship with service users that was intended to enhance client coping skills and lead to their increased self-sufficiency (Clarke 1993, 9).

Charity was underpinned by existing knowledge during the COS era. Science was called upon to help differentiate between the deserving and undeserving poor and to contribute to the efficient collection of data and in establishing personal contact (Philp 1979, 95). In 1950s and 1960s England, casework methodology began to be 'underpinned by the application of psychoanalytic theory' and provided a quasi-scientific basis for social work and its claim to professional status (Hollis 1972). Psychoanalytic theory provided social work with a 'semblance of theoretical coherence, which it has never since regained' (Jones 1996, 195).

As discussed above, even after the creation of the post-War welfare state, social workers continued to work in a variety of voluntary organizations and different local government and NHS contexts with little professional coherence (Clarke 1993, 15). Social work was a marginal and fragmented activity practised in disparate organizations with a range of client groups until after the end of World War II (Jones 1999, 37). It could be argued that this constituted a 'mixed economy of welfare' in that people in need of help could turn to family, private services, the voluntary sector or the statutory social services (Webb and Wistow 1987, 6, Adams 1996a, 24). However, in this 'mixed economy' the state was the 'defining factor' (Webb and Wistow 1987, 8) and this mixed economy existed by default rather than design. It did not represent a deliberate, coordinated effort to mix sources of assistance in the same way that the current efforts to achieve a 'mixed economy' of welfare are intended to diminish dependence on the welfare state.

The Seebohm Committee Report (1968) recommended the 'creation of unified Personal Social Services Departments (SSDs) and affirmed the claims of social work to professionalism' (Parry et al., 1979). The recommendation resulted in Local Authority Social Services Act (LASSA) (1970), which conferred upon social work a bureau-professional status and an organizational identity in the Personal Social Services. These initiatives were part of the trend toward community-based services. In the 1960s and 1970s, social workers were 'at the forefront of the movement towards "community care"' (Clarke 1993, 45). 'The Seebohm Report made the case that the most important aspect of the Personal Social Services is social care in the community, therefore implying that "field" social work [as opposed to institutional or residential social work] is the essential instrument for insuring its provision' (Adams and Shardlow 2000, 123). With 'social work's coming of age' (Howe 1986, 7) in the Seebohm era and their new found identity as bureau-professionals or semi-professionals in the structures of the welfare state, social workers developed a degree of power and discretion as 'street level bureaucrats' (Lipsky 1980) in SSDs because of their ability to interpret policy on a case-by-case basis.

Howe reported on the practice of social workers in welfare bureaucracies sixteen years after Seebohm and seven years before the implementation of care management (Howe 1986). One of the conclusions that can be drawn from Howe's research is that issues of discretion and the conflict between social workers and their managers predate the introduction of care management. Social workers reported feeling frustrated by the constraints on their practice (Howe 1986, 147) and felt 'over managed' even then, before the introduction of the more managerialistic practices associated with care management. Although the introduction of genericism was one of the purposes of the restructuring of SSDs, social workers still tended to form a 'bias within genericism' and prefer some client groups over others (Stephenson and Parsloe 1978, 172, Holme and Maizels 1978, 130 in Howe 1986, 12).

The Barclay Committee Report (1982) was an attempt to consolidate Seebohm but had little impact because by the time it was completed the post-War collectivist movement had waned. However, it was relevant to the developing community care policies in that it identified community social work as the way forward for social work (Sheppard 1995, Adams and Shardlow 2000). Social workers acquired a role in prevention and community networking in the 'patch'-based organization of the Personal Social Services (Davies 2005, 13).

Because social work's bureau-professional identity in post-Seebohm Britain was established to a considerable extent through legislation and established the framework within which social work was practised (Harris 1998, 845), it has been vulnerable to fluctuating political ideologies. '... The establishment of social services in 1971 was a Pyrrhic victory for social workers' (Henkel 2000, 126). State involvement has promoted the occupation's interests, 'But the state's very ability to define and create the work of the personal social services denies the occupation itself control over the content of its own practice' (Howe 1986, 146). Social workers have laid claim to specialist knowledge and professional expertise, but their professional identity has been established to a large extent, not by that claim, but by political fiat (Reade 1987, 126 in Clarke 1993, 15). Historically, British social workers have therefore owed their bureau professional identity to policy makers, rather than to their own esoteric knowledge base or a process of professional registration.

In the 1980s and 1990s, UK social workers were pilloried and scapegoated (Brewer and Lait 1980, Franklin and Parton 1991, Langan 1993, Langan 1998, Franklin 1999). Social workers were open to the criticism of excessive claims and limited achievements (Wilding 1982, 89). They had failed to produce knowledge or techniques that reduced social problems (Howe 1986, 147, Parton 1994, 26, Hopkins 1996, 28). The New Right believed that professionals had gained a monopoly through their place in the state bureaucracies where they controlled both the demand and the supply for welfare services, both the diagnosis of problems and the prescription of solutions (Alaszewski and Manthorpe 1990, 238). With the 1979 election of Thatcher, the Conservative government was in a position to act upon its distrust of professionals and curb their discretionary powers with new managerial controls (Hopkins 1996, 30).

Social Work Theory – From Psychodynamic Theory to Care Management

There were also trends within social work, independent of external political pressures, that made it possible to 'graft on' care management to social work practice in SSDs. Viewed historically, there is an observable shift in the use of theory and models of practice in social work, from a psychodynamic approach to other theories and models, including the Person Centred Approach (PCA), Systems Theory and the Task Centred Approach, which presaged the introduction of care management in SSDs. Each modified social work practice in SSDs and moved social workers from 'reflexive-therapeutic' roles to 'individualist-reformist' roles (Payne 1997, 4). Different theories were and still are used in different practice settings (Payne 1997, 40) or are mixed eclectically. Use of one theory did not necessarily preclude or replace another theory, but the introduction of each new approach made it easier for the idea of care management to be accepted as a model of practice in SSDs.

Psychodynamic theory, adopted in Britain in the 1950s and 1960s (Hollis 1972), placed social workers in the position of an 'expert' in relation to service users' problems. The role of the social workers was to interpret and address inner psychic issues for the benefit of the service user within a long-term therapeutic relationship. PCA (Rogers 1951) moved social workers away from their position as the 'expert' in relation to service users' problems. The PCA rejects the basic psychoanalytic principle that the past determines the present and focuses on the 'here and now'. The PCA makes the assumption that service users have within themselves the solutions to their own problems and will find these solutions as long as the social worker is genuine and congruent, conveys unconditional positive regard and is empathetic in their work with service users.

The application of ecological systems theory in the United States (Germaine 1979) had a major impact on social work in Britain in the 1970s (Payne 1997). Systems theory requires social workers to be aware of the different systems or networks within which service users function, such as their family system, the community systems, and systems which support individuals, such as police systems, health care systems and social service systems. The social worker would need to analyse with the service user which systems were working and which were not. The goal of practice would be to strengthen existing support systems or to create systems that had broken down or did not exist. Systems theory has relevance for social workers working as care managers because one of the goals of community care was to enable service users to remain as part of their community by creating or strengthening networks of informal and formal care.

However, neither systems theory nor the PCA approach gave social workers a rationale for active intervention. Like the psychoanalytic approach, the PCA could involve long-term therapeutic relationships, which became increasingly difficult to justify in the context of bureaucratic organizations. It was also difficult to justify the cost of these approaches because evaluation of their outcomes was complex. A systems theory approach could identify problems in systems, but it might not be possible for the individual social worker to address or rectify problems at a systems level.

The introduction of the Task Centred Approach (Reid and Epstein 1972) gave social workers a clear rational for focused, brief work with explicit time limits and the possibility of measurable outcomes (Payne 1997, 104). Combined with the PCA valuing of the strengths of the service user, the Task Centred Approach set out a method of working with service users in partnership, identifying problems and negotiating a joint plan with clear tasks for both the social worker and the service user, to identify and address the presenting problem. Partnership, which facilitated an empowering approach, was established in working toward mutually agreed goals (Ahmad 1990). It was a short step from the task-centred approach to the adoption of the care-management approach. The task-centred approach informed the care-management approach (Challis and Davies 1986, 45). Both are time limited. Both are intended to work with the service user to identify problems that need to be addressed.

However, the task centred model of work involved an elaborate review of individual tasks carried out by the social worker and the service user at regular intervals to reflect progress and setbacks in relation to established goals. Care management, involves an initial assessment of need by the care manager, intended to 'take account of service users' wishes (Griffiths 1988), which is a far cry from the Task Centred ideal of jointly negotiated plans. Care management does not rest on a social work theory or model of practice. It simply 'provides administrative systems within which social work may be more effectively provided' (Payne 1997, 55).

The direction of new approaches within social work, combined with social work's weak knowledge claims and ambiguous professional standing, allowed the imposition of care management upon social workers in SSDs (Alaszewski and Manthorpe 1990). Social workers' dependence on their externally created bureau-professional status, their weak knowledge claims, reflected in a degree of anti-intellectualism in social work education (Jones 1996, 191, Thompson 2000, 85), an absence of empirical data to demonstrate efficacy (Fischer 1973, Fischer 1978) and a weak professional status left social workers in SSDs powerless to prevent the changes introduced by the Thatcher government. These changes were marked by the increasing importance of NPM in the public sector (Clarke et al., 2000, Walsh 1995, Pollitt 1993), which brought quasi-market (LeGrand 1991) reforms, economic competitiveness and business contracts to SSDs.

In the late 1980s and early 1990s, care management was introduced and with it a new role for social workers. The Department of Health was greatly influenced in this by the positive research findings of the Personal Social Services Research Unit (PSSRU) at the University of Kent (Challis and Davies 1980, Challis and Davies 1985; Davies and Challis 1986; Challis et al., 1988) in their evaluation of care-management pilot projects in Thanet and Gateshead (Lewis and Glennerster 1996, 21, Means and Smith 1998, 111; Wilson 1993).

Care management was intended to change the culture of social work (Alaszewski and Manthorpe 1990) and was to be accomplished through 'a radical restructuring of social work' (Alaszewski 1995). SSD care managers were made responsible for managing care rather than providing care (Griffiths 1988). The emphasis in care management has become targeting, financial assessment and the co-ordination of care rather than the professional 'use of self' in a casework relationship over time (Phillips 1996, Means and Smith 1998, 122; Harlow 2003, 39). The discretion and power of Seebohm caseworkers declined with the increased responsibility and power of managers and their ability to judge professionals on the basis of performativity, or their ability to produce tangible outcomes.

The introduction of the concept of needs-led services was an important element of Care in the Community policies. Post-War collectivist service provision was criticized as expensive and service-led, that is, not designed to meet individual need. Services were provided and if they did not meet a service user's needs, then nothing could be done for the service user in the community, possibly resulting in admission to a residential facility. The Griffiths ideal was that service-user need would be the starting point for services designed specifically to meet those needs, including the identification of unmet need for the purpose of designing relevant services. This is a contested area, however, as some SSDs may prefer not to be aware of unmet need if its recognition implies additional cost in organizations that are already struggling financially.

The purchaser/provider split meant that these functions were fragmented, presenting social workers with a distinct change in role. 'The arrangements for delivering community care under the NHS and Community Care Act had a profound impact on front-line social work staff in social services' (Adams 2002, 97). In the Seebohm model, the same practitioner would meet a service user, assess their needs and attempt to meet identified need themselves, drawing on related resources as appropriate, in the context of an ongoing professional casework relationship with the service user. The purchaser/provider split involved the separation of functions formerly carried out by a generic Seebohm caseworker.

The Impact of Care Management on Social Work in the UK
– Poachers Turned Gamekeepers

Care management has had a significant impact on workers in England. Care management in the UK has meant that social workers working for SSDs have become gamekeepers, working on the inside of bureaucracies, protecting resources and containing costs. Issues related to the introduction of care management in the UK are relevant to social workers in other national contexts where it has been or will be introduced. The impact will vary depending on the history and culture of the society in which it is introduced and to what degree social work is recognized as a profession, but care management has the potential to fundamentally change the role of social workers. Social workers working as care managers should be under no illusion that they are working toward a more just society. They are simply drawn more tightly into a residual model of social services delivery. It is argued that the analogy of 'poacher turned gamekeeper' has relevance for the change in role experienced by social workers working as care managers in the UK. It is argued that the care management role will have a similar impact wherever it is introduces.

Social work is a socially constructed activity which is often tied to the state and which must therefore reconfigure itself according to political shifts. While some argue that social work is becoming an internationally recognised 'social profession' (Lyons and Lawrence 2006), others, such as Parton (1996, 12) argue that social work is subject to increasing 'diversity, uncertainty, fragmentation, ambiguity and change'. Lorenz (2004, 145) argues more specifically that it is care management that has begun to fragment the profession. It could be argued that both positions are relevant to the current debate. Where care management is introduced, there are commonalities in its practice. However, the introduction of care management fragments existing social work practice into different areas of social work including traditional 'provider' social work practices and 'enabling' care-management social work. The trend toward fragmentation of practice tied to budget controls is pertinent to the US social workers despite more solid footing of profession in the US than the UK, where professional registration is a recent development.

The care-management model of social work practice was introduced across England between 1990 and 1993. Ostensibly, it was based on pilot projects that were carried out by the Personal Social Services Research Unit in Thanet and Gateshead (Challis et al., 1988). It would therefore appear that care management was based on evidence from research and is thus an example of Evidence Based Practice (EBP) (Corby 2006, 28). However, the care-management model piloted in Kent bears little resemblance to the care-management model of service provision that was rolled out nationally, presenting a 'margin to mainstream' social policy research issue. The original indicators of intensive care management used in the pilot projects, such as devolved budgets, small caseloads and clear eligibility criteria were lost in the national implementation of care management (Challis et al., 2001). The controlled research parameters that existed in local conditions were not replicated in national programmes established on the basis of this research. The differences between the pilot projects and what was introduced nationally on the basis of these projects are discussed in more detail in Chapter 6.

Much has been written about the implementation of care management in the UK since its introduction in 1993 following the enactment of the National Health Service and Community Care Act (NHSCCA) (1990): (Challis and Davies 1980, 1985; Davies and Challis, 1986; Challis et al., 1988; Wilson 1993; Reigate 1994; Lewis and Glennerster 1996; Newton et al., 1996; Levin and Webb 1997; Rachman 1997; Webb et al., 1998; Department of Health 1998; Kirkpatrick et al., 1999; Ellis et al., 1999; Postle 1999, 2001, 2002; Baldwin 2000; Carey 2003; Means and Smith 1998; Dustin 2000, 2004; Bradley, 2005). Most of these studies highlighted the gap between rhetoric and reality and the dilemmas involved in implementation of care management. However, the impact of care management on the role of social workers has been discussed only indirectly with the exception of Rachman, Postle, Baldwin and Dustin.

Although care management has been adopted in various configurations across the UK (Stalker 1994), the focus of this book is on the impact of care management on social work practice in England, more specifically in inner London. Part II of this book presents the findings of research concerning the impact of the introduction of care management on social workers in England. These findings are relevant in other national contexts where care management has been or will be introduced. Care management and the marketization of social work have changed the practice of social work in the UK. 'It is not that the social work business gets in the way of "real" social work: the social work business has changed what "social work" is and what social workers do' (Harris 2003, 183). Social workers have 'become more specialised around assessment of resources and risks, the investigation of abuse and rule breaking, and the setting up and enforcement of contracts. It has developed into an arm's length, office bound, report-writing official kind of practice which leaves face to face work to others' (Jordan and Jordan 2000, 37). The business mentality required by care management 'has resulted in problems of the "fit" between the values and ideals held by many of the people who enter social work and quasi-capitalist rationality of the organizations within which they work' (Harris 2003, 185).

The re-organization of local government social services departments that established care management as a model of service delivery in the UK in the early 1990s has put social workers in a peculiar position in relation to the market. There is a strand of thought in social work that has been critical of the market because social workers have seen the effects of poverty in market-oriented industrial societies. Social workers have historically used their skills to help individuals who were disadvantaged by capitalism or suffered from the problems created by capitalism, that is, the necessity for the increased mobility of labour, break up of families and unemployment. In this context social workers acted as mediators, representing the needs of the powerless to those with power (Philp 1979). As care managers, they are purchasers rather than providers of services and thus have been made operators or key figures in the quasi-market of social care.

Radical social workers in the UK (Bailey and Brake 1975) thought that social workers should act to redress the oppression created by capitalism and work toward a more egalitarian society with a more equitable distribution of resources. This perspective was relevant to the 'patch' system and followed on from community development projects. Social workers stood with local people to improve their lives. It seemed that social workers could act as modern day Robin Hoods, taking from the rich to give to the poor. They should be 'poachers', advocating for the poor and redistributing resources from within systems of service delivery. As the radical social work movement made some advances, it was effectively damped down by Thatcher who set up management systems to take more direct control of social workers' activities. This was achieved by the Griffiths Report and the following NHSCCA in 1990 which ended the 'patch' system and meant a withdrawal of statutory social workers from community development work.

The introduction of care management reduced the scope of the social work task to assessing individual need and purchasing services. 'Care managers cannot advocate on behalf of clients because they have become implicated in the budgetary responsibilities' that are part of the care-management role (Harlow 2003, 36). The role of social work which emphasized preventive community-based work was curtailed. Work with 'the community' was replaced by the responsibility to develop individual social networks. The effect was to reduce professional discretion, deskill social workers, and make social workers more directly accountable to managers, putting them in a position where they were responsible for finding the lowest cost way to meet identified need for individuals within limited budgets. The registration of social workers in the UK from 2005 meant that social workers were individually responsible for their actions and could be struck off for bad practice. While registration of social workers is a positive professional development in that it raises the status of social work and protects the public from malpractice by individual social workers, it means that social workers must become more conservative in their actions and cannot risk taking practice risks which are sometimes necessary to facilitate change.

In the transition to managed care systems, policy makers clearly retained social workers' skills in negotiating with service users regarding the assessment of needs and risks. Skills used to help services users take advantage of state services were turned to the advantage of managers to contain cost. Care management has appropriated social workers' skills by involving them directly in applying business principles to social services delivery thus reducing state expenditure and maximizing the functioning of capitalism. Social workers who were Robin Hoods or 'poachers', taking from the state and redistributing resources to the poor, have been transformed into 'gamekeepers', watching over and conserving the resources of the state. Social workers are sometimes referred to as 'gatekeepers', but at least this term implied that there were gates to be opened to service users. The term 'gamekeeper' implies that the resources are to be protected from any outsider. Social workers who historically had a role in redistribution now participate in managing the system that protects resources. The caring element of social work has been replaced by complicity in the reproduction of oppression (Healy 2000, 3). Robin Hoods have become sheriffs and poachers have become gamekeepers.

Conclusion

Care (case) management has been adopted in several Western industrially developed countries as a way of making them more competitive in the international marketplace. Each national social service system has a unique history and exists in a specific political and economic situation, which means that care management will be adapted in slightly different ways. It has been suggested that care management will be increasingly adopted in industrialized countries in an attempt to be competitive in the global marketplace. The development of care management in the UK has been put in the context of the UK's historical, economical and political circumstances. It has been suggested that social workers within UK care management have become responsible for the protection of state resources. Given social work's post-World War role as part of the redistribution of resources, this is an uncomfortable position for social workers to occupy.

In Part II, the reaction of UK social workers to their work as care managers is explored.

PART II

THE MICRO PERSPECTIVE

Social Workers' Perceptions of their Care Management Role – Findings from Research

Introduction to Part II – Chapters 3 to 5

Part II reports the findings of research conducted in statutory Social Services Departments (SSDs) between 1998 and 2000 to assess the implications of the introduction of care management for social workers in the UK. Interviews were carried out in five London inner city SSDs. Eight individual team managers and eight teams of care managers were interviewed. At the time of these interviews, service delivery in SSDs was mainly differentiated into services for elders (people over 65 years old), children, and adults with physical disabilities. Individual team managers from three elders' teams, three children's teams, one hospital team and a review team were interviewed. The hospital team manager worked generically with a range of service user groups. The review team had been set up to review the 'packages' of services (or care plans) designed by care managers, which they themselves had not had time to review. Focus groups were conducted with four elders' teams, two children's teams, one adult disabilities' team and one review team. All interviews were audiotaped and transcribed. The data was analysed using 'framework' methods (Ritchie and Spencer 1994) to enhance transparency and verifiability and allow the location of responses within written transcripts. Direct quotes from these transcripts are used extensively in Part II to give social workers 'voice' in an area where they have often not been consulted. Speakers are identified according to the client group they worked with, for example, elders' team manager or member of an elders' team. *Direct quotes from interviews are printed in italics.* Data was generated regarding care managers' perception of their work from four perspectives: (1) the skills and knowledge needed to practice as a care manager, (2) the impact of care management on practice, (3) the effect of care management on service users and (4) the possible impact of the registration of social workers.

Findings regarding skills and knowledge needed to be a care manager are reported elsewhere (Dustin 2006), but a central finding was that care management requires a range of complex skills and knowledge. Some pre-Griffiths casework skills are still necessary to practice as a care manager, such as interpersonal skills, negotiation skills and organizational skills. However, new skills are required, such as risk management, the ability to construct a case and use IT, management of other professional input and use of accounting and budgetary systems. Knowledge needed to be a care manager included practical knowledge, such as knowledge of resources and procedures, and theoretical knowledge, such as hierarchies of need and human development. Pre-Griffiths casework skills and knowledge were found to be necessary but not sufficient to practice as a care manager.

Findings regarding the impact of care management on practice are reported in Chapter 3, findings regarding the effect of care management on service users are reported in Chapter 4, and findings regarding the possible impact of the registration of social workers are reported in Chapter 5.

The Impact of Care Management on Social Work Practice

Introduction

The purchaser/provider split and the mixed economy of care in the UK 'caused a fundamental reassessment of services and professional practices' (Levin and Webb 1997, iii) and 'signalled the most fundamental changes to the delivery of social care since the creation of unified social services departments' (Webb, Moriarty and Levin 1998, 1). In their new role as care managers, their day-to-day activities changed and their discretion was reduced, although not eliminated entirely, through management practices and strict adherence to procedure. Their activities became more prescribed and were marked by a greater degree of managerial control than before the NHSCCA (Dominelli and Hoogvelt 1996). Social workers were required to become aware of the cost of services and purchase the lowest cost service possible from a range of sources to meet service user's needs. They therefore became part of the commodification of services (Crooke 1994, 7), transforming care from an intangible service into a tangible commodity to be bought and sold (Ritzer 1996, 155).

The factors associated with the introduction of care management are consistent with the concept of McDonaldization in that Fordist management techniques have been applied to the service sector to increase post-Fordist choice. Overall, the issues which were identified by care managers as most significant to them include the following: rapid restructuring of SSD organizations; changes to their role and title; the rise of managerialism, including issues of efficiency, performativity and calculability with a parallel loss of professional discretion; a deskilling of social workers, including the loss of the capacity to engage in ongoing professional relationships with service users; the loss of a preventive role because of increased targeting of services; and a restriction of consumer choice because of block contracts with external service providers. Care managers expressed a range of reactions to these changes.

Changed Structures – The Restructuring of SSD organizations

It was necessary for SSD organizations to be reorganized to accommodate the changes required by the NHSCCA and the new purchaser/provider arrangements. For some care managers, restructuring was the most immediate cause of the changes they discussed. They could talk about the restructuring more readily than the legislation that led to the restructuring. Care managers were 'experiencing the pain of major organisational change but few of the benefits' (Hoyes et al., 1994, 14). Further, rapid organizational change affected their 'capacity for concern' (Downes et al., 1996) resulting in alienation and cynicism towards community care reforms (Means and Smith 1998, 120). Respondents were asked to comment on the restructuring that occurred when care management and the purchaser/provider split were introduced.

Most practitioners had found the restructuring distressing because of the rapidity with which change occurred. Restructuring was ongoing between 1993 and 2000, for example, a total of five restructuring processes in one local authority in this period. Practitioners in one elders' group expressed a feeling of not being in control of their work because of ongoing restructuring. At the point of their interview, they were in the middle of a restructuring to standardize procedures across their borough. A typical comment was:

> *Personally, I think it's been a disaster. The problem is they* [the structures] *keep changing all the time. You're not sure where everything is fitting in. It's not that I'm negative about change, but when you've been through so many, I'm not sure about anything.*

New labels were attached to existing teams or groups of people resulting in confusion. Practitioners felt destabilized.

> *No one has ever given me any direct information about the changes that have occurred recently, no one.*

This statement, from an elders' team member, reflected the feeling of not being consulted or informed about the changes and that managers were not interested in how the changes were affecting them.

Changes in Role and Title

Restructuring involved fundamental and rapid change, including a changed role and title. Different expectations arose from this different role. 'The task of social workers who are care managers is to assess on behalf of society what people need, not to be caring and kindly' (Payne 1999, 255). Practitioners were required to transform themselves from generic direct providers of services to specialist purchasers of services. Their activities as purchasers involved a prescribed sequence of activities, which included assessment of need, commissioning of services and reviewing these packages. Services were called 'packages of care' because it was likely that several services from different agencies would be purchased and delivered to a service user. The changes constituted a major alteration to the traditional Seebohm casework role in SSDs.

An elders' team manager who had practised as a social worker prior to the NHSCCA observed,

> *In those days, you did a lot more social work. These days, it's not about social work much of the time. It's about using social work techniques, the techniques of assessment, but it's a lot more about devising care plans based on budget limitations and eligibility criteria, which years ago you didn't think about. I qualified in 1983 and the job now bears no relation whatsoever to what I did then, none.*

From the perspective of most practitioners and managers, the changes were far reaching. Interpersonal work that had been the focus of social work became a minimal part of their work. This perception was shared by all practitioners, but expressed most strongly in an elders' team.

> *A major part of the job was taken away. It's turned around for me. I came into the borough in 1986. Now it's like another lifetime away from when I initially came into social work.*

A member of the disabilities team said that the most important element of the change for her role was the separation of need from provision of services.

> *It began with needs being very separate from services and the needs-led notion. There was that split which was quite difficult really, separating needs from the services and certainly, speaking for myself, the idea of having to negotiate figures and price everything up was really terrifying. It wasn't a skill that I had ever used. I've had to develop that.*

It was intended that social workers would need to understand financial management activities in order to realize the potential of community care arrangements (Caring for People 1989, 37). However, the expectation that practitioners, in their role as purchasers, were suddenly required to consider the cost of services and to be part of the budgeting and rationing process came as a shock to many social workers. The manager of an elders' team expressed a common view that considering the cost of services was a new experience.

> *Social workers are now key to the rationing process. I don't think they are necessarily very confident about it here in my experience and some people find it a real struggle to do it.*

A member of the disabilities' team went on to give one of the clearest and most positive interpretation of care management among those interviewed. She observed that,

> *We're the linchpin that holds all this together.*

She gave an example of her work with an adult physically disabled woman who had lived with her parents all her life and wanted to live on her own.

> *I've just moved a fifty-year-old woman who lived with her family. She has moved into supported housing. She's being supported by a network of services. I see that as empowering. It was her choice to do it and the family had to be supported to let her go. And then there had to be this support network to make it work. We were involved in bringing these services together. That was just fantastic results and managing the risk was a huge job.*

This woman's parents were elderly and could no longer carry out the physical tasks required to maintain her. She wanted to remain in the community. The care manager therefore coordinated her application for housing, the assessments of all the professionals involved and the organization of the delivery of their services. Her point was that she thought she was recognized as a professional in her dealings with the professionals supporting this woman to live in her home. Further with regard to this example, the interviewer suggested that this work required traditional casework skills, but that it was not just about working with this service user and her family.

> *Actually working with her and the family involved very little direct help to them. I had hold of it, but the actual day-to-day working with the family was what I mean about holding it all together. I made sure everybody had the same objectives to working with the family. We had different people going in working with the family and we were all on the same objective, but I actually didn't help them directly very much. I had very, very little one-to-one contact with the family except at reviews. I didn't do any of that work, but I was holding it together and making sure it was happening and keeping everyone to the objectives. I think that it is a role about empowering and that is a new role for the social worker and I think it links in with the professional judgement about what everybody else is doing.*

This statement is a quite positive view of the care manager role, which also highlights the differences between the traditional role of social workers and the role of care managers.

She thought it was a difficult but worthwhile role. In the discourse of community care where needs were to be separated from services, services to an individual service user could be provided by a range of service providers. It was the care manager practitioner who was expected to provide the linchpin or the 'joined-up thinking' and pull together a range of providers, professionals and non-professionals. The practitioner assumed a new role as manager of service provision, one that had not been part of the casework role. Care managers became responsible for managing or holding together each individual service user's system of care to meet the needs of that individual service user. Casework skills were useful in this role. However, the role also required skills that were not traditional in this role and for which practitioners were not trained (Caring for People 1989, 67).

Another change in role was the expectation that practitioners would monitor and review the services provided by people in a range of other agencies. This was a new role and one that caused some concern. One elders' team discussed the fact that some agencies from whom they purchase services went on to sub-contract that service to another agency. The practitioner did not have a daily monitoring role with the service user. The practitioner might purchase a service and not find out that the service had been sub-contracted until six weeks later at the scheduled review meeting. This situation concerned care managers in this team because they felt they were responsible for the service and yet there were providers of service going into a service user's home who were unknown to them and who had no clear accountability to them.

A change in title often accompanied the change in role. Social workers who worked as care managers in SSD care-management teams were not usually called social workers. They were usually called care managers, but the exact title varied from one local authority to another. The struggle over the title seemed to be symbolic of the change in role and was a contested area. The manager of an elders' team said that in his team the title was '*social worker/care manager*'.

I suppose that reflects a bit of an uncertainty, really, as to whether they are now social workers in the traditional sense or care managers in a new sense. I know there was uncertainty when it came to drawing up job descriptions. There was quite a lot of debate as to whether they should be called 'social work assessors' or 'care managers (social workers)'.

The disabilities team decided that they were not going to call themselves care managers. They wanted to retain some recognition for their social work role with the 'specialist practitioner' title. Although they recognized the pressure to become care managers in the sense that they could no longer carry out their casework role, the issue for them was that if they called themselves 'care managers', it would be recognition that they were no longer social workers.

We call ourselves 'specialist practitioners' and we are fighting for that and we tell somebody off if they call us a care manager because we feel care management is part of our role, but it's not all of it. But in a way, we're fighting a losing battle with that.

Rise of Managerialism and Constraints on Professional Discretion

Managerialism concerns the ideology that managers should exercise their freedom to manage and has been central to the political commitment to introduce markets to public services and to creating post-Fordist mixed economy of care (Clarke et al., 1995, Pollitt 1993). Modern Fordist management techniques used to produce tangible goods have been applied to the provision of intangible services such as social care. An important element of Fordist management is the belief that elements of provision must be quantifiable, auditable and 'calculable' or subject to calculation (Ritzer 1996). Managerialism is an important concept both with regard to the immediate effects of changes associated with care management and with regard to the longer-term issue of professional status of social work (Exworthy and Halford 1999, Spratt 1999).

Calculability stands in contrast to professional discretion that is based on intangibles, such as knowledge and experience. An inherent tension exists between professionalism and managerialism. Before the introduction of care management to SSDs, professionals defined need based on their specialized knowledge. When professionals were constructed by the New Right as obstacles to the introduction of care management (Newman and Clarke 1995, 23), managers gained the power to define need and to specify which needs would be met through control over spending (Clarke et al., 1995, 6). The negative effects of the technocratization of social work practice have been noted (Dominelli and Hoogvelt 1996, Hughes 1995).

In Chapter 1, the links were made between Fordist management techniques, managerialism and Theory X, the belief that workers resist work and that managers must be authoritarian in order to ensure that employers produce as much work as possible. Fordist management techniques such as time and motion studies, performance targets and performance indicators, referred to as performativity and historically used in factory settings, seem to be used increasingly to manage care managers in SSDs.

The working climate of practitioners was marked increasingly by their activities being directed by procedures introduced by managers. As one manager of an elders' team noted,

> *I suppose what's changed from the 80s and through the implementation of Community Care is that the union's lost it's teeth and people are resigned to the fact that there's no alternative. You get on with it or you get out. That's your choice. I think, people* [social workers] *often don't think too hard about what is happening because they couldn't actually come and do the job* [if they thought about it].

Managerialism was performance oriented and output oriented and did not encourage reflection.

> *You're having to think it out and it's become almost a secret occupation. You're a human being responding to really quite dreadful circumstances and dealing with people's human expression of them, whatever that might happen to be, and you do have to think about it. It is rare to find a supervisor who is there truly to enable you the individual and I do miss having interesting discussions. I personally would love a supervision where one can also have reflection and also be able to be honest about the issues you are facing, the way you're considering or resolving them, but it's very much down to targets and actions.*

The degree to which care managers felt they could exercise discretion varied from team to team. Discretion was reduced by three factors: the imposition of prescriptive forms, time management and authorization to spend.

Firstly, regarding the use of prescriptive assessment of need forms, practitioners spoke of being required to fill out detailed forms to assess need, which could be over twenty pages long. Use of prescriptive forms raised the issue of mechanistic assessments of need *vis-à-vis* professional discretion. References to repetitiveness of work and being on a production line were relevant to this point.

The issues of paperwork detracting from work with service users and the mechanistic nature of care-management procedures were themes that came up repeatedly. For example, a member of an elders' team said,

> *There's too much paperwork. To the SSD, there is sense in it, but in terms of the work you do, it makes little sense. Audit means having to write everything down. What's expected from a care management point of view is to go out, assess someone's needs, try and meet as many of their needs as possible by purchasing the services to meet those needs, review, etc. But social workers want to get to know someone rather than just seeing them as a list of tasks and needs. It's mechanistic.*

From a management perspective, however, the forms were useful in promoting equity. An elders' team manager said that having a checklist assessment form ensured that the same points were covered in every assessment. However, the manager of the review team commented that even though the forms must be used, it would be *stupid* for a practitioner to use the forms in a mechanistic way. This would seem to put care managers in a conflict in that they were expected to use the standardized forms, but they were blamed if they used them in a mechanical way.

The existence of the forms and how they were to be used seemed to represent the issues in the debate about the relative merits of managerialism and professionalism. Some social workers did seem to use these forms in a mechanistic way and they resented having to use the form. For example, a member of the disabilities team said, 'You go in and you say, "Sorry, this has to be completed"'.

For practitioners, these issues were often related to the issue of quality. They felt that the quantification of output and the pressure to work to deadlines and to complete work within specific time limits did not recognize the process that would lead to good quality assessments of need. Members of an elders' team observed that they knew of some teams that did manage to work within the given time limits, but their feeling was that work completed to strict time limits was not carried out adequately.

Secondly, regarding the imposition of time limits on assessments, the point was made that people were so different that it was difficult to put a time limit on understanding their needs, but they had to get through as many assessments as possible because the SSD needed to demonstrate that they were doing the work. In direct reference to the need to quantify work, a care manager from an elders' team said,

I think part of it is to do with the fact that they need the numbers.

The time periods allocated for assessments varied with the level of anticipated need presented by a service user. For example, in one team they were expected to do a basic general assessment in one hour and a high need assessment in three to five hours. It was the manager of this team who also used 'league table' charts on the wall indicating the number of assessments each practitioner (Modernizing Social Services 1998, 89) had completed within the allotted time.

Pressure of work was often related to a feeling that they were not able to spend enough time with a service user to establish 'real need'. This point is central to a feeling of not being able to do the work properly and related to a perception that the work they were doing was superficial.

Thirdly, budgets and the purchase of services were critical areas where care managers felt that they had least discretion. Care managers from an elders' team expressed high levels of frustration because they had very little power in relation to the final decision to purchase.

It's very frustrating. You've done the assessment. There is a clear need for the services to go in and the resources are not there.

In some teams the process of budget approval was subjected to two layers of approval. Care managers from an elders' team took assessments to senior practitioners for approval of the assessment and then they went to the area manager to approve funding, representing increased bureaucracy. Their original assessment could be modified or reduced at any stage. This factor reinforced their perception that their professional discretion had been undermined.

Members of the review team felt that the manager was very much in charge with regard to spending.

The manager decides. Every purchasing decision goes to the manager if it is below £100 and above £250 it goes to a panel.

In one elders' team, every expenditure over £30 had to be approved by the manager.

A manager of an elders' team said that there is sometimes no money available to purchase services because the budget had been exhausted. However, care managers were still expected to carry out assessments of need. There was an element of frustration inherent in the role of care manager in that they were required to carry out assessments of need knowing they would not be able to meet needs that they themselves had identified. This manager said,

> *The expectation is that people would still go out and do their assessments and do their identification of need, but what they can't say is that we can guarantee anything. They always need to get budget approval.*

In spite of managers' control of budgets, some care managers felt they could still use discretion. For example, members of the disability team expressed the view that there was the potential for discretion in their work. The conditions for this discretion to be allowed were that the manager respected them and that the social worker was able to '*make a case*' for their plan. They said that if the manager did not respect the worker, then the manager would just issue instructions to the practitioner.

In one children's team, there were elements of the purchaser/provider split, but in this team the care-management role was not as strict as in some adult teams. This children's team could both purchase and provide. They felt that one way they used their discretion was that it was up to their judgement whether to refer children to the Children in Need Team or the Child Protection Team. They commented that this decision on their part was partly determined by the level of resources. The services of the Children in Need Team cost more than the Child Protection Team. If a situation was borderline, between neglect and protection issues (if a child was neglected because their parents lacked resources to look after their child properly) they would ordinarily refer to the Children in Need Team.

However, if the resources of the Council were being cut back, they would refer to the Child Protection Team thereby constructing the situation as one needing surveillance rather than as one needing input of resources. In this situation, a family that might initially be regarded as being in 'need' because of poverty would have to be reconstructed or re-categorized as being abusive. This use of discretion on the part of the social worker would make an enormous difference to the family in terms of how they were perceived within the service system and in society and how they perceived themselves.

Members of one children's team spoke of social workers being more independent in the past than they were currently. However, one member of this children's team had worked as a social worker prior to restructuring of her role. Before then, she had '*always done what she wanted to do*' and she felt that she still exercised professional judgement '*more or less*' even after restructuring. She also expressed the view that ticking boxes does not mean that your creativity is taken away from you. She felt that she could use her skills and her discretion within the limits of the standardized assessment forms.

This view, expressed in a children's team, was in contrast to that of practitioners from most of the elders' teams who felt that the assessment forms did remove discretion and creativity. Members of one elders' team felt there was no discretion, '*no leeway*' and spoke of a lack of trust in them as professionals.

Theory X and Theory Y Management Approaches

While most managers seemed to use a Theory X approach to the management of care managers, some tried to retain elements of Theory Y management. An example of a Theory X manager, cited by an elders' team, was one who thought care managers should operate in a mechanistic output oriented way, that is, '*get in, get out and move on to the next one*'. Such strictures on working practices seem geared to producing the maximum output in tangible, measurable forms.

In teams where Theory X management practices were evident, there was an atmosphere in which measurement of work output was expected. Practitioners from the review team said they were required to '*write our figures down and keep statistics*' regarding their own work. Performance targets using specific quantifiable data collection techniques were part of this ethos in these teams.

SSDs varied in the degree to which they employed these management techniques. The manager of one elders' team, who used the factory analogy, had league tables on the wall in the form of bar charts that identified, by name, social workers who had completed their assessments within the allotted time. In another elders' team, practitioners had to complete time and motion sheets for a week to show what they were doing. The charts did not reflect other more intangible criteria such as quality of work, satisfaction of service users or whether they were reflective practitioners. This reinforced their feeling that

> *We are on the production lines very clearly.*

Practitioners who had worked as social workers prior to the purchaser/provider split felt the changes most acutely. A member of an elders' team, comparing her work before and after the introduction of care management, said,

> *In comparison, for me, when I first came to this borough, it was a very, a very joyful place to work because all these pressures weren't existing then.*

She no longer enjoyed her work as a care manager.

The manager of one elders' team, who had a more supportive Theory Y management style than most team managers, said she had maintained the same members of her team over a relatively long period of time. She thought that there was some loyalty to her because of her supportive management style.

> *I was appointed as manager of the old team* [prior to current restructuring] *in 1995. I've kept my staff until this year* [1999] *so it's longer than average.*

She tried to overcome the problems of care management by encouraging her care managers to reflect on and evaluate how they exercised their skills. She retained a perception that process was important in achieving output, rather than simply demanding output with no attention to the process leading to output. She felt that people were loyal to her because she used a more 'person centred' management style.

She was sympathetic to practitioners regarding the effect of changes and did what she could to maintain a supportive Theory Y approach to her management role. She was aware of the effects of routinized work routines on care managers.

> *It really makes people feel quite helpless. It is worse because all the intentions* [of the purchaser/provider split] *are sensible and valuable, but the enacting of it, it really makes people feel quite helpless. If there isn't a sense of depression, there's a sense of boredom.*

She held regular group supervision sessions with her team during which she encouraged people to talk about their work. She saw this as a way of avoiding a '*closed door*' or managerialistic way of working. She tried to show them that she was interested in the process that they were experiencing in doing their work, not simply in an outcome at any cost. The manager of this elders' team was clearly operating from a Theory Y management perspective, as indicated by the following quote from her.

> *If there's an issue, I want them* [care managers] *to come and talk with me about it. That can be difficult because, in this new world, I think there is more value on managers who close their doors than on ones who leave them open. You talk to people; you deal with the issues they have. All those human components of the bigger management picture are the ones that are either allowed to breathe or endlessly get crushed. I think what I do is, I think I can inspire people to think it's worthwhile. It's a bit of a gift that has developed over time and held people together and given them some sense of* [purpose]. *I think as a manager, I've always been more person focused than is perhaps compatible with the organisation that has lots of procedures and fact manuals. Again* [these things are] *from the olden days. They are still there and determining how we should work. But for me, the only reason to do the job is that what you do is really designed to be of true assistance to the people you're working with.*

Stress and Conflict

Care managers experienced stress and conflict as a result of their attempts to negotiate the competing demands represented by managerialism and professionalism. Practitioners were not asked specifically about stress related to their work, but the issue arose spontaneously. A member of an elders' team put it as follows:

> *Personally, I think you need to be able to manage stress because it is an incredibly stressful role. You have to become much more adversarial. You really have to stand your ground and I hate it. That's not what I came in to do. It's management rather than caring. We need to be supportive of each other. I know a lot of people who wouldn't be able to do this job. I sometimes think I should go and work as a labourer, on my own. It gets like that.*

The manager of this elders' team acknowledged the stress for practitioners.

I think most professions are going through a difficult period. There are lots of conflicts and care managers are then caught in the middle of restructurings and changes. People complain about too many things to do, too many bits of paper to process, endless changing rules and regulations, not enough time to do the job efficiently, money difficulties, on and on.

Care managers talked about conflicting demands on a number of levels. The conflicts involved mediating the following: the difference between what they thought they should be doing and what they were doing; the difference between what they would like to have been doing and what they had to do; the difference between service users' needs and what could actually be provided; and the difference between what they felt they were trained to do and the expectations of SSDs. This last conflict was expressed in one elders' team as a culture of SSD's *'which is "anti" everything you were trained to do'*. Additional areas of conflict were conflict with other professionals, especially with regard to hospital discharge plans for the elderly and the conflict between what service users think they should be able to do and what they can actually do.

A further area of conflict was expressed in a children's team. This quote reflects the conflict of interest that typifies the care-management position.

Social workers are caught in a conflict between two different sides, their responsibility to the organisation to provide services at the right price and also their responsibility to the clients to see that those clients' rights are guaranteed within the service.

Deskilling – A Decline in the Level of Skill Required for the Job

Deskilling is a concept that describes a working situation wherein there is a decline in the level of skill required to do a job (Ritzer 1996, 115). This description of care management as deskilling is relevant to social workers who became care managers (Dominelli and Hoogvelt 1996, Wilson 1993). Care managers in specialist teams felt less deskilled than care managers in generic elders' teams. Specialist care managers could use higher levels of discretion and engage in more detailed assessment work than generic elders' care managers (Ellis et al., 1999, 274).

Respondents were not asked directly whether they felt deskilled, but rather, were asked to talk about how the purchaser/provider split had affected their work. They themselves used the word 'deskilled' to describe the impact of care management on their work.

Many practitioners spoke of a sense of having lost a major element of their earlier social work role in the transition to their role as care manager. Assessment of need and risk management were recognized as important skills that they used as practitioners within care management. However, they felt that within care management, there was a loss of scope to apply the casework skills they thought they possessed. This sense of loss was most apparent among those respondents who had practised prior to the legislation enacted in the early 1990s to implement the purchaser/provider split.

Both team managers and care managers expressed a feeling of loss. The following quote sums up the feelings of several practitioners.

> *My best skills are wasted. The social worker that you were, that you should have been, that's gone by. There's been a mistrust about our skills and what we do and a lot of skills that we have had which have now been shelved basically, for example, doing inter-personal work.*

The manager of the hospital team summed it up by saying that risk assessment was a refined skill, but the rest of the work was essentially clerical. Even recently qualified practitioners, comparing what they were trained to do with what they were actually doing as care managers, felt they were limited in the application of their skills. The feeling of being deskilled was associated with the clerical nature of their role, mentioned above, and a loss of satisfaction because they could not establish an ongoing relationship with service users and they did not have a role in the direct provision of care.

> *It's not just the actual kind of task itself which is quite dry and arid and uninteresting or pretty awful. It's just that all the other stuff you actually get the satisfaction from in the job has been squeezed out.*

Regarding the feeling of being deskilled, one person from an elders' team remarked that,

> *It's mad to feel bad about talking to a service user beyond the time allocated for a needs assessment.*

This issue of loss of relationship with service users will be discussed further below, but suffice it to say here that this loss is associated with a feeling of being deskilled and a loss of satisfaction with the work care manager practitioners carry out.

In some respects social work skills were used, but were focused in new ways. For example, they said that they could not use counselling skills with service users because providing counselling services was not within their role as care managers. The interpersonal skills that they developed in the course of their training and experience were used in assessment interviews. However, rather than using their interpersonal skills to provide direct support to service users, they said they used these skills in negotiating costs and conditions with service providers. In both ways, interviewing service users about their needs and negotiating with service providers to meet the needs, practitioners could be said to use their interpersonal skills, but could not be said to be doing formal counselling.

Relationship Building

One of the biggest impacts of the change from caseworker to care manager practitioner seems to have been upon the relationship between the worker and the service user. Within the casework, the expectation was an ongoing relationship with service users. 'The relationship is the soul of social casework. It is the principle of life which vivifies the processes of study, diagnosis and treatment and makes casework a living warmly human experience' (Biestek 1957, v). Central to the ideal of casework has been the 'use of self' which involved a normative professional relationship (Toren 1972) and was intended to strengthen and empower the service user. For the social worker, the 'self' is a tool to be used in the interaction service users. 'Use of self' implies an ongoing relationship over a period of time between social worker and service user. However, 'the social worker's use of self is lost from the equation if he or she is simply the co-ordinator of services' (Harlow 2003, 39).

The caseworker may have referred the service user to other services and may, in fact, have purchased services for the service user. From this perspective the care manager role retains elements of the casework role. However, the difference between the two roles is that the caseworker maintained ongoing contact with the service user throughout the process, whereas the care manager might only have direct contact with the service user at specific points, for example, in the initial assessment and at periodic reviews.

A focal point in most discussions was the issue of relationships with service users. The quality of relationships was different within the care-management model than it was prior to the introduction of this model. Practitioners did not feel that they could develop a professional relationship with service users. The role of the care manager was to assess, purchase and monitor providers to ensure they were giving the service they were contracted to provide. Care management removes the 'emotional content of practice and the significance of relationships' from practice (Harlow 2003, 38). Care managers' role was not to provide counselling or establish ongoing normative relationships with service users.

Members of all teams, except the children's teams, discussed the difficulty for practitioners in establishing or maintaining a relationship with service users. The following comment reflects the perception that interaction with service users was minimal.

> *The reality is, you don't have a lot of time to have a very big interaction with service users. Doing interpersonal work ... has now been sort of shelved. The interpersonal stuff that gets you involved* [in social work] *initially is squeezed out. A full casework relationship is a luxury. I think you can do it* [have a relationship] *to an extent, but it's much more difficult. Face to face contact is a minimal part of our job now.*

Members of children's teams still seemed to do direct work with children and families. However, for one children's team, the most important element in their work was that time was needed to establish a relationship with children and their families in order to facilitate the right decisions. They did not feel that they had the scope to develop the kind of relationships with service users that would lead to the most beneficial outcomes.

> *We're taking decisions about a child's life. The responsibility is great. We need time and a relationship to do it well. The purchaser/provider split has disempowered that kind of discussion and involving clients in decision-making.*

As observed earlier, respondents from several groups referred to percentage figures as to how much time they spent with service users themselves. When figures were referred to, the amount of their time spent with services generally cited was between 20 percent and 25 percent. The rest of their time was spent in filling forms, writing reviews, filling out invoices and doing related paperwork. Of course, telephone work and meetings and other work not involving direct work with service users also took up much of their time.

In an elders' team, the view was expressed that practitioners could no longer look at the 'whole' person. They did not have the time to get to know an individual and thus really know what their needs were. This perception was linked to the issues of pressure of time and the feeling of being deskilled referred to above. They felt that their purchaser role was totally service focused, that is, focused on tangible purchasable services rather than on the service users themselves. A member of this team said, '*It's the feeling side of the person that seems to be ignored*'.

Managers themselves were aware of the difficulties care managers experienced in coming to terms with their role and commented directly on how the new role had affected the care managers in their team. The manager of the review team referring to the loss of an ongoing relationship with service users, said, '*I think that it is actually devastating for the workers.*'

She commented that it had been harder for older workers who started their careers prior to the 1990s than for recently qualified workers for whom this was the only model of work they had experienced. While she herself, as manager of the review team, was very positive about the greater efficiency and effectiveness of the service she was managing, she did acknowledge that, '*We have lost something*'.

A practitioner in an elders' team described an experience which demonstrated the changed relationship between social worker and service user. When she first came in to social work, the satisfaction she got from her job was caring for people. As a care manager, she now understood that this was not her role.

> *When I first came here, I had a man who was grossly obese, cardiac problems, incontinent, but he wanted to live by himself. This man knew he was going to die soon, but he wanted to die at home. My job satisfaction at that time came from popping in at his house on my way home from work because I felt that one day care workers would find him dead, but I would not do that now.*

Another group member asked her if that was because she wouldn't have the time to visit him now. She said, '*I just would not*', implying that the culture of work had changed. There are a number of contradictions in this narrative. The speaker said that she visited this man regularly, but would not do it now, implying that the current constraints on her work would make an ongoing relationship of this kind unacceptable. But she went on to say that even at that time, her supervisor criticized her for visiting the man. Therefore, even in the pre-purchaser/provider split model, she should not have been having such an intensive supportive relationship with this service user. She also said that she now realized that she should not have been visiting him in the way she was, but '*It was the feelings I had*'. At the time, she felt that she should look after him in that way and she used her professional discretion to do so.

This example would seem to illustrate the point that social workers come into this area of work because they think they will 'work with people'. However, even before the purchaser/provider split, an ongoing 'caring' relationship, such as the one this practitioner described, was inappropriate from an organizational or bureaucratic perspective. The difference between the pre-care-management SSD organization and the organizational requirements of the current care-management structures may be that the structures of management were 'looser' prior to the 1993 implementation of the NHSCCA. Social workers were not supervised as closely. Social workers had more discretion and were trusted to do their job, so they had scope within their work to develop helping relationships with service users. One of the consequences of the various restructurings that have gone on since 1993 is that manager surveillance of practitioners has increased to such a degree that there is now '*no leeway*', in the words of a respondent from an elders' team, for social care managers to have an ongoing relationship with clients in the way many thought they would when they entered social work.

This change in the relationship between worker and service user related to loss of satisfaction with the work as well as a feeling of being deskilled. A member of an elders' team said:

> *For me, sometimes you just have to switch off and do your work. Not in a mechanical way, but it's almost like sometimes, you feel like the aspect of job satisfaction is gone. You know, you're doing the work and you still feel committed, but sometimes, on the worst days, it just feels like a job, and it shouldn't feel like that.*

Several care managers expressed the need for adequate time and a relationship with service users in order to assess need properly and get help them accept the services they need. For example, a member of an elders' team said,

> *If we went into a relationship and got to know them and were able to give them a choice... then we would be able to empower them. It takes time to tell them* [service users] *what they can do and what they can't do and a one or two-hour assessment doesn't allow that. It also takes time to help service users adjust to new circumstances.*

When a complicated package of care is delivered with several people coming and going from a service user's home, the acceptance of this new way of living needs an adjustment on the part of the service user. The kinds of changes that go along with having services come into a service user's home can seem minor, but involve a change in lifestyle for a service user. While it is positive that they are able to stay in their own home, having these services coming into their homes represents an intrusion into their lives, which they must deal with successfully in order to benefit from them. If the service user had friends and family to talk through these changes, they could help the service user adjust. If the person was socially isolated, it was necessary for the practitioner to take this role with them. A member of an elders' team said,

People [service users] *actually need time ... and talking to people and having to explain, it's quite complicated trying to explain to people. That doesn't seem to be taken into* [account], *the time-scale thing, that you can't actually drag the clients along the time-scale that people* [i.e., managers] *would like.*

This speaker felt that there was a valid reason to consult with a service user who is faced with making the transition from living at home to living in a residential facility.

You can't get around that. It has to happen or things fall apart.

On the whole, most respondents felt they should be spending more time with service users both to assess need and facilitate the introduction of services. The manager of an elders' team said, '*It's always easier if you've got some kind of working relationship.*' They wanted to have at least a working relationship with service users and felt that service users often wanted to have more of a relationship with social workers than was possible in the care-management model.

Loss of Preventive Role

Although a survey of senior managers found that targeting services to those in greatest need threatened preventive services (Levin and Webb 1997, v), an unanticipated finding in this current study was the strength of feeling from practitioners with regard to their perception that they could no longer do preventive work. Practitioners felt that they could do more preventive work prior to the introduction of the care-management role. The perception that social workers should do preventive work is linked to the modern precept that knowledge could be used to improve society and contribute to progress. Prevention could be seen as a positive aspect of the social work surveillance role. Prevention, or the improvement of society, was no longer a part of the social work activity in their role as care manager. As care managers, they were simply part of a rationing process. Whether social workers ever worked in a preventive capacity could be debated, but from the perspective of most practitioners interviewed, this was the case. The issue arose in the first interview with an elders' team so subsequent groups were asked to comment on the issue. The short term perspective of needs assessment within the current care management model does not seem to allow a preventive approach and is consistent with the view that care management was introduced to primarily to cut expenditure (Lewis and Glennerster 1996).

Respondents from several teams said that one of the problems that they saw with care management and the purchaser/provider split was that they no longer felt that they could do preventive work. A comment from an elders' team member was,

The problem is that the amount of preventive work we should be doing, we don't do.

The manager from the hospital team who had been a social worker for over 20 years, referred to the 'buzz' of the 1970s. He said that social workers thought they would '*make a difference*' in people's lives. By this he seemed to mean that social workers thought they could contribute to the improvement of society. This relates to their perception that their role before the introduction of care management was preventative. They now had to wait until an individual's circumstances reached crisis point before they could do an assessment. The risk had to be significant enough to warrant a judgement that without service input harm would result. Targeting of services meant that only those most at risk could be considered for service, consistent with the wider policy shift from universal to selective service provision.

Respondents said that a service user's situation must be in crisis to warrant even an assessment. A related issue seems to be that the care-management role required practitioners to focus on one individual service user at a time. It would seem that there was no scope in the care manager role to address structural issues, the focus of radical social work in the 1970s, which they felt would have been preventive. An elders' team member said,

> *I think if I were to establish a relationship and do more preventive work and if we could get to know people, it would help. It takes quite a long time to find out what they can do and what they can't do because quite often, we are doing a reduced assessment. We do an assessment of an hour or two and that doesn't give you enough time. I think if we went into a relationship and got to know them and were able to give them the choice, then they we would be able to empower them.*

When asked directly whether social workers could take a more preventive role before the introduction of the purchaser/provider split, a member of one elders' team thought they could do preventive work.

> *It was easier then. The time was there. The resources were there. That was what the assessment team was about in a sense, the preventive work, so we got in there early. And at that time there was a preventive budget. So there were certain things we could do.*

Members of one elders' team made the point that tightly targeted services with stringent eligibility criteria and the absence of early intervention or prevention was costly in the long run.

> *I think part of the original intention was to ensure that you were getting cost-effective service, but in reality that's often been translated into the cheapest services. Then people do deteriorate. The preventative work goes by the board and people deteriorate and then you have to put in a much bigger package of care because you haven't had the [input] at an early enough stage.*

One children's team reminisced about the Barclay 'patch' model of service delivery. They said that under the 'patch' system social workers knew their area and met with local teachers and vicars to discuss local problems and they could do preventive work. Currently, within care-management structures, they felt they no longer knew the community.

> *I cannot pretend to say that we can do anything to improve the lives of people on the estate. If this estate blew up tomorrow, you'd feel shameful that you'd come into this office every day for years, but you didn't know the people.*

In one elders' team, practitioners sometimes had to reduce or withdraw existing services to a service user, consistent with Levin and Webb (1997) findings. Service users with an existing set of services provided according to one set of eligibility criteria could have these services reduced when the eligibility criteria was tightened up as part of a subsequent SSD budget cut. Respondents felt that there were often insufficient resources put in the first place, but sometimes existing services had to be withdrawn. The issue was not only the inability to do preventive work, but continuous budget cuts, which they thought were also costly in the end. The manager of an elders' team raised the issue because she thought it was a practice that most people did not know about.

> *I think the other thing you need to be aware of now as well is that practitioners are often going out now and reducing people's packages because that is now part of their role. If people haven't had their review for a couple of years, say, they may not actually need the service that was put in ... or in fact the eligibility criteria might have changed.*

Taking services away from elderly people was an uncomfortable and unusual role for practitioners to be in. She said that care managers in her team were upset at having to withdraw services.

> *It's quite difficult for care managers to tell service users that the criteria had changed and that they were no longer entitled to a service.*

She also thought that these budget cuts and the withdrawal of service were a false economy in that services would cost more in the future as a result of not putting in services at an early stage to prevent deterioration in the personal independence and social functioning of service users.

> *I think it's appalling when you have a situation where we are taking people out of services. Basically we know that in six months time they are back down again because they're now in distress and we'll probably have to put more resources in because we should have continued with what we had originally put in.*

Needs-led, Service-led, and Resource-led Services

The care-management model of service delivery was intended to be needs-led rather than service-led. Care management was central to the operation of a needs-led model of service. Care managers were expected to identify service users' needs without regard to existing services. Post-War and Seebohm welfare arrangements were criticized for being service-led because service users were provided with existing services whether or not these services were appropriate to their needs. Respondents were asked whether they thought care management was needs-led, service-led or resource-led, in light of budget restrictions. Two further issues related to needs-led services were whether care managers could spot purchase and whether unmet needs were being recorded so that services could be commissioned to address these unmet needs.

A children's team made the point that services were not service-led because there are hardly any services left after the imposition of budget cuts. Needs could often not be met because services were not available to meet identified needs. They did not feel that care management was needs-led.

Only one team, an elders' team, could still spot purchase, consistent with a needs-led approach and enhancement of service users' choice. Members of this team observed that spot purchasing facilitated a needs-led approach, but that spot purchasing had generally been replaced by the use of block contracts. The following quote from this team expresses a commonly held position among practitioners.

> *We've actually gone full circle now and we are at a stage where things are now going back to being service-led.* [The budget is] *becoming smaller and the client group is not becoming smaller. It's meant that basically we have had to say this is the service level we have got so either you fit in it or you don't. The market, the independent sector, hasn't flourished as initially thought and so, whilst we can assess specific kind of needs, the services aren't there for them so therefore, you're left with a service model rather than a needs model.*

Members of the disabilities' team made the point that the market model had not produced with a plethora of services from which to choose. If care managers could have 'spot purchased' services from any source to meet needs, this would have enhanced choice both for the service user and the care manager purchasing services for the service user. However, block contracts and service level agreements with specified agencies had restricted choice because care managers could only purchase from agencies approved by their SSD Contracts Department. This quote from a member of the disabilities team summarizes the view that block contracts have created a service-led approach:

> *The purchaser/provider split was brought in for political reasons, but apart from that, I felt it's around providing the services and choice which I think in my experience initially was the case. There was lots of freedom to be creative, to make one-off spot purchases. Since then as time's gone by, we've moved away from that. Block contracts have come in which are around economies of scale, saving money, getting more for your money. So you are going to be service-led. The general principles were great in terms of putting service users at the centre of the process, but choice has been limited by service level agreements and block contracts.*

On the positive side, the purchaser/provider split widened the range of services from which to purchase, consistent with attempts to create a needs-led post-Fordist service. The manager of an elders' team felt that there were advantages in the purchaser/ provider split and that services now reflected local communities better than before the purchaser/provider split. He said that meals-on-wheels could now be purchased from local voluntary organizations representing minority ethnic communities. Service users could be provided with culturally appropriate meals rather than receiving SSD meals-on-wheels. SSD meals were characteristic of Fordist service led organizations which were not able to meet the needs of the various groups living in the community. However, the point remains that, although the range of allowable sources of providers had been expanded, care managers were required to purchase from an approved list of service providers and therefore from this perspective, provision was still service-led.

Approval of agencies as providers from which care managers could purchase services was an important part of the needs-led model. Separate teams, sometimes called Contracts Departments, inspected and approved agency services for purchase. It was reported by at least one care-management team that SSDs sometimes did not have the resources to approve private and voluntary services properly or to maintain a surveillance of these services once approved. One example was mentioned wherein agencies were approved without a visit because the Contracts Department did not have enough staff to visit them. A related issue was that once an agency was on the approved list of providers, the mechanisms for removing a poor agency from this list were not straightforward. Ongoing approval should have been actively maintained. However, some practitioners knew of poor agencies that were still being used apparently because the failings of these agencies had not been communicated to their Contracts Department. Their own role in the surveillance of external agencies did not seem clear to them.

The recording of unmet needs should be carried out in order to develop services, but this happened unevenly. The manager of the review team was clear that she wanted unmet needs recorded so she could create services to meet these needs, but she said that the practitioners in her team were not recording unmet needs. They would discuss unmet needs in team meetings. She therefore felt she was aware of unmet needs through verbal discussions, but that it was not being documented. She had identified a specific cultural group that was not taking up services and had employed a worker from that group to document where there was a need for services that was not being met and the reasons.

Range of Reactions

Care management was implemented locally, with each SSD introducing the changes in its own way (Newton et al., 1996, Lewis and Glennerster 1996). Teams represented in these studies expressed a range of reactions to the changes, which were mediated by a number of factors, for example, the philosophy of the SSD, the perspective of their own team manager and the client group with which they worked. Children's teams were affected by the purchaser/provider split, but not to the same degree as the teams that worked with elderly and the disabled people. Specialist teams felt more positive toward care management than generic elders' teams.

Members of an elders' team seemed most affected by the changes. They seemed to feel destabilized and expressed the view that they had little control over their work.

It's down to budgets and you don't have any control over it.

At one point in the group discussion, one person made a positive statement about the changes. He said, '*It's not all bad. There are some good things happening*'. The rest of the group challenged him strongly on this point. He defended his position by saying that research is being done to see if the changes were improving services delivery. They challenged him again by saying that no one had asked them anything. They were not aware of any research. They said that whatever research is being done did not reflect the difficulties, the psychological effects, the choices that had to be made in care management. They expressed the perception that no one was interested in their situation or the stress it was causing them.

The issue of not having control over their work arose because of the realities of resource constraints. Practitioners often referred to their perception that while they were responsible for assessing a service user as needing a specific service, they did not have direct access to the resources that would pay for the services. This process appeared to make practitioners feel that they were not in control of their work.

Members of a childrens team referred to the changes in policy with regard to children in care as '*basically little adjustments as we go along, so there isn't a whole body of policy. It just gets updated when it needs to be*'. They did not experience the major restructuring of adult services, so they did not feel as destabilized as care managers in adult services.

In spite of the criticism of the changes and discomfort that the changes had brought about for practitioners, there were some positive comments on them. A member of the disabilities team thought that the care manager role clarified the role of social workers. '*In some ways, it's been quite good. It clarifies the roles.*' Members of this team felt the role had been clarified in that there was more uniformity in the role of care manager than there was in the pre-Griffiths social work role.

A member of a children's team felt that because of scandals in SSD services, it was widely accepted that social workers could no longer offer a good enough service as genericists. '*Some people resented the change from generic work to specialisms, but many people wanted that change.*' She felt that social workers needed to specialize in order to know enough about their area to practise effectively.

Another member of the same children's team said clearly that she did not regret the loss of relationships with service users. Her position was that service users do not want relationships with practitioners and that the traditional professional relationship was more for the benefit of the worker than the service user. She felt that service users just want the services they can get through the assessment of need, carried out by the practitioner. She said she liked the care-management role.

> *I love the fact that it is just a referral system. That suits me, not having to get involved and literally just pointing people in the direction of other people who specialize in certain things, although I can really empathize with people who came up in the era where you did a lot of direct work.*

Although it is in some senses a simplistic interpretation of care management, she liked the role because she did not have to engage in an ongoing relationship with service users. She liked being something of a technician rather than getting involved in the 'warmly human' casework model of social work. She was also, however, sympathetic with people who did not like the assessment and referral care-management role.

A colleague in this children's team, expressed a much more common position, which was that,

If it's about just sitting at a desk and saying 'Well Children and Families can [do certain]
*work ...' then I don't want to be part of something like that because I think that's incredibly
deskilling really.*

There were some positive observations about the management practices. While some
care managers in elders' teams lamented the pressure to produce tangible outcomes
and the seemingly artificial time constraints put on assessments, members of the
second children's team felt less pressured by the changes. This team felt that tighter
legislation and guidelines should not be criticized because, in the end, the basic
elements of good service were results and output, not a relationship or a process.

*I think in terms of the guidelines and the deadlines and all that, those things are there
to improve service to clients and to actually improve our professionalism, for instance,
not delaying things to do with children. That's in the Childrens Act and that's extremely
important and that, in fact, is something which I as a social worker and as a manager
would underline. I wouldn't undermine that by saying it's managerialism. Because if it's
improving the service to the client, that's what you're working for.*

Conclusion

This chapter has explored the impact of care management on social workers.
Managers' and practitioners' comments have been cited on the following topics:
the restructuring of their departments, changes in their role from caseworker to
care manager, the increased role of managers and what this means for the use of
professional discretion, increased levels of stress and conflict for workers, deskilling
and the decreased scope for a professional relationship with a service user and loss
of a preventive role.

In work with children as well as adults, there was so much pressure on services,
that is, 'the sheer weight of referrals coming into the system', that the threshold
for intervention has moved upward (Little 1995 in Campbell 1997, 246). It is
more and more difficult to be judged eligible for a service. Because systems are so
proceduralized, it is relatively straightforward for the criteria at which services are
given to be moved to higher level (Neate 1996). This process defeats the purpose
of prevention, which surely must be ethically valid in work with both children and
adults, as well as saving resources in the long term (Chappell 2007).

Finally, an important point was raised by managers and practitioners. The
intention of needs-led services has not been fulfilled because block contracts are
necessary to provide economies of scale in service provision. A range of small
flexible services has not emerged because large providers are less expensive and
provide more predictable, standardized care than small independent providers. This
finding may explain to some degree why the intention to provide service users with
choice and establish needs-led services has not been fully realized.

Chapter 4 considers social workers' perspectives on whether service users have
been empowered by care management.

Chapter 4

Consumerism, Choice and Empowerment in Care-managed Services

Introduction

This chapter reports findings regarding care managers' views on the construction of service users as consumers within the discourse of care management, including whether they had been able to increase service users' choice and whether they felt that as care managers, they could empower service users. One of the main reasons for the introduction of the NHSCCA (1990) was to provide services to vulnerable people in the local communities, rather than placing them in remote and depersonalising institutions and to widen choice with regard to the kind of services they received and the way in which those services were delivered. A further thrust of this legislation was to try to change the perception of service users. Service users were to be considered as consumers in a mixed economy of care rather than patients or clients subject to the discretionary power of 'experts'. The intention was to introduce consumer choice in a market of service providers. Care manager assessments were the key factor in identifying need and enhancing choice by purchasing services from a range of SSD and non-SSD providers.

Respondents were asked whether care management had enhanced service user choice, whether they thought service users had been empowered, whether service users had more rights now then they did before the introduction of care management, and their impressions of how service users perceived the care-management process. Finally, they were asked whether service users were now regarded as clients, consumers or citizens (Adams 1996a).

Efforts to Increase Choice

Needs-led services were central to the rhetoric of Community Care policies. While increasing choice for service users was the intention, there were problems 'inherent in maximising choice for individuals and their carers at the same time as taking into account the local availability and patterns of services' (Beardshaw 1990, 1). The purchaser/provider split was intended to make the care manager 'feel distanced from in-house provision' and under less pressure to recommend SSD services over non-SSD services (Means and Smith 1998, 124). However, it was recognized that putting care managers in the position to both assess need and represent the SSD as the funder of services could put them in conflict (Stainton 1998, 139). Saving money for the SSD could 'put pressure on professional standards' (Baldock 1999, 106).

Spot purchasing was used to enhance choice in the community care pilot projects in Thanet and Gateshead (Davies and Challis 1986; Challis et al., 1988). However, it was observed early on that placing purchasing decisions at the level of care managers and team managers encouraged a system of spot contracts or purchases which were user-centred, but which could have the effect of undermining the financial viability of small independent sector providers (Means and Smith 1998, 133). 'Experience to date suggests that choice has not been greatly increased' (Manning 1999, 87).

Both care managers and managers agreed that choice had been enhanced in some ways, but had reservations about how much choice service users actually had. The members of an elders' team said,

> *In the early days of community care, it did initially open up a lot of opportunities for people in terms of independent living. They had choices about staying in the community, but now because the whole emphasis is on saving money, we've got to keep services at as low a cost as possible, then you can't provide the quality of services any more to keep people safely at home or to give them any real choice, basically, but I think we do provide better services than before the community care policies.*

Specifically, choice had increased for elderly service users with regard to the choice between residential care and care in their homes. Members of an elders' team said that service users now have a right to an assessment and could no longer be '*kidnapped*' from hospital to residential facility without consultation or against their will. With regard to choice, however, both managers and care managers raised the issue of the way in which service 'block contracts' limited choice.

Originally, it was envisioned that care managers could 'spot purchase' meals from local restaurants to enhance service users' choice about the food that was delivered to them. The manager of one elders' team said that,

> *In the early days when money wasn't so tight, I think there was more innovation around than there is now. I certainly remember care managers paying a neighbour to go in and provide meals for people and cafés taking meals in.*

Another elders' manager said that services were provided by '*preferred agencies*'. These service level agreements with 'preferred agencies' meant that the SSD had investigated the service and that it met the required standards for service provision. Insurance matters would also presumably be covered in such an agreement. It seemed that the original ideal of providing choice through 'spot purchasing' had not been possible because SSDs had to take responsibility for services provided. Although the bureaucratic procedures required were cumbersome and limited the discretion of care managers, they ensured SSD accountability. A member of the disabilities' team said,

> *The general principles were great in terms of putting service users at the centre of the process, but choice has been limited by service level agreements and block contracts.*

Service level agreements and block contracts have been discussed earlier with regard to the issue of needs-led versus service-led models of service provision. The needs-led model implied that needs would be identified and choice of services facilitated.

Provision of meals-on-wheels for elderly and disabled service users raised interesting issues regarding choice. Prior to 1993, the meals-on-wheels services were provided exclusively by SSDs. The manager of one elders' team said that in-house meal-on-wheels were not ethnically sensitive. He said that with the introduction of care management, agencies outside the SSD had been approved for delivery of meals-on-wheels if they had been vetted and approved by the SSD and had service level agreements. Care managers could then purchase meals-on-wheels from voluntary private or not-for-profit organizations established by ethnic minority groups. These agencies provided the service and then invoiced the SSD. He felt that in this case, the market had enhanced choice '*a bit*'.

In other elders' teams, however, practitioners said that in their SSD they had to justify to their manager the reasons for a service user's choice to receive meals-on-wheels from voluntary agencies. Presumably they had to justify a service user's choice to receive this service from a voluntary agency because this cost more than in-house (SSD) meals-on-wheels. The policy in their SSD was that service users would be provided with in-house meals-on-wheels unless there was a good reason for them to receive meals from elsewhere. The onus was on care managers to justify purchase of non-SSD meals-on-wheels. This position would seem to contradict a policy that encouraged choice.

A relatively simple policy initiative to provide choice to service users with regard to receiving meals-on-wheels from a non-SSD agency generated a high level of bureaucracy in SSDs. This process involved creating new Contracts Departments to vet, approve and establish block contracts with agencies from which services could be purchased. Care managers had to have a good understanding of what the service user wanted and be able to match that with the possible range of services available in order to enable choice. It was care managers who were the key to making this choice possible within the system as it operated. However, if care managers had to justify service users' choice to receive a non-SSD service, then this would seem to discourage choice or at the very least, make it the care manager's responsibility to facilitate choice. This is an example of the conflict of interest inherent in the care-management model wherein care managers both assess need and represent the SSD as the funder of services (Stainton 1998, 139).

Two elders' team managers agreed that choice was enhanced '*a bit*' by Community Care policies. As one said,

> *I think we started out with the premise that services should be needs-led. I think the reality of life is that they are much more resource-led. I don't think they're as service-led as they used to be in the olden days* [pre-Griffiths]. *You can purchase from external sources. Having said that, the external agencies that we purchase from are usually those that are on our approved list, so if you don't get on the approved list* [you won't get used]. *It's not as open as it was in the early days of Community Care where you'd have spot contracts with neighbours, for example. We haven't done that for a very long time.*

Some consumers of children's team services seemed to have little choice about the services that are provided to them. One children's team questioned the very idea of choice. The manager of a children's team also took this position.

The difficulty with terms like 'service user' is that it implies that people have a choice about their involvement. It's OK when a mother is motivated, but when a mother denies a problem, how do you empower that person?

Users of children and family services are often 'users' of this service against their will. The term client would seem more appropriate in this service because an element of power was implicit in forcing some families to accept the intervention of care managers.

Empowerment of Service Users

Empowerment of service users (Payne 1995, 175) and choice were central objectives of Community Care policies, although contradictions can exist between these two concepts because they must be implemented within resource constraints (Horder 2002, 116). Empowerment has been defined in various ways. 'Empowerment involves helping people to gain greater control over their lives and their circumstances' (Thompson 2002, 90). One perspective on empowerment is 'concerned with how people may gain collective control over their lives, so as to achieve their interests as a group' (Thomas and Pierson 1995, 134). This is not a perspective that would be relevant to care managers who work with individuals. A more relevant definition of empowerment for care managers would be, 'a method by which social workers seek to enhance the power of people who lack it' (Thomas and Pierson 1995, 134) or 'to make someone stronger and more confident, especially in controlling their life and claiming their rights' (Pearsall 1998, 605). These last two definitions relate to empowerment in working with individuals. Strengthening service users' coping capacities is a normative role, which is difficult to achieve in care management where care managers often have a minimal ongoing contact with a service users. Empowerment in the sense of making sure that service users are enabled to claim their rights is an instrumental or informative role (Adams 1996b, 57) and one that is consistent with the care-management role.

Empowerment can be used in the political sense or the economic sense. 'Empowerment involves establishing the legitimacy of user-determined goals as an attribute of citizenship' and is therefore a political concept (McDonald 1999, 152). The term 'empowerment' is also used in the context of consumerism and refers to the process by which service users are helped to take greater responsibility for their own lives (Orme and Glastonbury1993, 189). However, claims made by advocates of consumerism for empowerment are suspect (Adams 1996a, 23).

Empowerment is not a straightforward process (Adams 1996b, 10) and is circumscribed by a number of factors. In the context of scarce resources, some people's choice can restrict other people's choice (Manning 1999, 84), thus empowering one person may disempower another. Respondents were asked whether, in their experience, service users had been empowered.

Respondents felt that they needed more time to work with service users, firstly to assess their needs, secondly, to allow them to consider their options and thirdly, to help them through the process of change. They thought it took more time than they were permitted to get to know the service user well enough to establish their needs. In order to empower service users to make choices, they needed to spend more time explaining the options to service users so that they could make informed choices. They also needed to have time to help the service user through the process of accepting the changes that they experienced. A member of one elders' team said

> *The time is taken away from you to ensure that the client is receiving what they are supposed to get, monitoring it regularly yourself. You need to have a relationship to empower people, but in most cases, it's a one-off visit.*

There was another example of this perception in another elders' team:

> *If we went into a relationship, got to know them and we were able to give them a choice, then we would be able to empower them. It takes time to tell them what they can do and what they can't do, and a one or two hour assessment doesn't allow that. It also takes time to help service users adjust to new circumstances.*

A care manager who was a district nurse in an elders' team agreed that service users needed time from care managers to adjust to the changes involved in service provision.

> *I once spent a whole day moving a man from his home to a residential facility. He needed time to accept and adjust to this fundamental life change.*

Another member of an elders' team expressed the same view.

> *People actually need time and talking to people and having to explain, it's quite complicated trying to explain to people. That doesn't seem to be taken into account, the time scale thing, that you can't actually drag the client along the time-scale that people would like. There's a valid reason to counsel someone taken from their home into a residential home. It has to happen or things fall apart.*

Some managers were sympathetic to this point; for example, the manager of a children's team said that,

> *It is very difficult because the time is limited and the number of cases that social workers actually carry now is too high. Caseloads are far too heavy. If you're working with a reasonable caseload* [ten in a leaving care team] *then maybe you can spend some quality time.*

The manager of an elders' team, who was most sympathetic to care managers, had tried to soften the effects of the managerialization of services. He said,

> *It's the same increasing depersonalization of services. What people* [service users] *say they want is simplicity and knowing who they speak to. And preferably, they want the social worker to hang about* [in their job] *for a while so that they know the organization. It's always easier if you've got some kind of working relationship, a pleasant, amenable sympathetic working relationship with the other party.*

This manager of this elders' team was aware of the need for throughput and output of work. However, she was concerned about the depersonalization of work, that is, the 'sausage factory' analogy alluded to earlier. She expressed the same concerns as care managers regarding the need to have a working relationship between care manager and service user. She did not agree with the narrowing of the care manager role to assessment only. In the above quote, she also addressed her concern that care managers were not staying in their job long enough to understand the organizations. This comment was in the context of earlier comments in her interview about the increasing tendency for agency workers to come and go from care-management positions. She felt that agency workers could not get a proper grasp of services on offer in order to make these services available to service users.

The consensus among care managers in elders' teams was that they were not allowed to spend enough time with service users to give a good quality service to them. For example, if a service user did not understand what was going on or could not adjust to the changes involved, the service would be rejected or further problems would result. The care manager was the only professional involved who was in a position to coordinate all the services that might be going in to a person's home. Each of the separate services would only be concerned to provide what they were paid to provide. The role of the care manager was to hold all these potentially fragmented services together. They had the '*linchpin*' role described earlier in the disabilities' team. Part of this role would be to help the service user understand what was going on. This took time, depending on the ability of the service user to take in and accept the information given to them. In rigid managerialized service delivery systems, care managers seem to struggle to maintain this essential contact with service users.

One elders' team felt that they could not empower service users because the resources were not available to purchase services to meet their needs.

> *How can you have more choice and rights when the resources aren't there to meet need?*

However, members of another elders' team talked about empowerment from a different perspective. They used the phrase '*that's life*' to describe the fact that scarce resources are a reality. From their perspective, needs were potentially unending, and no SSD would ever have the resources to meet all service users needs. Rather

> *Empowerment is about being honest and giving information so that service users can make informed choices. It isn't about giving them everything they need.*

Some care managers felt that care management did empower service users. The review team felt that simply telling people what was available, an aspect of the instrumental role (Toren 1972), and offering them choice was empowering.

> *You are empowering service users because you are putting in a certain package. You are empowering them even if you just tell them what is available. They have the choices. Put the choices before them and they have to power to decide. So you are empowering them by making them realize that they have rights.*

This quote raises two issues. Firstly, telling service users what is available raises images of a service-led model of service, as if the services were already in place and the service user simply had to decide which one to choose. This would be contrary to the needs-led model. Theoretically, if an appropriate service was not available to meet the need identified, a service could be created, although as discussed above with regard to meals-on-wheels, this is harder to accomplish that it might seem. Secondly, regarding service users' rights, few actual rights exist, aside from the right to an assessment if the service user meets the criteria for an assessment. The service user also does not have the right to a service that the SSD cannot afford. Therefore the issue of the right to a service is not fixed or uncontested, as the word 'right' would imply. These issues will be discussed more fully below.

When asked 'Do you think that service users are empowered within the purchaser/provider split?' one elders' team manager said,

> *It is difficult to answer that question. It is empowering to stay in your own home.*

Another elders' team manager said that elders had not been empowered, '*but there are some plans ahead to do that*'. The plan she referred to was for home carers to train elderly people for independence in their own homes upon hospital discharge so that they did not need as much home care in the long run. One might wonder whether this plan was to empower people or to save SSD resources, but as long as both goals were being met, there could be little objection to the strategy. This could be considered a 'win–win' situation in which the SSD could save money by avoiding costs of institutional care and the service user could be empowered to maintain their independence by living at home.

There is a policy assumption that service users will want to stay in their own homes, and indeed most people do (Twigg 1999, 357). When an elderly person wanted to receive care at home and this could be done safely, there was congruence between individual choice and policy objectives as this was a less costly option from a policy perspective. However, if an elderly person wanted to exercise the choice to move to a residential facility, they would have had some difficulty exercising this choice because of the cost implications. There might be some situations in which a service user might genuinely want to live in a residential facility for a variety of reasons, for example, because they felt more secure knowing that staff were available to look after them in an emergency, or because they wanted the companionship of other people which would not be possible if they were living alone. If this service user did not meet the criteria for residential care because their physical needs were not great enough to justify the cost of residential care, then s/he would not be able to exercise their choice to stay in a residential facility. In this situation, the care manager might believe that the service user was so anxious about staying alone in their own home that good professional practice would be to recommend that they live in a residential facility. However, because of the pressure of keeping costs down, they might not be able to justify the recommendation because the service user did not meet the criteria of physical need. From this perspective, the service user choice would be limited because of cost considerations.

The disabilities' team took the position that care management facilitated independence. They believed that care management was an improvement over casework, because casework created dependency on the part of service users. They said that within care management, people were encouraged to speak up for themselves, express their needs and be part of the decisions that were made about their lives.

However, these care managers said there was a dilemma in asking service users to say what they needed. Having facilitated service users' saying what they thought they needed, care managers sometimes had to go back to the service user and say, '*Oh, sorry, you can't have that*'.

It was for this reason that care managers had to be guarded. When doing an assessment, they had to be careful not to promise service users that their needs would be met because they might not be able to get agreement from their manager to purchase the services that the service user needed. They had to say things like, '*We'll get back to you*'. *We can't use phrases such as 'Well, yes, you are entitled to...*' These comments from an elders' team convey a sense in which laudable policies to enhance choice hit the reality of cost constraints.

The issues of choice, empowerment and having the time to make decisions were related. Often service users were asked to make choices quickly. Elders' teams thought that pressure on elderly people to decide quickly what they wanted was disempowering. Members of one elders' team said,

> *The whole philosophy behind Community Care was about empowering the individual and about increased choice, but it never ever translated that way.*

Members of another elders' team agreed

> *A good fifty per cent of our work is dealing with people who are being discharged from hospital. You've got lots of pressure from the hospital to get them out or get a decision made as quickly as possible. Everything forces them to make a decision quickly and we're under pressure to get them out as well. There was once time when you could say, 'well, I'll take you to see this home and I'll take you to see that home and you can choose which one you like'. Now, it's 'this is the one we and your relatives have identified. Go and see it and if you like it, you can go there'.*

The first part of the above quote regarding hospital work is consistent with research that indicated that hospital social work achieved a higher profile nationally and locally as a result of the NHSCCA (Levin and Webb 1997). Service users often needed time to weigh up the implications of their choices for themselves. Care managers thought that to be rushed into making fundamental decisions about where they might be spending the rest of their life was disempowering to elderly people. It is understandable that hospitals want to clear beds for other people to be admitted and treated. However, to see hospital care as a conveyor belt with people coming in at one end and going out the other end, without considering their social/psychological needs, would be disempowering to them.

Both care managers and managers observed that the care-management service delivery model was providing better services, but to fewer people. This reflects conventional wisdom related to selective, targeted services (Fitzpatrick 1999, 261). Their advantage is that they can focus services on those who need them most (Lewis and Glennerster 1996, 163). The manager of the review team thought that,

Elderly people are getting a better service, but only those who meet strict eligibility criteria. The criteria are so strict that only a small percentage get any service. Some say that the service is better to the elderly, but fewer are getting a service because eligibility criteria for an assessment has been tightened up.

The community care policy of targeting services to fewer but higher risk service users is evident in these views. This issue is linked to the issue of prevention observed by respondents earlier. Targeting diverts resources that away from prevention.

In the review team manager's SSD, there had been an outreach programme directed at elders living in the community, which resulted in increased applications for assessment of need.

In this SSD, we have not restricted eligibility yet. Anybody who wants an assessment will get it. We put leaflets through everybody's door and the Occupational Therapist referrals went up two and a half times their normal rate. In the future they will focus on higher need levels because of reducing staffing levels.

However, only those assessed as needing services that also fell within the income criteria would have been given services. This manager said that in the future the service would probably be targeted to service users with higher levels of need because of staffing cutbacks. It would seem that here the phrase 'targeting services' was a euphemism for 'restricting services'.

The managerialistic practice of standardizing assessment forms was thought by one team to have been empowering to some service users. There were items on the assessment form for the second elders' team that required the care managers to ask questions about the service user's race and culture. The members of this team thought that considering the service user's race and culture explicitly had been empowering. Requiring all care managers to raise the issue meant that care managers could not overlook the issue or allow it to be pushed off the assessment agenda. It also enhanced equity, in that all service users were asked their preferences and needs in the context of their culture.

The manager of the review team cited another managerialistic practice that was empowering service users. She thought that more attention was paid to making sure that the service user signed the confidentiality forms and their care plan. She thought this was empowering to service users. A signed care plan meant that the service user was involved and understood what was going to happen regarding service provision. The practice of giving copies of the assessment of need and care plan to service users was empowering because it was written in language they could understand, perhaps for the first time in their experience of social care provision, especially if they were elderly. However, there still existed the possibility that a service user could be rushed into signing something they did not understand because they were stressed or confused.

The issues in the children's teams were slightly different from those in the elders' and the disabilities' teams. When asked whether she thought her team could empower service users more within the care-management model, the manager of a children's teams said,

Some you can [empower] *and some you can't. I suppose you have to assume you can, otherwise you'd wonder why you'd be in the job, wouldn't you? I'm realistic enough to know there are some people who are so damaged, so disturbed, so deprived that you can't empower them. I find it hard just off the top of my head to think if we empower more or less. The ultimate protection of a child is empowerment. Sometimes we must threaten the mother to empower the child.*

Extending this line of reasoning, members of a children's team said that there is a power dimension to their work and sometimes it is empowering to say 'no' to service users to prevent dependency. They gave an example of empowerment by refusal of a service wherein a woman had requested that their team put her baby up for adoption. The care manager involved felt that the mother and baby had bonded and that the mother did not actually want to give up her baby, even though that was her expressed wish. The woman's request was therefore refused. The team worked with her to resolve the problems she was having. The care manager involved felt this refusal was empowering because the woman later said that she if she had succeeded in having her baby adopted, she would have regretted it.

The manager of a children's team discussed the situation in her team when a group of refugee children had come into their SSD. On their arrival in the area, they had been placed in SSD residential facilities because they had nowhere to live. This manager said that they were not given choice. '*They have been expected to fit into a regime and a culture that is quite alien to them.*'

She said that as a team they discussed the issues and came to the conclusion that they should have gone to the private sector to set up a housing unit run by people from the refugees' country of origin. This would have been an ambitious plan that was not possible or fundable and demonstrated the limits to choice.

The manager of a children's team expressed some doubts as to how much they could empower their service users.

The Children Act defined the relationship between the SSD and parents and tried to empower individuals to take some control and some responsibility for the outcomes that they may be looking for. But the way it was interpreted by some SSDs, the emphasis was not put on ensuring that consumers had a voice.

Children's teams were often operating in a 'controlling' capacity rather than a 'caring' capacity. These team managers appeared to find it difficult to reconcile control and empowerment.

SSDs were intended to meet with communities to ascertain need (Department of Health 1991b, 41, Johnson 1995, 30) and unmet needs were to be recorded (Baldwin 2000). To the degree that these elements were in place, they would be empowering.

Service User Rights

After the establishment of civil rights and political rights, Marshall (1950) predicted that social rights would come to define citizenship in social democracies. Social rights are defined as 'provision of sufficient means for all people to engage in full participation' (Ellison and Pierson 1998, 48, Manning 1999, 53). The issue of social rights is also related to human rights in the climate of the human rights movement (Human Rights Act 1998; Editorial, *The Economist* 2001, 19). Plant (1992) has discussed civil and political rights in relation to the difficulty implementing economic and social rights. Civil and political rights are negative rights, that is, 'freedom from' interference. They are unambiguous and do not entail obvious costs, although it does require resources to administer and guarantee these rights. Social and economic rights are positive rights, that is, 'freedom to' health, education and welfare. They are ambiguous, open-ended and involve distribution of scarce resources. One problem with social and economic rights is that society cannot agree on criteria for the just distribution of economic and social rights (Plant 1992, 20). In order to implement social rights, professionals and bureaucrats in the public sector gain power to distribute resources in an 'ethical vacuum' as there 'cannot be any rules of justice to guide rationing of scarce resources' (Plant 1992, 20).

Therefore, two problems exist with regard to the implementation of social rights. The first is cost and the second is ensuring enforcement. Enforcing social rights would be difficult in the climate of New Right ideology, which is against the state becoming involved in anything more than the enforcement of civil and political rights. The decline in strength of organized labour and the growth of single-issue politics, or new social movements, has lessened the impetus toward government involvement in the guarantee of social rights (Manning 1999, 54). The rhetoric of community care policies was related to service users' rights as consumers in the market rather than rights as citizens in a political sense. Respondents were asked whether they thought community care had conferred more rights on service users.

Service users had a right to an assessment, but it was a qualified right. Practitioners felt that the right to an assessment was qualified by a number of factors, such as resources. The manager of an elders' team asked rhetorically, '*What does "right" mean?*' His comment highlighted the ambiguity of rights within the care-management model of service provision.

Managers, however, were quite clear that service users had the right to an assessment.

For example, the manager of an elders' team said,

There is a legal obligation to do an assessment on specific forms so if anybody challenged us legally about whether we'd done an assessment, the only way you could prove that is by actually having some paper to show that you had done the assessment.

The manager of the review team said that in her SSD, there was an active attempt to inform service users of their rights to an assessment. This resulted in an increased take-up of the right to an assessment of need. '*Anybody who wants an assessment will get it.*'

However, the right to an assessment itself was means-tested in some cases so the service user requesting an assessment had to fall within specific criteria before they were entitled to an assessment. A member of an elders' team said that in a SSD where he had previously worked, applicants for assessments were assessed for income first. If they fell outside the income criteria, the process was stopped and they were not given an assessment of need at all. This does not seem to be the case in the elders' teams interviewed here. In these teams, assessments were provided, but if the service user's income was above a certain level, they were not considered eligible for SSD services. These service users at least had the benefit of an assessment. They could then use that assessment to purchase their own services.

The manager of one elders' team made the point that service users had a right to an assessment, but they had no right to services. A needs assessment 'does not in itself give the individual a right to have those needs met' (Petch 2002, 227). This manager said that care managers could assess need, but *'they've never been able to guarantee anything. They cannot say if the need would be met as a result of the needs assessment.'*

She referred to the Gloucester Ruling in 1994 (Drakeford 1998), which ruled that SSD's did not have to provide services if they did not have the resources to do so.

Having said that, we'll see what happens with the Human Rights Act, won't we?

Members of children's teams raised the issue that children have a right to protection even if the SSD does not have enough money to provide this protection. Budgetary limitations could not be used as a reason not to protect children. They said that courts could order that services be provided for children at risk, and SSDs would have to find the money from somewhere to provide such services.

The manager of a children's team that prepared young people for independent living said that in her team they give a second assessment after the child arrived in their residential unit. This raises a question about what would happen if these two assessments conflicted, and which assessment would be considered more valid, raising the issue of conflict between care manager and provider (Levin and Webb 1997). The second 'provider' assessment would perhaps be more 'expert' of the two, but the care manager who conducted the initial assessment and purchased the service would, it seems, have the power to withdraw funding and remove the young person from the unit if the provider's assessment conflicted with the purchaser's assessment. The mechanisms for resolving this conflict seem unclear, especially with regard to how the service user's views would be taken into account in the resolution of the issues.

Another right was the right of service users to see their files. Members of the review team said,

They have the right to see their file, but it is quite limited. They can't just walk in and say 'I want to see my file' so it defeats the object.

The right to complain was raised by both care managers and team managers as a new and useful right acquired with the implementation of care-management policies. The right to complain did not seem to be taken up by some service users, especially elderly service users. Elderly service users sometimes complain passively, by refusing a service thereby putting themselves at risk. This process of complaining about a service by 'exit' (Means and Smith 1998, 83) would only be empowering if the service user was then able to say that they wanted to use another service instead. The concept of choice by 'exit' implies the availability of a range of services, which would allow the service user to exit a poor service and use a better service.

Theoretically, this would force poorer services out of business. No mention was made in the discussion by care managers of a service user not using one service and then going on to use another service instead. The impression they conveyed was that if a service user did not like a service they could refuse to use it, but they then put themselves at risk by not having any service at all. This would seem to reflect the reality of a relatively small range of available services, with service users needing to use the services that existed or none at all.

The manager of the review team said that she always told her care managers not to be afraid of service user complaints as long as they have followed the proper procedures. She said that she advised them to '*forewarn*' her if they thought that a service user might complain. She instructed them to give the service user her (the manager's) telephone number, and tell them their complaint would be listened to.

A manager of an elders' team said that the manager's reactions to complaints were much more rigorous after the implementation of Community Care policies. The NHSCCA set up complaints procedures in which complaints were taken more seriously than they had been before the Act. In the past, complaints were seen as some failing on the part of the person making the complaint. He said,

> *A complaint was seen as an indication that the service user couldn't relate to their social worker, or that it revealed a problem on the part of the service user. The feeling was 'this is why they have a social worker. Something is wrong with them'.*

This manager said that scenario would not happen now. He said that since 1993 he starts from the point of the customer's right '*even if they may be just "having a go"*'. He said that he was going to see a service user who was complaining about their social worker that afternoon. The service users had complained that his social worker was not qualified and was '*out of her depth*'.

> *That wouldn't have happened a few years ago. In the past, I would have talked to the social worker who would have said, 'Oh, that woman's crazy' and I would have written a standard letter.*

The manager of the review team told her care managers that they should not worry about complaints '*as long as they had followed procedures*'. Taken literally, this would mean that service users' complaints would not be acknowledged unless procedures had not been followed by their care manager. From this perspective, the service user could not complain about the personal qualities of the care manager. This stance on complaints would not seem to allow for the possibility that the care manager was rude or ill informed. It would seem that service users might have complaints about things that did not fall into the category of '*failure to follow procedures*'. The above example of a service user complaining that his social worker was '*out of her depth*' was such a complaint. It did not relate directly to the care manager not following procedures. The complaint was acknowledged and the manager was, commendably, taking action to investigate it.

This elders' team manager made two further points about rights. He said that service users with advocacy groups are more likely to have their rights recognized than those without such advocacy groups, and 'younger' elderly are more likely to demand their rights than 'older' elders. However, he also said that service users who knew their rights were more likely to influence the social worker to set up a package to meet their needs than those who do not.

The statements from this elders' team manager would mean that the most vulnerable service users are not being empowered. If this was the case, then the care-management model of service delivery has not been an improvement on previous models in securing services for these service users. Even with universal systems of service delivery, those with the greatest knowledge and influence gained most from the welfare system because they knew their rights and were in a position to demand them. It may be the case that service users who are most aware of their rights and have higher levels of education, income or stronger social networks still get the most out of the care-management system. This observation would be consistent with Stanley (1991) who found that those users who were able to articulate their own needs forcefully were most likely to be able to exercise choice.

There was agreement that service users were not aware of changes in professional roles and the service delivery system. One elders' team thought that service users have more rights within care management, but they are not aware of those rights. This theme ran through the discussions in almost all of the teams interviewed.

> *You say to people, 'I'm sorry, but I can't give you any information about this, or we don't do this any more'. They just can't understand why. They say, 'You're a social worker. Why can't you do it?'*

The relative roles of the professionals in the care-management system were often unclear to service users. Professional roles and boundaries between roles are quite important to the professionals involved. For example, professionals may get into arcane debates about whether nurses or social workers should be care managers. However, from the perspective of the service user, it may not matter who performs which role as long as their needs are met. In that sense, all professionals are 'helpers' from the perspective of service users.

The same point was raised in a children's team.

> *Nobody's out there telling our clients about the changes. Ten years ago, we were handing out resources left, right and centre. Now I say to people, 'Yes, ten years ago we would have helped you, but now you're going to have to try this agency or that agency.' And I feel terrible.*

None of the managers interviewed commented on the issue of service users' perception of the changes in the service delivery system. This may be because they did not usually have direct contact with service users, so this was not an issue that they dealt with on a daily basis.

Service Users Viewed as Clients Rather Than Consumers or Citizens

Community care policies attempted to change the discourse of care from a professional focus to a market focus. This involved the reconstruction of service users from clients to consumers. The issue of citizenship in relation to the construction of clients and consumers is complex (Jones 1992, Adams 1996a, White and Harris 1999, Salskov-Iverson 1999). The term 'client' would seem to imply a power differential in a relationship with an 'expert', with the client as the 'object of [a] professional therapeutically-oriented service' (Payne 1995, xv). Even having a social worker involves stigma (Payne 1999, 255), which would seem to make it difficult for users of social work services to be viewed as consumers. 'Customer' implies an individual buyer in a market. 'Citizen' implies equality of rights and responsibilities in a collective sense. 'The relationship between citizenship and consumerism ... is a complex and often contradictory one', not least because of the problem of equating economic principles of efficiency and political principles of citizenship (Symonds and Kelly 1998, 66). Payne (1995, xv) also observes that the term 'service user' is employed to denote an empowered user with rights to control over services provided in the context of community care legislation, but that this conveys a false impression of an 'empowered user'. In this discussion, the term 'service user' has been used because it is the most neutral term available. The terms 'client, customer, citizen' were raised with care managers and team managers to ask them how they thought service users were regarded in the current climate of care.

While respondents were aware that there was a policy to construct service users as consumers of services, most of those interviewed still viewed service users as clients who needed to be helped. One elders' team separated themselves from their organization's policies. '*This organization sees them as consumers.*' They further qualified this by saying that service users were definitely not citizens with rights. Although this team did not go on to say they saw service users as clients, this was implied.

Other teams were more explicit. The review team viewed service users as clients. One children's team saw their service users as clients, although they did not call them that '*to their face*'. The use of the phrase 'to their face' would suggest that they thought 'client' was a negative term. They thought service users could be clients and still have rights, but '*Calling them consumers is insulting because in Children and Families teams, half our clients don't want us to be there*'.

However, one member of this team said she had experience working in another SSD where they were required to refer to service users as customers.

> *When I worked in another borough, they actually made a deliberate shift from calling the user a 'service user' to calling the user a 'customer'. It actually changed the way you thought about the person you were dealing with. If you thought about them or saw them as clients, there was a power thing, whereas if they are customers, you actually thought about serving them.*

This statement raises the issue of language as symbol and as label, as well as the use of language to change the discourse attached to service users and the construction of their identity *vis-à-vis* care managers (Symonds and Kelly 1998, 8). For the above speaker, the words she used to refer to service users changed her perception of them. Words and labels were then important from this perspective. The words attached to service users both represented them but also shaped and changed behaviour toward them.

Managers commented more often than care managers about the terminology attached to service users. The manager of an elders' team said,

> *We're very much into a customer focus as a borough. There is pressure on us to use the word 'customer' from the chief executive.*

He said that every non-social work department in his borough used the term 'customer' to describe the users of their services. However, social workers still used the term 'client'.

Advocating for service users' rights implied seeing service users as citizens with rights. However, care managers' ability to advocate was limited within resource constraints and service users seemed to have few rights beyond the right to an assessment and the right to see their files. The right to services was constrained by resources so this right was not absolute.

One elders' team manager, when asked whether service users are now clients, consumers or citizens, had given some thought to the implications of the terms used to think about service users.

> *I think care managers think of them as clients. I think that implies 'doing to' them. I think it's kind of patronising, looking at it now. It never used to be years ago. That wasn't how you saw it. Well, maybe that was how we saw it. I think there's a move in social services departments in more recent years to look at people as customers. But also with the recent changes, we're actually talking about people as citizens with rights and responsibilities.*

She thought there was a tendency to make people dependent in the traditional social services. '*I think its much more positive working now. People who use the service are not thought of as different from anybody else who uses any council service.*'

This last comment seems to refer to the stigma that has historically been attached to the use of SSD social services. She implied that the use of SSD services to the elderly or to children should be perceived no differently from use of SSD parking services. This would support the conceptualization of service users as citizens with rights. From this perspective, service users should receive social services as a right, as 'citizens', rather than as an admission of failure or inadequacy, as 'clients'.

Similarly, the manager of a children's team reflected on the way that the three concepts of service users intertwined. She was speaking from the perspective of work with children. She started by saying that service users are citizens.

> *Children need some help in becoming citizens. The child is dependent on parents so the parent is the client. Parents need assistance to assume a citizenship role. Sometimes we need to teach parents how to assume the rights and responsibilities of citizenship. I see them as citizens. I don't see it as 'we're out to rescue them' [i.e., see them as clients]. Services are rationalized, but 'consumer' implies that service users can just 'come and get it' which is not the case. Much of our work isn't wanted.*

Services to children did not necessarily involve direct work with children. Social workers were often imposed on parents when parents were judged not to be looking after their children. Child protection work implied unwilling consumers. In these situations, it would not seem appropriate to refer to parents in these families as consumers. Care managers were also balancing the rights of the parents and the children. The manager of an elders' team used the term partnership, but where care managers were imposed on service users, the power balance would not seem to justify the word 'partner'. In this situation, the above manager alluded to the child being the citizen and the parent as a client. Care managers may need to see parents as clients being worked with in order to enhance the rights of the child to parenting that is 'good enough', a term used in work with children and families (Adcock 1985) to describe parenting that is 'good enough' to enable children to assume the role of a responsible citizen.

This seemed to be supported by the manager of a children's team. She thought that the Children Act (1989) defined shared responsibility between social workers, the SSD and families. However, she said the way the Act was interpreted by some SSDs meant that families did not have very much power.

> *I don't think the emphasis was put on ensuring that consumers had a voice, as in having Children's Rights services and other kinds of complaint procedures. If they* [families] *weren't happy, they had no mechanism for saying that. So 'you get what you get'. If you don't like it, well, there's no avenue for letting anybody know.*

She thought families were not really customers of services. She said, '*We should use the term partner, but the systems are not in place to make people feel they are partners*'. In this, she concurred with the manager of an elders' team who said that he felt the word 'customer' was not accurate because they, service users, were not buying the service. Rather, the care manager was mediating their demands. He thought that ideally, '*We should be empowering our service users to become partners*'. He said that the word 'partnership' implied more power than customer or consumer.

The term 'client' would seem to imply that the service users had a problem that was so great that they were not able to make choices or that they had forgone the right to make choices by their behaviour. It implied a power imbalance. The care manager as expert would seem to have the right to impose services against the will of the service user, because as 'experts' they 'knew best'. In such situations, the terms such as 'citizen ', 'consumer' or 'partner' would not seem to be appropriate.

The manager of the review team was against the use of the term 'consumer'. She said that in her team they use the term 'client'. They thought the term 'consumer' was insulting.

> *'Consumer' implies pounds, shillings and pence. That's much too easy and simplistic. My instinct is that they're still being seen as clients. I can't see anybody thinking they're consumers. Direct payments would make them consumers.*

The issue of direct payments to service users was raised by several respondents who observed that direct payments would empower service users. In theory, direct payments to service users would allow them to purchase their own services. They said that purpose of the Community Care (Direct Payment) Act 1996 (Department of Health 1996) was to assist people to maintain themselves in the community, which would, of course, be empowering in the sense that they could exercise greater control and responsibility in their own lives (Orme and Glastonbury 1993, 189) because the service user would be given resources to purchase their own services and employ their own carers. Direct payments are consistent with mixed economy of care policies and the enhanced personal responsibility of individuals for their own care (Twigg 1999, 356). The Act was meant to give service users greater say in their care. The manager of one elders, team said that direct services to disabled people were empowering. In this arrangement,

> *Care managers assess for the needs, and the service user purchases their own package of care. They have more choice and independence, but they also have more responsibility.*

The manager of an elders' team said that direct payments to young disabled people was empowering. The manager of the review team also mentioned direct payments as empowering.

> *I don't know of anyone who gets a direct payment, but it is being introduced and it has major implications. Giving people choice is empowering. The 'we know best' culture is changing.*

Perhaps the reason that the review manager did not know anyone who got a direct payment was that she worked with the elderly. When the Community Care (Direct Payment) Act came into force in April 1997, direct payments were restricted to disabled people under the age of 65. According to Twigg, this initial exclusion of people over 65 was a result of a fear that the cost of direct payments would 'escalate out of hand' (Twigg 1999, 356). In 2000, direct payments were extended to people over 65 (Department of Health 2000, Petch 2002, 233). However, when this interview was held, the extension of direct payments to those over 65 had not been implemented in this review manager's SSD.

The manager of the disabilities' team said he did not know if the NHSCCA was meant to change the status of service users or not.

> *I certainly think what they intended to do was maybe to try to and offer service users a better deal. I think we should consider service users as consumers. I think they are citizens with rights to maintain their physical and mental health and their well being in the community, with a right to choice as to how that's done, and how they're cared for and who does it.*

Conclusion

This chapter has considered managers' and practitioners' views as to whether the commodification of social services has resulted in increased choice for service users and empowered them in the quasi market of care. Opinion was divided as to whether service users were consumers, citizens or clients. The rhetoric of choice is central to care management. The reality for those interviewed was that services were predominantly resource-led rather than needs. However, whether or not service users have choice has emerged as a central issue in this study.

Empowerment of service users has been enhanced in some ways but not in others. Service users' rights appeared to be limited to the right to an assessment (in specified circumstances) and the right to complain. Children have the right to protection. However, service users are often not aware of their rights.

In order to enhance choice and meet individual need in the UK, SSDs were required by the National Health Service and Community Care Act (1990) to identify need in the community and to create or commission services in the community to meet these needs. SSDs were then expected to enhance the use of existing voluntary organizations and facilitate the creation of small non-profit voluntary organizations (operating on business principles) from which SSDs could then purchase services. This process has happened unevenly because it depends on SSDs being proactive and well organized in identifying needs and commissioning services in the community. In the main, needs-led services are only needs-led in that assessment of need is more stringent than it has ever been and it is set against a rigid criteria of what can be provided. A needs assessment does not mean that needs will be met or resolved. Social workers ascertain what the service user wants and then attempts to put together a 'package of care' by purchasing services from a range of providers. The 'package' is intended to be tailored or customized to the specific needs of the individual and to provide choice to service users. However, if services are not available, that is, if they are 'not on the menu', then it is possible that social workers have raised the service user's expectations inappropriately. Local authorities may react creatively to excess demand for services by simply raising the eligibility criteria to prevent more service users from being eligible for services, thereby defeating the purpose of meeting the needs of many vulnerable people (Brindle 2007, 1).

Increasing choice and an orientation to service users' needs were important arguments for the introduction of care management in the UK. However, there are ironies and contradictions in increasing bureaucratization for the purpose of increasing choice. Choice in McDonaldized care-managed social services organizations means that service users can have anything they like as long as it is 'on the menu' so choice is restricted. In terms of choice, service users in the UK are in much the same position as they were before the introduction of care management. The main difference is that criteria for defining need are tighter, the assessment process is standardized, service users are asked more formally what they think they need and block contracts are established with the private and voluntary sector. The availability of services is still limited by budgets; the reality is that availability is even more budget-led than it was prior to the introduction of care management. In theory, it is up to the social worker to find ways of meeting need in creative ways, but creativity is difficult to achieve when the social worker is on a treadmill of mechanically assessing need, purchasing services and reviewing packages of care.

In spite of efforts to construct service users as consumers of care or customers, most of those interviewed still viewed them as clients or service users. Efforts to construct service users as citizens or partners were limited. The potential of direct payments to enhance choice was raised, but was not used widely at the time of these interviews.

Chapter 5 addresses the views of managers and practitioners as to the issue of how care management has affected the professional status of social workers in the UK.

Chapter 5

The Professional Status of Social Workers Practising as Care Managers

Introduction

The purpose of this chapter is to explore perceptions on the introduction of professional registration in the UK. Registration was introduced shortly after the introduction of care management. Two contradictory forces were therefore at work: the deskilling of the social work role implicit in care management and the raised status of social workers through professional registration and a protected title.

Social work professional identity has historically been weak in the UK because it has not been a registered profession. Social workers' claim to professional status has been ambiguous because as bureau-professionals, social work has been subject to government definition of its roles. Its knowledge claims have been challenged in the postmodern questioning of the expert. Care management has deskilled social work. Care management 'present threats to the position of social work' (Sheppard 1995, 293) and questions have been raised as to whether or not care management is social work (Postle 1999, 219). Social work within care management is 'under erasure' (Pietroni 1995, 30).

Professional registration of social workers was agreed in Britain in 1998 (Adams and Shardlow 2000, 130). Registration has been viewed as possibly elitist (Orme 2001, 615) Bureaucratization and professionalization are both criticized by some (Meagher and Parton 2003, 13). However, registration of social workers would give social workers an enhanced professional identity independent of their bureau-professional identity established in the Seebohm era. It must be recognized that the proposal to register social workers was not initiated by a strong professional body to promote its own interests as in the prototypical professions, law and medicine, but has been accomplished through increased surveillance of social workers' activities. The advantages and disadvantages of the registration of social workers are explored, including whether or not respondents viewed registration as elitist. The possible use of registration to offset the potentially negative effects of managerialism will be discussed.

One of the questions at the outset of this study was whether social workers might prefer to work in the non-statutory private and voluntary sector in order to escape the increasingly managerialized public sector bureaucracies. The possibility has been raised that social workers would leave SSD social work for the private and voluntary sector because private sector service provision has been encouraged in the climate of right wing policies and free market philosophies (Cheetham 1993, 172, Van Heugten and Daniels 2001, 739). Care managers and managers were asked, from their perspective and given their experience of care management, whether they thought social workers would prefer to work as providers in the private or voluntary sector rather than as purchasers in SSDs.

Social Work – A Profession?

Historically, the professional status of social work has been ambiguous. Social work has been described as a semi-profession (Toren 1972) or a bureau-profession (Parry et al., 1979) because it consolidated its identity with the expansion of the bureaucracies of the welfare state. Social work is a minor profession (Schon 1983, 23) as opposed to the 'major professions' of law and medicine. Minor professions, such as social work are constructed differently in different times and places and are therefore unable to develop a base of systematic scientific professional knowledge. Social work suffers from 'ambiguous ends, shifting contexts of practice, and no fixed professional knowledge base' (Schon 1983, 46). This analysis of social work reflects the changing purposes for which social work has been used in a social policy context in Britain. The 'shifting contexts of practice' describes perfectly the reality of restructuring that took place to facilitate the introduction of care management in SSDs.

Two reasons have been put forward for social works' difficulty achieving professional status. The first is technological. Social work has 'hitched its professional wagon to science' and claimed to be able to predict and cure, yet the problems social work grapples with are not those which are amenable to cure so social work is accused of 'failing to deliver the goods' (Howe 1986, 147). The second reason is ideological. Social workers 'side' with clients and sometimes blame society for their service users' problems (Howe 1986, 148). This position has not endeared social workers to the state, which is in a position to give or withhold professional status to social work.

From the perspective of the sociology of the professions, social work is not a full or free profession, in the way that medicine or law are professions, because it has not successfully pursued a 'professional project' (Macdonald 1995). A 'professional project' is an agreement or a trade-off between government and a group of professionals in which government allows the profession a degree of freedom in return for a degree of control by the state. Registration and the granting of a protected title are part of such a trade off. Social workers were not registered in the UK when this study was carried out, although the registration by the newly created GSCC was under discussion when respondents were being interviewed. Respondents were asked whether they thought social work was a profession. More specifically, they were asked whether they thought that their role as care managers was consistent with social work professionalism.

In answer to the question 'Do you think that social work is a profession?' the consensus was that social work was a profession because it required training. The manager of a children's team said,

I think it is a profession because it requires training and qualification and with most professions, that is the basic requirement, that you undertake a particular kind of training and you get qualified to allow you to be able to do that field of work.

Similarly, the manager of the disabilities' team said,

Social work is still a worthy profession even though it does different things than it did twenty-two years ago when I came in to it.

However, there were several points of qualification to the position that social work was a profession. A care manager in an elders' team said,

I think that it's in a kind of professional crisis. In terms of what tasks seem to be valued and acknowledged by the central government and consequently by the institution you work for, the interactive and the personal skills don't seem to be valued. Personally, I feel that a lot of the stuff I do does not require a person to be a professional.

Some thought that care management diminished the professional aspects of social work practice. They thought that social work was a profession, but that care management was not a profession. The purchaser/provider split and the care manager role had blurred the professional boundaries in work with adults because care managers did not have to be a social worker. The manager of the review team said,

Social workers are professionals, but most people these days turn around and say that care managers are not social workers. I think social work is a profession.

The manager of an elders' team said,

I don't think care management is a profession because you don't need professional qualifications and care managers don't have a professional body or professional standards.

While some thought care management diminished the professional aspects of social work, others thought care management clarified the social work role. Managers of two elders' teams thought that social work had tried to be too many things to too many people and that it needed to focus its activities. They reflected on the past status of social work and said they thought social workers were regarded as being more professional since the introduction of care management. As the manager of an elders' team said,

As a profession, it's always been a bit suspect because it's been such a mish mash. It's tried to be poor man's psychiatrist, psychologist, mother, father, the lot.

The manager of an elders' team thought that care management had enhanced the perception of social workers. He felt that in their work with other professionals in multi-disciplinary settings, social workers practising as care managers were regarded as fellow professionals.

In the past, we always used to call it a semi-profession, but we never quite made it to being a full profession. But in the multidisciplinary setting, it is very clear to me that doctors and district nurses and people like that regard social workers as fellow professionals. I use the work 'professional' quite a lot. I talk about people's professional judgement, professional assessment, professional decision-making and so on.

The two teams that gave the least favourable comments about whether social work was a profession worked in the same SSD. One was an elders' team and the other was a children's team. A member of the elders' team in this SSD said that social work was *'just about'* a profession, meaning that social work was almost a profession. Lack of autonomy in their work and a sense that their work was not valued were two reasons why they felt they were not considered professionals. Because these two teams were located in the same SSD, it could be surmised that their perception of whether social work was a profession was associated with how they themselves were perceived in this particular SSD.

Members of the disabilities' team expressed the most positive views of care managers as professionals.

> *If we're pulling together the psychologist, the consultant, the psychiatrist and the occupational therapist, and if we were not professionals ourselves, how could we perform that role?*

Social workers working as care managers in multidisciplinary settings were positive about how their role was perceived. The manager of a children's team, however, sounded a note of caution regarding multi-disciplinary work.

> *Work has changed. It's a lot better. It's much more professional, but we need to start being a bit more proud of ourselves. Too often, a social worker is deferring to other people. Sometimes in court reports, even the most junior social worker writes a report and then the psychiatrist uses the information as if it is his.*

Consistent with the view that social workers are bureau-professionals, a member of a children's team said,

> *I see myself as an agent of the government because they've got all this legislation that at the end of the day, if I don't follow* [I will be in trouble]. *It's government law. I'm not just a council employee, but an agent of the government. Social work ceased to be a profession in 1970.*

This comment refers to the LASSA (1970) that led to the establishment of SSDs and the generalist role of social workers. Members of this team thought that in 1970 members of specialist social work organizations, such as the association of social workers who worked with the elderly and the association of psychiatric social workers, disbanded and gave up their identity as specialist social workers. There was not a proper social work council to work for the interests of social workers. A member of a children's team observed that,

> *All of them became members of BASW* [British Association of Social Workers]. *After that, they were just simply employees of whatever organization they were in.*

This respondent thought that when social workers were members of specialist organizations, it was their knowledge and their skills that was the basis of their status. After specialist organizations were disbanded, he thought that their allegiance was to the organization for which they worked and they protected themselves by joining unions such as NALGO. Thus respondents in this team felt that the attempt to unify social work into one profession with the introduction of BASW had not succeeded. They associated the abandonment of specialist professional organizations with the unionization of social workers working in SSDs. They felt that by unionizing, social workers had reinforced their identity as SSD employees, which detracted from their professional identity.

These comments relate to the issue of specialism and genericism within social work. Social work had developed specialisms prior to the Seebohm Report. The LASSA (1970) created a generalist role within SSDs. Following this Act, one of the biggest distinctions between social workers was whether they were field workers or residential workers. The purchaser/provider split contributes to a return to specialisms within social work and raises the issue as to whether this has fragmented the social work role. Members of a children's team felt that even before the introduction of the care-management role, the differences between social work in specialist fields was too great to warrant a single professional identity as social workers.

> *I'm sorry, but residential social work is not the same as fieldwork. A person that works here* [in a community-based children's team] *is not the same as an educational service social worker. Possibly, it's not about the profession of social work, but the professions within social work that need to be formed, the links that need to be made between the common factors.*

Asked whether the potentially fragmenting influence of a new specialism, that is, care management, would be overcome by the unifying effect of professional registration, a member of a children's team said,

> *I don't think you can unify social work. I believe that there's no such thing as social work. It's a construct, so therefore the fact is that there's no agreement as to what social work is or what constitutes social work or what should be part of social work.*

This statement expresses the socially constructed nature of social work. Social work does not exist as a tangible reality. The respondent thought that that social work training attempted to unify social work, so that even if not all social workers did the same thing, they all had the same body of knowledge. However, in the end, he said rather cynically, that we don't even have a common body of knowledge and that social work attempts to create a unified professional identity 'will just be a desperate collection of people who are desperate to get a place in the market'. It could be argued that both unionization and professionalization are different routes to the same goal, which is a place in the market. Relating social work to the market, whether through professionalization or unionization would be consistent with the culture of late capitalism.

Virtually all of the respondents thought that greater professional status was desirable. None thought registration was elitist. Only one member of the review team thought that some social workers would not want to be seen as powerful professionals in relation to service users and would not want to consider themselves as professionals. There was only one response from one member of one team that took this position.

Discretion, Indeterminacy, Trust and Accountability

One difference between casework and the current care-management procedures was that within casework, social workers were providing services. This was qualitative activity, wherein simply visiting the service user was part of provision. Under care management, they were assessing and purchasing, which were more tangible and 'calculable' (Ritzer 1996) activities. Time limits could be put on completion of assessments and a tangible result, that is, a completed assessment form was produced. It was more possible for management to make social workers accountable for their activities within care management than it was within Seebohm casework. The ability of care managers to calculate and quantify elements of a service has made care managers more 'manageable' (Ritzer 1996). Measuring activities and calculating whether activities had been carried out was related to the surveillance activities associated with new managerialism. The effect on these care managers, however, was to make them feel less trusted and disempowered as professionals.

Sheppard observed that social workers need to balance the needs of technicality and indeterminacy. Technicality referred to issues such as tick-box assessment forms. Indeterminant knowledge refers to the perception that professionals work in areas of uncertainty which 'because of the special skills of the professionals involved, can only be understood and assessed by those with the requisite skills and knowledge – those from the same profession' (Sheppard 1995, 275). Indeterminacy was related to discretion and professional autonomy and was limited by managerial control. Sheppard noted that professional autonomy could not take place to the exclusion of technicality or organizational requirements but that if professional indeterminacy was viewed by politicians as being too great, it was likely that deprofessionalization of that practice would occur.

Social workers' power to interpret policy in the Seebohm era SSDs contributed to the New Right's perception that social work power needed to be curbed by the introduction of greater management controls.

Some care managers said they felt that they were not allowed any professional discretion. Reduction of their discretion was one of the reasons they thought they had been deskilled. In the elders' team where members consistently voiced the most negative comments about the introduction of care management, one member said,

> *We have no leeway. If you don't feel empowered yourself, it's quite difficult to empower others.*

They did not feel trusted by management. They acknowledged the need for accountability but felt that the need for accountability sometimes verged on paranoia.

Their example was with regard to procedures related to visiting service users.

> *Whatever you do, wherever you go, you write it down. If you go out, if you cross the road and see this elderly lady, you have to write 'visited Mrs So and so' because everything is double-checked. But when we were in the Home Care Team [prior to the introduction of care management], if we were in X Street visiting two or three residents, and then decided to visit another three or four, that was fine, just to pop in and say hello and see if they*

were ok. Everybody trusted you. Accountability isn't necessarily a bad thing, but it's just that you sometimes feel that it's been taken to an extreme where there's almost a paranoia about what you are doing.

Members of the disabilities' team made the point that if the manager trusted a professional, the manager would allow that professional to use their discretion.

I think we use a certain amount of professional discretion, depending on the sort of manager you have or the sort of relationship you have with that manager. If the manager has a view of you as a capable, confident professional, obviously [they will allow you to use your discretion]. *If your manager doesn't think of you like that, then maybe they're going to give you as little discretion as possible and just give you instructions.*

A care manager in one elders' team gave an example of a conflict with her team manager over the time she was allowed to do an assessment. The conflict was between a team manager in a highly managerialized service and a care manager who thought that professionals should be allowed the discretion to do what good professional practice required. The care manager in this elders' team discussed how these issues were inter-linked for her and the way in which she experienced frustration with the constraints imposed upon her. She said that pressure from her manager led her to try to do the assessment within the prescribed time limit against her own professional judgement. When she failed to do the assessment within the time limit, and told her team manager that she had needed more time to do it properly, her manager's response was to blame her for not requesting more time to do the assessment. The manager said that she could always take more time to do an assessment if necessary. The point for the practitioner was, however, that she did not feel that she should have been put in the position of having to justify to the manager why she took 'extra' time. The practitioner essentially had to ask permission from her manager to do what was expected from her as a professional. She felt she was not trusted as a professional to use her discretion to complete the assessment properly.

For one elders' team, care management was mechanistic. When managerialized services were run bureaucratically, to tight procedures with activities being prescribed in a mechanistic manner, the human element which attracted social workers to the job became marginalized. The term 'mechanistic' denotes factories and conveyor belts, which connoted a Fordist approach to the provision of services.

What's expected from a care management point of view is to go out, assess someone's needs, make a list of their needs, try and meet as many of their needs as possible by purchasing the services to meet those needs, review, and it goes on and on like that. What care managers want is to get to know someone rather than just seeing them as a list of tasks and needs. It's mechanistic.

For one children's team, the issue was identified as one of independence. They felt that social workers were more independent in the past. It would seem that the teams that felt most circumscribed by management were elders' teams. Children's team care managers seemed to feel that they were allowed more discretion than elders' team care managers. However, this children's team felt that even they could exercise less professional independence within care management than they had before the introduction of care management.

The manager of an elders' team observed that care managers had less discretion currently than they did in the early days of care management because care managers could spot purchase then. Initially, they could use their professional judgement to buy one-off personalized services for individual service users. She felt that this allowed them to use their budgets creatively. As they currently did not have direct access to budgets and they could no longer spot purchase, she felt that the creativity that could be used to design packages of care was no longer possible.

The manager of the disabilities' team said that the work they did required structures but it also needed a degree of flexibility. This manager worked in a SSD where Total Quality Management (TQM) had been introduced. TQM was introduced in this SSD because it was the wish of the newly appointed Director of Social Services. Every aspect of SSD activity was subject to quality management controls.

This disabilities' team manager gave an example of the use of forms to direct supervision, which illustrated TQM as an exaggeration of Fordist management practices. The supervision form was to be used for every social work supervision. Use of the forms could be seen as advantageous in making sure that each supervision conformed to an ideal of what should happen in a supervision session. However, if the content of the supervision deviated from the standard form, the supervisor was required to fill out a separate form to indicate that they had discussed something that was not included on the original form. This would seem to be an extreme form of standardization of the content of supervision sessions and an example of managerialism. Even if these forms attempted to capture everything discussed in supervision, it is unlikely that this would be possible, given the qualitative and subjective nature of the issues that arise in social work.

When asked what TQM does to social work discretion, he said,

> Well, that's a big question. There was a tradition of discretion in traditional social work. Discretion is still around, but social workers have to make sure what they're doing is within procedures. I don't think there's any harm in people being quite clear what they're doing, but I think sometimes you do need to be a bit flexible because we're dealing with human beings, after all.

The manager of one children's team made a point that addresses the conflict between professional discretion and accountability to bureaucratic managerialized procedures.

> Councillors and senior managers have never really understood is that if push comes to shove, the allegiance of the social worker will be to their client, not the organization. There is a temptation to bend the rules for the client. I think at the end of the day, they'll always go with what's best for the client, and they will struggle in SSDs. I think that's the definition, really, of a professional in the bureaucracy. It's really hard. Where do your allegiances lie?

What can be drawn from this quote is that managers thoughts in terms of the collective and social workers were oriented to the needs of individuals. Social workers valued the individual and thus valued discretion to shape procedures to fit individual need. Managers, on the other hand, were protecting the overall structures, especially budgets, from the misuse of the individual service user. There was thus an inherent conflict between professional care managers and team managers that manifested itself in different ways in different SSD circumstances. For example, one manager of an elders' team seemed to be in conflict with the professionals on his team, whereas another manager of an elders' team took a Theory Y approach to management that created an environment in which her team members knew they were valued.

Several care managers and managers felt that social workers could still exercise discretion. According to a member of the review team,

> *You do have a certain say in how you deal with problems and which way you manage them. Everybody's got their own individual way of working.*

An experienced care manager in a children's team who had worked in local social services for many years before the introduction of care management felt she still did what she wanted. She was the only care manager in this team who had worked in this SSD children's team since before the introduction of the purchaser/provider split. She said, '*I worked in this team before 1993 and I always did what I wanted to do. I still do, more or less. Ticking boxes doesn't mean your creativity is taken from you*'. The manager of an elders' team agreed. '*How you carry out the process is something you've still got control over.*'

The manager of a children's team said,

> *I feel you use your professional discretion all the time as long as you are doing it within the confines of the work you are doing. I would hate to think that anybody was working and didn't feel they were able to use their initiative and their discretion in undertaking their work. I feel there are other constraints which you have to work out which sometimes make it difficult for you to use your discretion.*

The manager of a children's team went on to gave the following example of how she planned to use her professional discretion to protect a young service user from a potentially damaging decision by management.

> *I suppose the most live example I'm dealing with at the moment is a young person who is accommodated and has been in the care system since the age of eight. Her father has recently died. She asked the department for assistance to go and deal with her father's burial. She was told she'd be getting a one-way ticket home. And that's it now for me. That's not dealing with the needs of that young person. What they* [management] *are saying is that your mother is there* [where the funeral was being held] *so therefore if you are going to go and be dealing with your father's burial, you might as well return to your mother. She's saying, 'That's not what I want. I want to go and deal with how I'm feeling about the death of my father who I haven't seen since the age of eight.' What she's been told is that we* [management] *are not prepared to buy her a return ticket. We'll buy her a one-way ticket.*

This funeral was taking place overseas. Management's position was that this young person should return to live with her mother and stay with her mother after the funeral. There would be a range of emotions, including grief and anger, for this young person to work through before she could be successfully reunited with her mother. Many issues would have to be resolved for her, not least of which would be the issue of why and under what circumstances she had been separated from her parents at the age of eight.

This respondent used the phrase '*And that's it for me now*' to indicate her anger at management for not considering the emotional needs of this young person. It could have been that management was trying to save money, not only on a one-way ticket, but in the wider sense of trying to end their financial responsibility to this young person altogether. This was an example of a conflict between managerial interest in saving money and professional concern for meeting the emotional needs of this young person. This respondent was a team manager who had previously practised as a social worker. She was ready to do battle with her manager to get a round-trip ticket to the funeral of this young person's father. She was using her initiative to resist procedures that she thought, given her experience and training, would be damaging to this young person. It is also an example of the care manager thinking of the individual rather than the collective.

Migration to Other Fields of Work

The starting point of this current research was that not only were there more employment opportunities in the private sector and voluntary sector, there would also be more opportunity to practise traditional provider-oriented social work in this sector (Cheetham 1993, 172). There were some indications that social workers would leave practice in the public sector (Jones 2001, 55) because they were demoralized by managerialism and the emphasis on budgetary considerations (Lavalette and Ferguson 2007, 2). 'The reining-in of public expenditure has provided the impetus for some practitioners to move out of the statutory provision in the independent sector' (Hopkins 1996, 33). The issue to be explored was whether social workers who worked in the highly managerialized SSDs would be driven out of SSD purchaser work and into the provider sector where they could practice from a more traditional casework perspective (Van Heugten and Daniels 2001). 'A free market global economy of social and health care opens the possibilities for social workers to operate as entrepreneurs offering their services to state or private agencies and clients' (Niemala and Hamalainen 2001, 13).

There was some confirmation that social workers might be leaving statutory social work (Audit Commission 2002, Russell 2002) because they are overwhelmed by government targets, bureaucracy and paperwork. Stress levels were reported to be higher in public sector jobs than private sector jobs.

There is some irony in the fact that care management was introduced to create efficiency and yet the staff turnover levels created by government bureaucracy were 'grossly inefficient' (Foster 2002). This finding highlights the inefficiency of efficiency in the same way that Ritzer noted 'the irrationality of rationality' in McDonaldized service-sector organizations (Ritzer 2004, 134).

The downgraded status of social work in statutory care-management teams has been related to an increase in freelance work (Douglas and Philpot 1998, 3). The Department of Health (1998) reported that between 1993 and 1996, 9 per cent of the SSD workforce social services left social work each year, yet the majority of staff interviewed in this study expressed a preference for working in the statutory sector. Respondents were asked directly whether they thought that social workers working as care managers would leave SSDs to work in the private and voluntary sectors because of the introduction of care management.

Almost all of the respondents indicated that there were shortages of social workers in care management. The reasons for these shortages were loss of social workers through restructuring and through social workers leaving the profession because of dissatisfaction with care management. One children's team thought the increasing shortage of social workers had resulted in a trend toward the employment of foreign-trained social workers and agency workers on short-term temporary contracts.

The manager of an elders' team said that more private and voluntary work would be available than statutory work because SSDs would '*farm out*' more work to the private and voluntary sector rather than providing services in-house.

> *I think there will be people working much more in private and voluntary sectors than in local government. A lot more services will have been 'farmed out'.*

The manager of an elders' team said there would be more commissioning of services by the statutory sector and less direct provision of services so the private sector would grow. She thought this would give the private sector the scope to attract skilled social workers.

Members of the review team, who did assessment work with elders, thought social workers would move to work in the voluntary sector because it was more satisfying. They said they would rather be providers because '*It's more hands on. I think I'd rather be working with people*'.

One manager of the disabilities' team thought it was possible that if services were provided in the non-statutory sector and social workers were trained and registered, they might move to the private sector, but this was '*possible, not probable*'.

He thought that some people might want to become privately employed care managers and that registration of social workers would therefore become important. He thought that registration would provide a check on people's practice. It may be that the combination of care-management practices, the registration of social workers and the increased availability of employment outside the statutory sector will facilitate social workers working outside SSDs to a greater degree than would been possible before the combination of these factors.

The manager of an elders' team also thought that it would be possible that social workers would move to the private sector as self-employed assessors. He said that if assessments were considered a provided service,

> *There's no reason why the staff need to be directly employed by the SSD. They could contract to provide so many assessments over such a period of time so that's probably on the cards, although most social workers probably see themselves as SSD employees.*

The manager of a children's team said with regard to whether social workers would leave the SSD sector that

I don't know about in children's work. It may happen in adult community care services If workers are thinking that all they're doing is assessing and filling out forms and not doing any of the nitty-gritty social work then I can see that, but I can't see that happening in children's services because we're still providing that direct social work.

She thought that if all work went to the private sector, the qualified social workers might go to the private sector, but '*I don't see that coming*'.

A member of one children's team said,

I would say I do think about the relationship we build up and who we involve in a child's life. How we work with families is fundamental and if that goes out of social work, then I'm out of it.

She thought that in the voluntary sector, there was more room for therapeutic work and long-term work, which she would enjoy. For example, SSDs did not do reminiscence work with elders, group work with older people to validate their identity through discussion of their common memories (Link 2007). She felt there was still enough direct work with children in her SSD position to contribute to her staying. However, if that element of her work were to be contracted out to the voluntary sector, she said she would leave her SSD post.

In contrast to these positions that it would be possible for social workers to move to work in the private provider sector, all the rest of the respondents, both care managers and managers, thought that social workers would not leave statutory purchaser work in SSD social services.

When care managers in the disabilities' team were asked whether social workers might move to the voluntary sector to take up provider roles, a response from the disabilities team was '*But they're not doing that*'. The manager of the review team, when asked the same question, said '*absolutely not*'. She said that provider agencies from the voluntary sector had engaged in what has been referred to in the business world as 'head hunting'. These private agencies had approached her and members of her staff and asked them to come and work for them as private agency social workers. She thought that neither she nor her staff wanted to take up the jobs offered by private sector agencies. However, her comments stood in contrast to members of her own review team which indicated (above) that they would consider working in the voluntary sector because it was more satisfying work. She gave three reasons for social workers staying in the statutory sector.

They wanted to stay in the statutory sector because they wanted to upgrade their skills. They don't want to be pigeonholed as residential workers and there is a deep distrust of the private sector.

This manager thought social workers would stay in SSDs and not move to the private sector because firstly, there were career progression opportunities within SSD social services departments that did not exist in the private sector. They could upgrade their skills and job security was greater in SSD employment. Secondly, elders' work in the private sector is in the residential sector and social workers did not want to be pigeonholed as residential care home workers. Thirdly, social workers would not go to work in the private sector because they distrusted the private sector.

The manager of both an elders' team and a children's team said that people were leaving statutory social work. However, they were not leaving the statutory sector to take up positions in the private and voluntary sector. They were leaving the profession altogether. The manager of an elders' team spoke of trying to fill a vacancy in her team. She could not find anyone to fill the post and referred to a 'famine'.

> *As it just so happened, there was a famine. You could not get workers. You could not get a qualified social worker through an agency. So that was when I first found out that people were leaving the profession.*

Members of a children's team said,

> *When I left my course, a lot of the social workers left and did other things, like one of my friends runs her own cleaning company now. Another's gone on to be a veterinary. Others have gone into counselling and therapeutic work in the provider sector.*

Some of these examples were of social workers leaving social work for completely different fields of work.

Members of an elders' team expressed the opinion that there was a policy intention to get rid of SSDs completely. They thought private agencies were being groomed to take over SSD roles.

> *I believe that there is a move to get rid of social services as it is. National Children's Homes and MIND are being groomed to take over statutory work.*

If that happened, then most social workers would work in private agencies.

A manager of an elders' team said that last year she lost two staff, not through restructuring, but because,

> *They no longer liked the way they were being asked to work and the pressure just to move people about. The restructuring was their particular Waterloo. They just couldn't take any more. I can think of other people who are thinking again* [about staying in the profession]. *If the future is less certain, people think of their next career move. People are leaving the profession.*

UK General Social Care Council – Advantages and Disadvantages of Registration

Registration with a professional body is an important element of professional identity. Registration creates a protected title, which can only be used by those who have achieved the qualifications necessary to entitle them to registration. Social work in the United Kingdom was not a registered profession until 2005. Prior to 2005, anyone in a social work post could call him/herself a social worker. The occupation of a social work post identified one as a social worker, regardless of qualification. In the mid-1990s momentum toward creation of a professional body for social work began to grow. Implicit in this idea was the registration of social workers with this professional body, thus making 'social work' a registered and protected title.

The 'professional project' describes the attempt of professions to strike a deal with the state which facilitates reciprocity with the state, allowing profession bodies to control their internal professional matters in exchange for some external regulation by the state (McDonald 1995). The establishment of the GSCC contributes to furthering the 'professional project' of social work in that it requires social workers to register and thus enhance the status of the profession. However, it must be recognized that the registration of social workers has not been initiated by a strong professional body to promote its own interests, but rather has been accomplished through increased surveillance of social workers.

Respondents were asked about the advantages and disadvantages of the registration of social workers with the GSCC, including whether they thought that registration of social workers would be elitist.

All of the respondents welcomed registration. It was observed by several respondents that historically, the absence of registration procedures has been a problem for the profession. In earlier discussions, respondents had questioned whether social work was a profession or a white-collar occupation because social workers were not registered. The issue of social work's not having a professional body was a theme of discussion in several teams. A member of one elders, team thought that,

> *One of the problems* [with social work] *is that there's never been a concerted effort to present itself as a profession. There's no body to represent us. There's no registration.*

Another elders' team took the same view:

> *If we don't have a body, an independent body, to steer it, to regulate it, then it is not a profession.*

Six advantages of registration were discussed. The first was the establishment of a protected title. Secondly, it would create parity with other professions such as nursing and teaching. Thirdly, although social workers could be struck off for bad practice, this was thought to be a good thing because it would help the profession establish a benchmark of good practice to which all practitioners would be expected to adhere. Fourthly, registration would help social work as a profession to resist political and managerial practices and it would strengthen individual practitioners *vis-à-vis* their managers. Registration would mean a professional body would protect professional interests. Fifthly, managers thought it would help them pressure for 'qualified only' hiring policies within SSDs. Lastly, for practitioners, it would contribute to greater employment flexibility and job mobility. It would make self-employment feasible because professional identity would be established by registration regardless of the post held.

The main disadvantage was that it could be difficult to separate individual bad practice and organizational bad practice because social workers' practice is so embedded in organizational procedures, a reflection of social work's bureau professional status.

Three further issues were raised. Firstly, registration would need to be national and compulsory. Secondly, social workers would need to pay to be licensed and would need professional insurance. This would be a disadvantage in that it would add costs to being a social worker, but it would be an advantage in that it would provide protection from malpractice suits and dismissal from employment. Thirdly, managers thought registration might change employment practices, especially with regard to the need for police checks.

Issues relating to social work's 'professional project' (Macdonald 1995) were discussed above. Firstly, regarding the issue of a protected title, there was a consensus that allowing anyone to call her/himself a social worker had been a problem for the profession. Respondents in several teams were concerned that currently there were no restrictions on who could call themselves a social worker. For example, members of both a children's team and elders' team both expressed the view that, '*Anyone can call themselves a social worker*'. They thought social workers should be registered and welcomed registration of social workers as an enhancement of social works' profession status.

The second advantage it was thought that social work registration would put social workers in line with other professions such as nursing and teaching. The disabilities' team thought that there were strong professional bodies in other fields which stood up for their interests and which gave them some power. They felt that this was in contrast to social work, which did not have a strong professional body. They thought that registration would be good for the accountability of social workers and for the protection of social workers. It would also allow the professional body to dissociate itself from bad practice, develop the concept of social work as a profession and give social workers a professional identity. A member of an elders' team said,

I think it would be a good thing if social workers were licensed in the same way teachers are licensed. I think it would validate the profession. Registration would be good for the public to see.

Thirdly, respondents agreed that registration would set standards and potentially empower service users to challenge individual social workers. Individual practitioners could be struck off for bad practice. A member of a children's team said,

It's about making a declaration that you are a member of an independent body that has values, ethics and regulations and that you could be struck off. There's been so much scandal about social work. It might give service users more power because social workers would be more personally liable. It's about professional accountability, isn't it? It's about regulation. If we want to call ourselves professionals then that would be the obvious way. I think it's one of the criteria of defining a profession.

The manager of the disabilities' team made a similar point. He felt that registration would help to establish national standards of good practice.

The GSCC would be good because it would make us accountable not only to the SSD, but it would make us look more closely at our standards because standards, and how standards are implemented, vary from SSD to SSD. I think it would be good to have standards all over the country. I mean, there are good and bad social workers and there are social workers that I'm afraid to say should never have been allowed to qualify. They just make it by the skin of their teeth and their practice isn't suitable. I think people should be made accountable regarding either offences against the person, or malpractice. Social workers should be accountable to both the profession and the SSD. Agency workers sometimes slip through the net.

Fourthly, registration would help social work as a profession resist political pressures and it would help individual practitioners resist managerial practices that were not in the best interests of individual service users. Several responses indicated that registration would help social workers as a professional body to maintain standards and resist political and managerial efforts to change the role of social workers or to compromise social work values. It was thought that registration would give social workers, as a body, the power to bargain with government and not to be compelled to change their role whenever it pleased the governmental party in power. It would mean that central government could not, in the words of the manager of an elders team, just '*dump*' things on social work. New working conditions could not be imposed on social workers without some consultation with the professional body. The GSCC would be able to take a stand about things that were important to professional values.

Several care managers and team managers made the point that professional registration would also help social workers resist managerial dictates that were contrary to professional values and strengthen practitioners position *vis-à-vis* their management. This view was consistent with those expressed earlier that registration would assist social workers to maintain their professional identity and values in the face of increasingly managerialized and procedurally directed SSD care management.

Members of one elders' team were sceptical about the value of registration; however, they thought that it would provide social workers some voice in determining their role in society. '*It might go some way to protecting our roles for us* [which are] *constantly being chipped away at.*'

Fifthly, managers thought registration would help them advocate for policies that restricted employment to qualified social workers. The manager of an elders, team thought that registration would be valuable for a number of reasons.

I think it's a good thing. It would enhance professional status. It would make my job easier in terms of standards. Being registered implies a lot of other things.

He thought registration might prevent bad practice. He did not think it would be elitist from the public's point of view. He said that care management was a very responsible position, being at the centre of this supportive network for service users. It would be a stimulus to individuals to maintain high standards because

They could potentially be brought before the GSCC and could be struck off. It would probably firm up our own existing 'qualified only' [employment] *stance of the chief executive. They need to be registered and recognized because they do such a difficult and responsible job.*

Lastly, patterns of work seem to be changing and registration would verify qualifications and help social workers retain their professional identity. Several respondents referred to an increasing trend toward social workers becoming free-lance, self-employed social workers or acquiring short-term fixed-contract work through social work employment agencies. If social work becomes a more self-employed or agency-based activity, then registration with a profession will be important in verifying their qualifications, demonstrating that they uphold expected standards of practice and establishing their identity as a social worker. There was speculation among respondents that registration would contribute to greater flexibility and job mobility for individual social workers and could facilitate greater self-employment among social workers because their identity would be established by registration, not by holding a social work post.

The manager of an elders' team made a salient point about how registration would affect the identity of social workers. '*If social workers become self-employed, registration will be more important to guarantee standards.*'

Registered professionals would be accountable to the profession '*if something went drastically wrong*', a comment made by the manager of the disabilities' team. Registration with the GSCC could facilitate accountability to the profession rather than to the organization. Registration would allow social workers to have an identity as social workers outside the structures of SSD social service departments. Professional identity would be strengthened and not depend on social workers' place in the bureaucracy of SSD social services.

Although respondents were generally positive about the idea of registration, several cautionary points were raised. The manager of a children's team was not optimistic about the introduction of registration.

> *I don't know if it will make any difference. I honestly don't really have a strong view about it.*

The main disadvantage identified was that it could prove difficult to separate individual bad practice and organizational bad practice because of social workers' bureau professional status. The manager of a children's team thought that individual social workers could be scapegoated by organizations. They could be held responsible for poor organizational practice. She observed that that there needed to be a separation of individual accountability from organizational accountability.

> *I don't know if it [registration] is elitist. I'm not sure it bothers me one way or the other because I'm not sure it will actually achieve that much. There's always going to be a tension between protecting children and interfering and sometimes we're going to get it wrong. The problem with childcare tragedies is not individual bad practice, but organizations' bad practice, fatigue, fear, overload. Being struck off is not the issue. I think it potentially leads to witch-hunts. It's an easy ploy for managers to blame someone, when they may have had too many cases.*

Four further issues were raised with regard to registration. Firstly, registration would need to be national and compulsory. If this could be accomplished, it would raise the standards of work and the status of social workers '*immensely*', according to the manager of the review team. A similar comment from the manager of a children's team was that,

> *Everybody should be on this register. But it would have to be monitored and it would be down to the registering body to monitor and to put information on that register. If it wasn't, then it's a failing on us and we're failing the service users who may then go on to buy a service from this person who* [could] *cause them difficulty.*

The manager of the review team thought that registration might be good but it would have to be compulsory to be effective.

> *But it's got to be like nursing that you've got to enrol. It isn't a choice. You've got to have certain policies and procedures that you must follow. It's got to be national and it's got to be actually followed through by each borough. And until that happens, I don't think we'll be seen as professional because there are so many of these new terms like care manager/ social workers.*

Secondly, registration raised the issue that practitioners would need to pay to be licensed and they would need professional insurance. This would be a disadvantage in that it would add costs to being a social worker, but it would be an advantage in that it would provide protection from malpractice suits and unfair dismissal from employment.

> *If social workers could be struck off, they would need personal insurance.*

This comment, from a member of an elders' team, contained two important elements. There was acceptance that social workers could be struck off throughout groups and managers interviewed. It was agreed that this would go some way to guaranteeing professional standards and improving the image of social workers generally. A concomitant factor raised in this group was that if social workers were individually liable for their work and faced the possibility that they could be struck off, they would need to pay for insurance to cover legal protection in the event that they were accused of malpractice.

Members of the review team thought that registration would be a good idea and that it would improve the perception of social work. They observed, however, that it would involve cost to individual social workers. '*We would have to pay to be registered.*'

Thirdly, registration could change employment practices of social services agencies. Before registration, a system of police checks was the best way for employers to assure themselves of an applicant's 'safety to practice'. Clearly, applicants had to be suitably qualified for a job. However, employment with a SSD social services organization also depended upon police clearance, so qualification was a necessary, but not sufficient, condition of employment. Employers had to wait for police checks to come through, which could take six months, before hiring social workers. With registration, it was thought that employers could hire quickly based upon the applicant's registration with their professional body.

Finally, some discussion related to the issue of social work's 'professional project'. The manager of one elder's team had not heard of the GSCC. Her initial reaction to the idea of registration was

I think it would be a valuable thing. I think they've got to give a lot of thought to what this organization intends to say about the future. That's going to be so much affected by what social workers are allowed to be in the future, what is seen to be serviceable to Great Britain, Plc. I don't think it will help to protect us in any way because at the moment as far as the government's concerned, these things are not negotiable. We've been sloppy for long enough and we're going to shape up.

This comment relates to the 'professional project' (Macdonald 1995), the trade off between society and professional bodies, that is, the balance between what is good for society and what is good for the profession. This manager was making the point that the government would not condone activities on the part of social work that it did not view as beneficial to society. There would have to be a dialogue between representatives of the government and representatives of the profession as to professional developments. However, if social work had a professional body, it would at least have professional representatives to engage in such a dialogue, which is something that has not existed historically, and indeed, could not take place without such a body.

None of the respondents thought registration was elitist. The manager of the review team observed that there were hardly any *'radical'* social workers left to take such a position, a reference to the 'radical' social work movement of the 1970s (Bailey and Brake 1977).

Conclusion

This chapter has discussed the professional status of social work and presented the views of managers and practitioners as to whether social work is a profession in the UK. Care management has decreased the 'human' intangible elements and 'indeterminacy' and discretion inherent in a traditional case role. Likewise, it has increased the 'mechanistic' technicality, that is, the tangible, identifiable elements of social work practice. It was found that contrary to predictions that social workers would prefer to work in the private and voluntary sector, most social workers interviewed preferred to work in the statutory SSDs, in spite of their reservations about their work in SSDs. The reasons given for preferring to work in SSDs were to do with greater security of employment and opportunities for training and promotion that existed in large local authority SSDs. Some said that they would not want to work in the private sector because they were suspicious of the effects of the profit motive on the provision of care.

At the time these interviews were conducted, between 1998 and 2000, registration was being proposed, but had not yet been introduced. Some thought social work was a profession and others thought it was not. Virtually all those interviewed thought registration would bring about greater professional status for social workers. No one thought that professional registration was elitist. The advantages and disadvantages of professional registration for social workers were discussed. All those interviewed welcomed professional registration.

PART III

CONSIDERING THE MACRO
AND THE MICRO

Looking Back – Looking Forward

Introduction to Part III – Chapters 6 and 7

In Chapter 1, Fordism and post-Fordism were set in the context of modernity and postmodernity. Postmodernity was defined as an exaggeration or an intensification of modern principles rather than a rejection of modernity, especially at the level of the organization. The use of the McDonaldization thesis suggests that the current discourse of social care is post-Fordist because there has been an exaggeration of Fordist management techniques and production principles applied to the production of intangible goods to produce tangible outcomes and enhance consumer choice (Ritzer 1996). The McDonaldization thesis has been applied to an analysis of developments in the fields of medicine education, leisure, sport and fast foods (Ritzer 1996) and to religion (Ward 1999). For the purpose of this study, the McDonaldization thesis has been applied to the provision of social care.

In Chapter 1, a theoretical framework was put forward to analyse the changes in the SSD social work role. Postmodernity as late capitalism has been used to provide a perspective on issues related to the change in social work role marked by NPM, commodification of care within the quasi-market, contractualism and the decline in trust of professional knowledge and discretion. Concepts associated with McDonaldization, which are efficiency, predictability, calculability and control, have become central to the provision of social care. These concepts have been used to define the exaggeration of Theory X Fordist managerialism to produce post-Fordist working conditions for care managers and post-Fordist consumer choice for service users.

As was suggested in Chapter 2, changes in the role of social workers must be seen in the context of changing political and socio/economic climates. Care management was introduced as part of a discourse, or system of meaning, marked by New Right faith in market solutions to social problems, distrust of professionals and the need to contain welfare spending in a climate of international economic competition. Government has increasingly been required to fit the cost of social services within the broader need for government to make Britain financially competitive in the global market place (O'Brien and Penna 1998). The main aims of the NHSCCA were to contain cost and enhance service user choice within an increasingly targeted and selective model of social care. Care management was to be the key to achieving these aims.

Chapters 3, 4 and 5 respectively reported the views of managers and practitioners on the skills and knowledge needed to practice as a care manager, the impact of care management on practice, the effect of care management on service users and (4) the possible impact of the registration of social workers.

Chapter 6 summarizes the findings of research presented in Part II and locates social work in care management as a feature of post-Fordist welfare provision. It is argued that care management retains elements of case work, but represents an adaptation of social work to conditions of late capitalism. This argument is supported by comparing Philp's (1979) definition of traditional social work to social workers as care managers, using the four main features of the McDonaldization.

Chapter 7 revisits theoretical perspectives discussed in Chapter 1. Issues of whether social work is a modern 'science' or a postmodern 'art' are discussed in relation to care management. The complexities of working as a social worker in the current global corporate era and 'how we should go on' in light of the 'irrationalities' introduced by McDonaldization are addressed.

Chapter 6

Care Management
as the Commodification of Care
within Postmodernity as Late Capitalism

Introduction

A multiperspectivist approach, including social policy and social theory has been taken in the analysis of the development of care management and the impact that care management has had on social work practice. In Part II research with practising care managers working in inner city London was analysed in order to gain insight into how they viewed care management. These are in some senses unique to these respondents because they worked in a UK setting where the process of professional registration of social workers was in its initial stages. Social workers in other national settings such as the US have long had a system of professional registration. The almost simultaneous introduction of care management and registration in the UK may be unique to the UK, but the way that care management affected social workers who were not registered and then became registered after the introduction of care management may have some resonance with social workers in other situations.

Care management as a system is a modern McDonaldized bureaucratic response to postmodernity as late capitalism. The increasingly rationalized delivery of social services is the hallmark of these systems. Social work arose in the context of capitalism so practice has always involved conflict and mediation between those with resources and those without resources. Social workers working in these McDonaldized systems of service delivery struggle with the issues of narrowly defined financial efficiency and cost containment and issues of professional accountability and good practice.

McDonaldized care management treats delivery of social services as a business and attempts to apply financial (instrumental) rationality to the process of conserving scarce tax-based resources. Internationally, social work practices may be converging with greater communication and transportation between countries. However, social work practice must always adapt to different national and local settings, that is, the historical legacy of 'place' and the existing political and cultural conditions of the time.

McDonaldization is a very modern phenomenon based on rationality and efficiency, yet it has come to prominence in what some feel is a postmodern era of uncertainty, rapid change and cultural relativism. Parton (2004, 35) has argued that rather than this being paradoxical, it is to be expected. With greater uncertainty, people welcome the seeming certainty and predictability of McDonald restaurants.

You will get the same hamburger at McDonald's no matter what part of the world you find yourself in.

McDonaldization applied to care management, however, still seems to be a paradox. A service user will not get the same service from every care manager, although this might be the ideal. No two services will be the exactly same; and yet from a bureaucratic systems' perspective this seems to be the ideal. This level of uniformity will not be achieved, unless it is a system where robots serve robots, but this is neither desirable nor possible.

The McDonaldization of the social care sector has produced post-Fordist working conditions for social workers, characterized by fragmentation, deskilling and superficiality. Fordist management techniques have been used to create the appearance, but not the reality, of post-Fordist consumer choice. Post-Fordist consumer choice has been enhanced by care management to some degree, but has failed to bring about the consumer choice that was anticipated in the rhetoric surrounding the implementation of community care policies. Social workers working as care managers experience the tensions inherent in implementing needs-led services which are not entirely needs-led and attempting to enhance choice for service users where there is often little choice.

Choice in the Quasi-market of Social Care

The rhetoric associated with the introduction of care management was that market principles could improve services to service users. A new discourse of social care was created consistent with the commodification of caring in the current phase of postmodernity as late capitalism. New Right policy makers have attempted to appropriate market mechanisms and harness the advantages of the market to provide social care. This new discourse is evident in attention to cost in the quasi-market, where competition between providers is encouraged and recipients of service users are constructed as customers with choice. A reference to 'Britain Plc' by one team manager captured the intent on the part of government to contain the cost of care and enhance Britain's financial competitiveness in the global marketplace. Market principles have been increasingly employed in the provision of social care. However, these efforts are full of tensions, contradictions and anomalies from the perspective of those who operationalize the system, the respondents in this study.

It is argued that one of the problems with this new discourse is that care cannot be subjected to genuine market forces such as competition and efficiency because markets respond to demand expressed through buying power and ultimately, markets respond to profit and loss. In the care sector, the relationship between cost and provision is contrived. Provision of services is not driven by market forces, but by centrally established budgets and eligibility criteria.

Respondents did not believe that cost has been driven down by competition. The introduction of competition among providers of care was an attempt to employ market principles to force providers to lower costs in order to be accepted by SSDs as block providers on their list of approved services. However, the ideal situation, with numerous agencies competing to provide services, thus driving down the cost, had not materialized according to respondents. Instead, the reverse seemed to have happened. The perception of respondents in this study was that agencies providing similar services had colluded to keep prices at commensurate level.

Service users are not customers. Eligibility criteria justified withholding services from all but those most at risk of harm. SSDs do not have to provide services if they do not have the resources to do so (Drakeford 1998). Service users are empowered to say what they need, but they do not have the power to purchase what they need. Rights in the real market place are dependent on purchasing power and service users do not have their own purchasing power. Power to purchase is not even with the care manager. It is with the care manager's team manager. Therefore the service user is rather far removed from the purchasing decisions that would allow them to be considered customers.

Care managers and service users struggled to fit their perspectives into the structures of the quasi-market provision of social care. When care managers did an assessment of need, they knew that the service user might not be able to have all their needs met. They were sometimes unwilling to encourage service users to identify needs that the care manager knew would not be met. What service users said or did not say depended on their knowledge of their rights within the system of care provision. Service user expectations were influenced by social factors such as age, gender, ethnicity and previous experience of SSDs. In the assessment of need process, the care manager and the service user engaged in a dance around the issues, both constrained by their respective perceptions of what was desirable *vis-à-vis* what was possible. Care managers' interaction with the service user was influenced by their knowledge base and their commitment to professional values as mediated by their employment, a central feature of which was their ability to contain cost. They recognized the tensions that were inherent working in a system that claimed to be needs-led when needs were only one factor in the equation of social care.

The Ideals versus the Realities

The rhetoric that accompanied the introduction of care management was that it would be needs-led. Previous studies have concluded that care management is not needs-led (Lewis and Glennerster 1996, 88; Kirkpatrick et al., 1999, 717; Stainton 1998, 140; Payne 1995, 204). Care managers in this study did not consider care management needs-led, in the same way that they did not think that service users were consumers. The reality from their perspective was a service-led and resource-led system of social care. It was service-led because of the introduction of block contracts and the need for service providers to have service level agreements with SSD's in order for care managers to purchase services. It was also resource-led because services could not be provided if the SSD did not have the resources to provide services.

An analysis of whether services are needs-led or whether they continue to be service- and resource-led was central to issues of choice and empowerment of service users. Respondents agreed that the degree of choice that could be exercised by service users had been enhanced to some degree by the introduction of the quasi-markets associated with community care. However, choice was limited by organizational constraints, funding constraints, and a conflict of interest wherein care managers both assessed need and purchased services as representatives of the agency that funded the service.

Assessment of need and the ideal of needs-led services appeared to allow post-Fordist consumer choice in the market of care. This appearance was deceptive because choice was constrained by a number of factors: for example, the capacity of a SSD to identify unmet need and commission services, the communication of information to care managers so they know what services have been approved for purchase, the skill of the care manager to work in partnership with the service user and identify the most relevant needs in a time-limited encounter, the availability of budgets, the existence of relevant services and the discretion of the team manager to approve the cost of a package of care recommended for the service user.

Service users could express what they thought their needs were, but there was no guarantee that their expressed needs would be met. The care manager brought an awareness of these issues to the assessment process, which all influenced the outcome for the service user.

Practitioners and managers identified four reasons why care management was not needs-led. Firstly, practitioners were not recording unmet need as discussed above. Ideally, unmet needs should be recorded by care managers, collected centrally and used to commission new services to meet these needs. Early in the implementation of community care policies, there was a policy discussion about the recording of unmet needs. At first, unmet needs were to be identified, recorded and addressed in order to create services that were more responsive. It was then feared that recording unmet need would create unrealistic demands for services (Drakeford 1998, 225). Team managers sometimes complain that care managers do not collect unmet need (Baldwin 2000), but within the current climate of managerialistic controls, it would not be difficult for managers to obtain this information if they really wanted it. While technology has been employed to increase surveillance of care managers, technology does not seem to be used effectively to collect information regarding unmet need.

Secondly, service provision was still not needs-led because local authorities defined the criteria of need, not service users. If a service user identified a need that did not fit the agency definition of need, then the need was not recognized as a legitimate need. Service-user choice was considered, but was only one of a number of factors to be considered in the final decision about the provision of services.

Thirdly, budget restrictions meant that the model of service provision was resource-led. Resource availability was a major factor in assessment practice (Baldwin 2000, 56). As one manager said, she wanted her care managers to '*think money*' consistent with the ethos of late capitalism.

A further development with regard to the issue of resource-led services was that care managers were required to assess need even when it was known that the SSD did not have the resources to fund services. Care managers were also sometimes required to re-assess need when eligibility criteria changed, a process which could lead to the withdrawal of services from services users.

Fourthly, services continued to be service-led because of the introduction of block contracts and service-level agreements. Services purchased as a 'block' from established providers had the effect of limiting the services from which a care manager could purchase. From this perspective, the model of provision was still service-led as purchase could only be made from existing approved sources consistent with the findings of Kirkpatrick et al., (1999, 717).

In spite of the feeling that a genuine needs-led model had not been established, there were positive developments associated with the attempt to establish a needs-led model. Respondents reported that there was now a wider range of services available from which to purchase than there was before the introduction of community care policies.

Care Management Pilot Projects in the UK – A Margin to Mainstream Research Issues

Evaluative research contributed to the establishment of care management (Challis and Davies 1980, Challis and Davies 1985). However, care management as practised in this study bears little resemblance to the pilot projects carried out (Means and Smith 1998, 112).

The Thanet and Gateshead pilot projects carried out at the PSSRU were established to evaluate the feasibility of care management as a model of service delivery (Davies and Challis 1986, Challis et al., 1998). These projects demonstrated the cost effectiveness of social workers with small caseloads and devolved budgets in preventing the institutionalization of elderly service users. These projects demonstrated that elderly people could be maintained in their own homes with intensive service provision, thus allowing them to remain in the community and avoiding the costs of institutionalization. It cost less to care for elderly people in their own homes than in residential or nursing facilities. These small-scale research projects were used to justify the introduction of care management on a national basis. In the implementation of these pilot projects as a national programme, a transition from margin to mainstream, Fordist management practices were applied to care management in order to contain cost and enhance post-Fordist choice. In the translation of these small-scale research projects to a national model of service deliverers, positive features of the pilot projects were lost. There was a subversion of the original intent in four ways.

Firstly, the original pilots were preventive in nature. This intention was turned on its head when care-management services became selective and targeted to those most in need. This has meant that in practice, care managers are only assessing need where the threshold of need is high. They are therefore dealing with crises, rather than putting services in early, which would prevent crises. Respondents agreed that care management was not preventive. Availability of service was based on strict eligibility criteria, which meant that only those most at risk can be considered for services. A service user's situations must be at breaking point in order to justify even an assessment to consider purchase of services. The implementation of the pilot projects reversed the original principle of prevention in the delivery of services.

Secondly, in the pilot projects budgets were devolved to social workers to allow them to 'spot purchase' in a cost effective manner. In the national implementation of care management, budgets have not been devolved to social workers, but have been devolved to the team managers of social workers. All respondents were clear they were in a position of negotiating between the needs of the service user and the budget restrictions of the organization. While care managers could assess need and recommend purchase of services, there was no guarantee that their recommendation would be approved by their team manager. This put care managers in a position of ongoing conflict between the needs of service users and SSD budget restrictions.

Thirdly, work with service users was needs-led in the early pilot projects in order to enhance service-user choice. In the implementation of care management nationally, services returned to a service-led model. Social workers could purchase services flexibly, or 'spot purchase' in the pilot projects and indeed in the early stages of care management. For example, in agreement with service users, social workers could purchase a service from a neighbour or contract with a local restaurant to bring meals to a service user. In the implementation of care management, this flexibility was lost. Respondents reported that while choice was expanded by allowing purchasing from both SSD and private/voluntary services, choice was then restricted by the need to purchase services 'in block' from approved lists of service providers. Care managers could only purchase from providers that had contracts or service level agreements with the SSD. These contracts guaranteed the service and the cost of the service. This was advantageous to the SSD because there were assurances that the 'preferred providers' met the quality standards and service specifications of the SSD. This was also advantageous to the providers because it made them more financially viable. Choice became restricted to the availability of services provided through block contracts. SSDs could not allow spot purchasing by individual care managers because the SSD was responsible for the service that was purchased. The SSD had to protect itself from accusations of negligence so it was obliged to approve agencies dealing with service users. This then reduced service-user choice and made the model service-led rather than needs-led. This has restricted the flexibility and choice that was envisioned in the early pilot projects. The use of block contracts reinstated the service-led model because care managers could only purchase from existing approved services.

Fourthly, caseloads were small and specially selected in the pilot projects. The reality for respondents was that caseloads were high which meant that care managers could not spend time with service users to empower them by helping them make informed choices or negotiating the changes they faced, or indeed always review services to see that care packages were being implemented. An example of this last point is that the Review Team interviewed for this study was established exclusively to review care packages because individual care managers could not keep up with reviewing packages of care that they had established. There was evidence in one team that the agency contracted to provide services had subcontracted to another agency without telling the care manager. Respondents in this team were concerned about this development. They did not think it was empowering for service users to have subcontracted workers coming into their home who were not accountable to the care manager.

Care management was introduced ostensibly because its effectiveness was demonstrated in these early Thanet and Gateshead pilot projects. However, the decision to introduce care management was a political decision. The case management model that was introduced nationally bears little resemblance to the model evaluated in these pilot projects. In hindsight, 'It is unfortunate ... that social services case-management was not evaluated in randomised controlled trials before its implementation in the UK' (Marshall et al., 1995, 409). The randomized controlled trials carried out in 1995 by Marshall et al. demonstrated no significant differences between groups of homeless mentally ill people who were care managed and those who were not care managed. Further research of this nature needs to be conducted to establish the effectiveness of care management.

McDonaldized Social Work as a Response to Conditions of Late Capitalism: Efficiency, Predictability, Calculability, Control

On the basis of existing literature and the findings generated by research discussed in Part II, there is strong weight of evidence to suggest that care management has had a significant impact on social work practice and professional standing. However, it is argued that social work as care management in McDonaldized SSDs is still social work, even though it has been adapted to fit in a society characterized by commodification of late capitalism. One of the policy intentions behind the introduction of care management was to make social care more businesslike (Harris 2003) and to bring the benefits of the market to the delivery of social services. It was found that elements of Fordist management practices were introduced to the management of social workers who worked as care managers to increase efficiency, control, calculability and predictability of outcome in the social care sector (Ritzer 1996).

It is argued that the McDonaldization of the social care system has exposed social workers to an intensification of Fordist management techniques for the purpose of achieving post-Fordist consumer choice. The resulting commodificaton of the social care sector is consistent with the realities of postmodernity as late capitalism. It is further argued that the creation of the SSD McDonaldized social care sector has contributed to the transformation of the Seebohm normative caseworker into the Griffiths instrumental care manager. However, registration may allow social workers working as care managers to maintain their professional identity.

Care managers have been substantially affected by the McDonaldized principles of efficiency, predictability, calculability and surveillance (Ritzer 1996). However, care managers retain elements of traditional social work, that is, mediation, negotiation, integration and surveillance (Philp 1979). Care management is analysed in terms of these two frameworks and the conclusion drawn that care management is a specialist field of social work practice adapted to the conditions of late capitalism.

Efficiency

Care management and the purchaser/provider split mimics the division of labour used to produce efficiency in the production of tangible goods in a factory setting. The attempt to save money through efficiency, or getting the most benefit from the money spent as reflected in Best Value policies, is the closest approximation to the to the late capitalist market ethos possible within the delivery of intangible care services. However, it is argued that one of the problems associated with the attempt to quantify 'care' as a commodity to be bought and sold in the mixed economy of welfare is that 'care' does not produce a profit so profitability cannot be used as a calculable criterion for efficiency.

Efficiency is therefore aspired to by other means. Respondents reported that one method was the use of time and motion studies. Some care managers were asked to record what they were doing and how long it took to complete each task. Workers were compared in terms of how fast they could complete assessments. Bar charts were displayed on office walls comparing practitioners' performance regarding how many times social workers completed an assessment within the allowed time. Measurable performance targets were set for individual practitioners. These management practices concerned practitioners because these indicators did not take into consideration the inputs, the intangible skills and knowledge and the time, necessary to produce desirable outcomes.

Managers valued the efficiency that care management brought to the work of social workers. However, some managers recognized the impact that care management had on social workers and felt that social work had '*lost something*' with the implementation of care management.

Ironically, efforts to improve efficiency in the delivery of social services have resulted in the 'inefficiency of efficiency' (Ritzer 1996, 142). High turnover of public sector workers has been brought about because workers are overwhelmed by government targets, bureaucracy and paperwork, resulting in 'grossly inefficient' turnover levels (Foster 2002). The high number of agency workers in a care-management team was not considered efficient from an organizational perspective because one of the criteria of a good care manager is knowing the resources available for purchase. It takes time to develop that knowledge. Therefore, managers and colleagues spend time helping agency workers develop this knowledge only for them to leave at the end of a short-term contract. The process starts again with a new agency worker.

Predictability

In McDonaldized organizations, procedures are used to enhance predictability. Standardized assessment schedules seem to have been introduced by most local authorities to guide the assessments of need conducted by care managers. Care managers now routinely use a standardized form to assess need following a set menu of scripted questions (Harris 2003, 2). Efforts to introduce predictability to the care management process can be seen in increased standardization of care manager activities, for example, standardized assessment forms and standard time limits for assessments. Use of assessment forms added to the workload of practitioners and was seen by some as an affront to their professional discretion (Baldwin 2000, 48). However, the forms had the potential to provide tangible 'audit-able' indicators of assessment outcomes. Assessment forms had the advantage of verifying the work performed by their teams, establishing care management as auditable and calculable service.

Prior to care management, assessment of need was considered a professional activity that was left to individual professionals to carry out. Care management required the use of assessment schedules that itemize every issue to be raised with service users in the assessment of their need. Procedures became more prescribed. In one local authority, which had introduced Total Quality Management, there was a procedure for every activity, including a protocol for supervision of social workers. Assessment forms are deskilling because they represent an effort to centralize and concretize the intangible skills and knowledge of social workers and deliver them back to social workers as if they did not know how to assess need.

Flattened featureless products and services are produced through scripted interactions with service users, for example, through assessment protocols (Jameson 1984b, 61). The assessment schedules that care managers are required to use represent scripted interactions with service users that can lead to a level of superficiality in communication between care managers and service users (Harris 2003, 2). It is argued that the danger of proceduralizing every activity is that it dulls the sensitivity of care managers to the use of theory and moral implications of their activities, as was illustrated by the example of services provided to immigrant young people discussed earlier. The managerialistic 'checklist' approach constrains the construction of service users' needs and can exclude information critical to adequate needs and assessment (Dill 1993).

There was some indication that the intensified of procedure made the use of theory difficult. While qualified social workers are introduced to theory in their training, the need for theory was minimized by adherence to procedure. Some respondents felt that common sense was important in care management. Professional common sense is different from lay common sense and that, while social workers may not be able to readily articulate theory, theory forms the underlying rationale for their work if they are drawing on 'unconscious competence'. Some respondents thought that explicitly 'theory driven' practice was dangerous if it became dogmatic or doctrinaire and did not balance the material realities of service users' situations with organizational constraints.

The need for predictability meant the routinization of work. Some respondents reported that care-management pressures made them feel that their work was superficial and that they could not offer the quality of work they would have liked to offer. The issue of pressure to work quickly and artificial time limits on work was related to their perception that they could not establish 'real need'. They did not seem to have the scope for professional discretion that would have allowed them to take more time to establish what they considered as 'real need'.

The degree to which they use these forms mechanistically varied among respondents, but the standardized assessment form represents an attempt to ensure that all relevant issues are explored with all service users. Team managers thought it was empowering for service users that issues of ethnicity were addressed with all service users currently because it was an item on the standardized form. They also thought the management practice of ensuring that all care plans were signed by service users was empowering to service users. Individual care managers could not use their discretion to decide who was capable of understanding and signing their care plan and who was not. This point raised the possibility of service users signing their care plans whether they understood them or not, which would defeat the point of the exercise.

Calculability

Some things are not calculable, but in the Western world in the current era of late capitalism, if an entity cannot be calculated then it does not exist. A good example of this is the issue of the environment. All people in the world depend on a healthy relationship with their environment. Issues of global warming are hotly debated. Yet attention to environmental problems is not taken seriously unless it is 'costed out' (Stern Review 2006).

Calculability refers to the capacity to calculate resources in terms of inputs and outputs. It involves constructing services that were previously considered intangible as tangible, measurable, auditable entities. Calculability was introduced into care management in the business-like process of attaching cost directly to services. For example, one team manager said that she wanted her care managers to be able to '*think money*', even though they found it difficult. Caring activities have been subjected to stricter costing mechanisms and measurement of the time it takes to accomplish tasks and deadlines by which tasks must be completed, on the assumption that time and motion studies can be applied to caring activities.

The emphasis was on work that can produce tangible and measurable outcomes that could be calculated. Practitioners said that managerialism and the pressure to produce auditable outcomes resulted in superficial work because it did not acknowledge the intangibles such as the skills and knowledge necessary to produce tangible outcomes. While some care managers regarded assessment forms as an impediment, or an obstacle to 'real' social work, managers needed assessment forms completed to demonstrate that work had been done and to ensure equity and audit. One of the main aspects of the role of team managers was to control budgets, so they had to have control of inputs and outputs that could be calculated.

Practitioners felt that the paperwork necessary to ensure the audit of work was a problem because it reduced the time they had to give to service users, even when it was clear to the care manager that the service user needed the time. Social workers who had practised social work within a more traditional casework model felt frustrated by the paperwork, audit and mechanistic approaches associated with managerialistic control, which was oriented toward calculable outcomes rather than the process that went into producing the outcomes.

Control

It was found in this study that control has been accomplished through managerialism, which included tighter monitoring and auditing of care manager activities. Managerialism has reduced the use of professional discretion associated with the Seebohm bureau-professional social work role in SSDs (Lewis and Glennerster 1996, 143). This loss of discretion is consistent with the fact that creativity is not valued in McDonaldized organizations (Ritzer 1996, 130). Managers' control over the activities of practitioners was increased by various means. While the role of social work has developed within the bureaucracies of the welfare state, and social workers were accustomed to following procedure, procedures had become more prescriptive in the current care-management model of service delivery. Respondents said they felt deskilled by prescriptive managerially imposed procedures and thought that procedures were an indication of a lack of trust in them as professionals.

In a situation of uncertainty or indeterminacy (Sheppard 1995, 275), professional knowledge regarding client need is required to make a judgement or a decision as to the best outcome for the service user. However, managerialistic practices strive for control. Control over uncertainty is gained through procedures, thus limiting the need for professional knowledge, creativity or discretion. Control over the process of an assessment is gained through formulaic, scripted assessment forms, which can be monitored. The managerialistic practices that have accompanied the introduction of care management have tended to reduce professional discretion through directive procedures and close inspection or surveillance of care managers' working practices. Many respondents felt that their discretion was reduced by the need to follow procedures strictly, but this varied. Care managers in children's teams thought that they had more independence in the past, but that they still had more discretion than care managers who worked with the elderly.

The ultimate control of care managers was, however, control over spending decisions. The main function of the care manager was to assess for need, purchase services and monitor provision of services. However, they had little control over purchase of services, which was central to the operation of care management. They could advise that a service user needed to have a service purchased, but the decision had to be made by their team manager. Respondents in this study found it frustrating when they identified service-user needs and then could not get funding to meet the needs, a finding consistent with that of McDonald (1999, 147).

The extended use of modern computer technology has contributed to managerial control of the service delivery system, bringing predictability and calculability to the process. Computers make the perfect bureaucrats because they are impersonal, impartial, predictable and dependable (Ellis et al., 1999, 271). Computer-aided assessment programmes, referred to by Ellis et al., (1999, 276), and the capacity to electronically track employees' activities, exemplify the use of technology to control and survey workers' activities.

A positive point put forward by one manager in defence of managerialistic practices was that of equity or fairness, insuring equitable practices. Managers stood in a position of regulating the resources in the relative interests of all the individuals in a specified group. Eligibility criteria represented an attempt to distribute resources fairly or equitably. Managers were therefore thinking collectively and equitably. In order to distribute resources equitably, systems and procedures were in place to ensure that this happened. It was the monitoring of these procedures that practitioners experienced as surveillance of their activities. Practitioners thought individually about the interests of the individual they were representing. This conflict between managers thinking about the collective and practitioners thinking about individuals may explain some of the conflict between managers and practitioners and some of the negative comments from practitioners about managerialism.

Managerial control and the loss of professional discretion seemed to contribute to high staff turnover. Most managers used varying degrees of the Fordist Theory X output oriented, performativity management style. Some managers tried to operate a supportive and participatory Theory Y process-oriented management style that acknowledged qualitative elements of practice. While some managers tried to manage in a traditional process-oriented way rather than an outcome-oriented way, it was difficult for them to maintain this approach to management in the current McDonaldized climate of service delivery. The manager who used a Theory Y supportive management style with her care managers felt she had a lower staff turn-over than team managers who used a Theory X style of management.

Continuity between Casework and Care Management: Mediation, Integration, Representation, Surveillance

In spite of the reality that care management has been significantly affected by the McDonaldization of social care, it is argued that care management retains essential elements of casework. In the examination of the literature regarding social work's history considered in Chapter 2, it is clear that social work activities change in response to changing social contexts. The introduction of care management clouded the identity of social workers' already ambiguous role. However, as one respondent pointed out, social workers do different things at different points in history and in different areas of practice, but they are still doing social work.

Since the introduction of the NHSCCA, social work has experienced significant change in the context of its work such as the introduction of quasi-markets, managerialism and efforts to make service delivery efficient, predictable, calculable and controllable. In spite of the imposition of Fordist management measures and the frustration of being part of the effort to maintain the appearance of choice without the reality of choice, it is argued that social workers working as care managers continue to approximate the role of social workers as delineated by Philp (1979). Although care management is almost unrecognizable as social work because its activities are so different from casework activities, continuities with the casework role can be seen by examining care management in terms of four fundamental aspects of the social work role: mediation, integration, representation and surveillance (Philp 1979).

Mediation

Social work activities have been different in different historical periods, but a main feature of its underlying role is mediation. Social workers typically mediate between formal 'systems' and individual 'lifeworlds' (Lorenz 2004, 146). Social work's early role was mediation between the rich and the poor (Philp 1979). Its Seebohm role was to mediate between the state and the family (Howe 1996, 81). Mediation is an activity fraught with difficulties for the profession. As Howe point out in his early study of social workers working in the bureaucracies of the welfare state, mediation can be regarded negatively as 'conducting scurries on the margins of society, robbing the rich to give to the poor' (Howe 1986, 148). The introduction of care management has restricted the scope of social workers' ability to mediate between the individual and society, or in Habermas's terms, between 'lifeworlds and systems' (Lorenz 2004, 146–7). It could be argued that its current care management role is mediation between the individual and the market, mediating between those who need services and those who can provide services, and in the process adapting existing knowledge and skills to the current context of postmodernity as late capitalism.

Managing conflict is inherent in mediation, and this is especially true in the care manager role. Mediation between the needs of the service user and the structures of SSDs is a core care management role. Further, care managers mediate between service users and providers. Conflict exists at a number of levels: conflict between casework and care management models of work, conflict between the rhetoric of needs-led services and the reality of service-led/resource-led services, and conflict between their responsibility to service users and their responsibility to the SSD which employs them. There was also potential for conflict between assessment of the purchaser and the second, more in depth, assessment of the provider. Most notably, social workers were in a conflict of interest positions because they both assessed need on behalf of service users and they were accountable to their SSD employer for conserving scarce resources. Mediation skills were important in care management.

Integration

A fundamental aspect of the social work role is integration, which describes two aspects of the role: integration of the 'whole' person and integration of the individual into society. Firstly, social workers have tended to consider service users' circumstances holistically rather than focusing only on their medical or emotional or financial or housing needs, all of which were the focus of separate professional groups. Secondly, social workers work toward the integration of marginalized or disempowered service users by creating or facilitating social networks. It is argued that this traditional aspect of the social work perspective makes them valuable as care managers.

In fact, in spite of the criticism of New Right Care in the Community policies, they were consistent with the fundamental social work role of integrating the individual into society. It could be argued that Care in the Community policies have strengthened the ability of social workers to integrate service users into the community, keeping them in their own homes where possible and preventing their marginalization in institutional settings.

It is interesting to consider the relationship between integration and fragmentation in care management. The casework role included both assessment and provision in a seamless ongoing relationship. Care management fragmented the role of the social worker between the assessment/purchaser role and the provider role (Wilson 1993, 112).

However, one element of the role of care manager was to overcome the resulting fragmentation of provision created by allowing, indeed encouraging, care managers to purchase from a range of providers, that is, from both SSDs and private/voluntary sector providers. If services could be drawn from a range of sources, the role of the care manager was necessary to hold the services together in the interest of the service user, to hold together the fragmented service delivery system. One team referred to their function as the '*linchpin*' that held services together, which conveys the reality that they were holding together a fragmented range of services.

One could argue that care management is social work in that it integrates a number of services for the benefit of the service user. Social workers feel that they have been deskilled by the fragmentation of the social work role, similar to the deskilling that occurs in factory settings when a 'whole' piece of work carried out by craftsmen was fragmented into 'piece work' in order to bring about efficiency. This argument supports the position taken here that social work has been affected by the McDonaldization of the social care sector. Social workers can only use some of their traditional skills in care management. They have lost the capacity for an ongoing professional relationship with service users and they have lost the capacity for professional discretion. However, they still perform an integration role in care management that is fundamental to the social work role.

On the other hand, care management has perhaps operated in opposition to social worker's looking at the 'whole' person in an ongoing professional relationship. Care managers reported that they could not look at the 'whole' person, nor could they establish 'real need' because of the pressure to work to deadlines. Practitioners observed that manager surveillance of practitioners had increased to such a degree, that there was now 'no leeway' for care managers to have an ongoing relationship with clients in the way many thought they would when they entered social work. These factors contributed to a feeling of being deskilled and a loss of satisfaction with their work. The exception to this experience was described by the manager of the residential unit for children leaving care, wherein her staff worked with the 'whole' child and tried to avoid buying services for them because they did not like having a range of service providers '*interfering with their life*'.

Representation

Care managers continue to represent those without power to those with power, a basic social work role. They present a case for a service user to their team manager so that it can '*be prioritised against all the others*' and they must '*stand their ground*' when they represent the needs of the service user to their team manager. This was described a new skill. However, it was only a new skill in so far as it was practised in a new setting. As care managers, they needed to represent the needs of their service user as being within the eligibility criteria and they needed to know where to purchase services at the right price so that the package of care will be approved.

However, their discretion to use their own interpersonal/professional skills is limited by adherence to procedure and by their ability to apply their knowledge of human need to the construction of an argument for service provision. It is here that social workers experience conflict, stress and frustration. Eligibility criteria screen out all but those most at risk. Budgets are restricted. Care managers have no role beyond purchasing, so if money is not available to purchase, they are left with an awareness of need, but with no way to resolve the need.

Advocacy is an aspect of representation. In their mediation role, social workers traditionally have advocated on behalf of the disadvantaged with those who have the power to help them. However, advocacy in the traditional sense was not possible for care managers because the structures for decision-making were quite prescribed. Within care management, social workers had to be more adversarial than in their casework role. Social workers could not advocate for service users when they operated as care managers (Humphries 2003), hence the use of the word 'adversarial'. Care management has resulted in a blame culture with little sense of shared responsibility and required a more adversarial style of work (Kirkpatrick et al., 1999, 721–722).

Adversarial skills were important in getting services for people when resources are restricted. Care managers were often in a position of having to '*stand their ground*' and defend their argument as to why the service user must have a service. This skill was also needed in reviewing a care plan and demanding compliance from service providers. If a provider agreed to provide a service and then did not comply, the care manager needed the skills to demand that the provider fulfil their agreement. In this activity, they were representing the demands of the SSD to the provider. The care manager role still involved representing the service user to the SSD and the SSD to the provider, but the representation role has been altered consistent with the McDonaldization of the social work sector in the context of late capitalism.

While care managers can become adversarial in challenging team manager decisions, there is little scope for advocacy, in the sense that they apply their knowledge and power beyond the limits allowed by their role as a care manager employed by a SSD. If care managers became too assertive in advocating for service users, they could jeopardize their employment. Fordist management techniques have not only curbed social work professional discretion; these techniques have also tied social workers directly to the goals of the SSD organization. Care managers were assessing need for the same organization that provided funding to meet needs. This was a conflict between their professional responsibility to meet service users' needs and their responsibility to their organization as employees to minimize cost. Their own viability as employees depended upon their ability to purchase at the lowest price and conserve scarce SSD resources. They had to be careful how far they advocated on behalf of a service user and were therefore in a conflict of interest situation.

Surveillance

Surveillance has been part of the social work role in the modern sense of the panoptican (Foucault 1979) since its origins in the 1800s (Walton 1975, Thane 1982). Surveillance and gatekeeping were implicit in the early casework role in that they had the power to distinguish between the deserving and the undeserving poor. Casework incorporated surveillance of individual service users by maintaining a relationship over time to allow the social worker to assess whether the service user was responding appropriately to the social work intervention. This could be interpreted as a negative role and one that is sometimes uncomfortable for social workers. However, the power to watch over or 'survey' the individual is an undeniable aspect of the social work role in, for example, child protection or mental health when service users may be at risk to themselves or others. Surveillance of society (by those with the power to survey society) has increased with advancements in managerial control and the increasingly sophisticated use of technology. Care managers have acquired a new surveillance role in the review process. They 'survey' applicants as to their eligibility for services; they 'survey' the input of providers to ensure that they are providing the services they were contracted to supply to the service user. However, the consumerist language associated with care management obscures their gatekeeping and surveillance role (Harris 2003, 136).

Surveillance could also be interpreted in a positive sense as prevention. In the modern sense, it could be understood as surveying society for the purpose of working toward social progress and ensuring that people who needed help received it. With the introduction of care management, some care managers felt strongly that they could no longer work preventively and felt a loss of this positive surveillance role. Their concern regarding loss of preventive role is reflected in the narrowed scope of their activities and the loss of their ability to look more broadly at their local communities. They were no longer expected to 'know' their communities in the Barclay 'patch' sense of working with community networks. Because they could only work with individual service users whose needs are severe enough to meet eligibility criteria, they were always working with people in crisis (Carey 2003). If budgets were not sufficient to meet needs as presented, service users had to be left to deteriorate further in order to justify the cost of intervention. This frustrated positive surveillance efforts or a sense on the part of care managers that they were contributing to social progress in the modern sense.

Further, social workers are themselves subject to increased surveillance (Parton 1996, 112, Moffatt 1999) as trust in professionals has declined (O'Neil 2002). Social workers survey service users and managers survey social workers. In the mid-1970s, the New Right identified the power of professionals as one of the obstacles to the restructuring of the public sector. NPM in the public sector was a tool to right the wrongs of the old welfare state (Newman and Clarke 1995, 23, Exworthy and Halford 1999, 2). A greater emphasis on efficiency, effectiveness and economic public services and responsiveness to consumers has been an objective of the managerialization of SSD social services (Exworthy and Halford 1999). The concept of managerialism has been described as an increased focus on procedures, systems and policies of social services (Spratt and Houston 1999). These procedures have enhanced the ability of managers to monitor and control the activities of care managers, facilitating increased surveillance. The focus of managerialism is on targets and performance indicators of a largely quantitative and calculable nature. This focus on quantitative measures has been at the expense of measures of a qualitative nature, which would allow a focus on casework values of relationship building and the empowerment of clients (Spratt and Houston 1999).

Surveillance could be considered a feature of the current regulatory state wherein the state has withdrawn from the direct provision of services, encouraging a mixed economy of care (McDonald 1999, 28, Means and Smith 1998, 126–35). This withdrawal from direct provision has been accompanied by an increased regulatory or surveillance role for the state. Research regarding the changing roles and tasks of social workers within community care policies found that care management 'has led the work of social work care managers to be both more manageable and more managed' (Levin and Webb 1997, iv). Regulation of those who provide services (Taylor-Gooby 1999, 558) has increased to ensure that services delivered in this mixed economy of care meet agreed standards. Surveillance and the importance of managers have increased as expectations have been formalized, making expectations of professionals more explicit and limiting the scope of their discretion.

Care managers' work can be monitored through observation of emails and their work on care planning computer programmes. Managers have greater control over care managers to direct their work through assessment forms and time limits on work. Eligibility criteria was so strictly observed that social workers lost the discretion to decide who should have a service and who should not have a service. In their gatekeeper role, they could 'shut' the gate by not recommending a service, but they lost their discretion to 'open' the gate to services unless they could demonstrate that the service user met the criteria for service and they could convince their care manager that the services warranted the input of resources.

From the Seebohm Normative Role to the Griffiths Instrumental Role – McDonaldized Care Management as a Specialist Role within Social Work

Care managers have been exposed to the McDonaldization of the social care sector and have experienced an increase in Fordist managerial control over their activities in order to achieve efficiency, predictability, calculability and control in service delivery. One of the reasons for the introduction of these measures has been to increase post-Fordist consumer choice, although the reality of increased choice for service users was questioned in this study. In spite of the new conditions within which social work is practised, it is argued that care management retains elements of social work, as analysed from the perspective of Philp's (1979) model of the social work role, and that it has become a specialist area of practice in response to conditions of late capitalism.

Care-management practice is patently different from casework practice. Respondents who practised as care managers questioned whether it was social work. It has been observed that social work may be 'under erasure' (Sarup 1993, 33, Pietroni 1995, 34) in the sense that the term 'social work' is 'inadequate but necessary' to describe care management.

An important part of the difference is the increase in instrumental powers and the decrease in normative powers (Toren 1972) available to care managers. The quality and purpose of relationships between social worker and service user changed with the introduction of care management. The most significant difference between Seebohm casework and Griffiths care management identified by respondents was their ability as caseworkers to establish a professional relationship with service users, the normative role. Social work in Seebohm SSDs allowed some casework and the use of interpersonal skills to be applied in direct work with the service user. Respondents felt this was not possible within care management where role of the care manager was to assess, purchase and monitor, not to provide a casework or counselling relationship.

The Seebohm caseworker could exercise the professional normative 'use of self' to enhance service users' coping skills. This activity is not within the role of the Griffiths' care manager. The care manager's instrumental role involves knowing the service system and using it to the advantage of the service user, by telling them what their choices are and ensuring that they get the services they need within the constraints that exist. Some respondents felt they could exercise some discretion within restricted organizational parameters established by policy makers and subject to team manager control over budgets, but overall most respondents did not feel they could exercise discretion on behalf of service users and therefore felt deskilled and frustrated in their ability to empower service users.

However, it is argued that the fundamental social work role is identifiable in both casework and care management. Care management requires a postmodern 'patchwork of ideas' (Rosenau 1992, xiii) including traditional and new skills. Traditional elements of social work such as communication skills and the skill of engaging quickly with service users are combined with the new skills of budget management and coordination of care. Practice in a new service delivery context without an acknowledgment of traditional skills and training in the new skills is certain to make social workers feel deskilled. If social work is going to continue to be practised within the care-management framework, then the essential social work role needs to be recognized and valued, while at the same time assisting social workers to adapt to the current climate of practice.

Care management was generally not valued by social workers who preferred the normative role to the instrumental role. While they were practising in a narrower, more specialist manner than they had as generic social workers, they themselves did not feel that they were working in more depth or with a more specialist knowledge base.

Respondents reported that much of their work was administrative and clerical, that there was minimal contact with service users and that it was difficult to establish or maintain a relationship with service users within care management. These factors contributed to a feeling of being deskilled and a loss of satisfaction with their care manager role. Although it could be argued that knowledge of what constitutes 'need' could be regarded as an area of specialist knowledge, this was not the perception or the experience of respondents. Team managers valued the skills of social workers working as care managers, but their emphasis on tangible outcomes seems to have led to a feeling on the part of care managers that their social work abilities were not valued.

Care management has become a significant area of work in restructured SSDs. Care management is important to the service users who receive care-managed services. When care managers successfully meet needs, they empower service users to maintain independence in the community. However, it seemed difficult for social workers to work in a context dominated by a market ethos. For example, social workers had difficulty viewing service users as consumers of care and for the most part, continued to view them as clients who needed help. It would seem preferable that social workers who value empowerment be employed as care managers than for social workers to avoid care management and leave decisions about service users to be made completely on the basis of market principles.

Theory X management, associated with the production of tangible products in factory settings is not appropriate to management of professionals for whom work has an intrinsic value. 'In part, managerialism fails because it is founded on suspicion and reductionism with respect to professionals; as professionals are self-serving, management must continually be seeking ways of controlling them. The premise is dubious.' (Cutler and Waine 1994, 148). A Theory X output-oriented performativity management style is discouraging to professionals who value the skills, knowledge and experience that contribute to positive outcomes for service users. Team managers in this study did not seem to value social workers' knowledge. They wanted care managers to '*think money*' rather than theory. This is consistent with the questioning of metanarratives by both postmodernists and New Right politicians (Rosenau 1992, 165, Sarap 1995, 155) and the rise of the market. Yet several managers said that they would rather employ trained social workers than untrained social workers. If team managers could value the process that leads to good outcomes, it would help social workers to value what they do in relation to the outcome. Professional registration may help social workers in this regard.

Care managers' role is part of a trend away from the generic Seebohm casework role toward greater specialism. Care management has created a clear role within the McDonaldized social care sector. Within the care-management role, assessment and purchasing skills have become a specialized instrumental area of practice, but a speciality that was not valued by care managers in this study. Because they could not exercise a normative casework relationship with service users, most care managers in this study did not value their care manager role. It would seem that if care management was viewed as an important discrete area of practice, rather than as a deskilled version of the Seebohm casework role, it would change the perception of care management.

Conclusion

This chapter has summarized issues raised in relation to theory, policy and findings from research carried out to assess the impact of care management in the UK. Issues are addressed regarding whether choice has been enhanced for service users and whether service users in the context of care management are customers or clients. The ideals *vis-à-vis* the reality of care management have been discussed. The research that led to the implementation of care management was examined. It was found that the early pilot projects that supported the introduction of care management in the UK bear little relationship to the care management.

Finally, it has been argued that care management has had a significant impact on social work practice in the UK. Measures have been introduced through care management to make social work efficient, predictable, calculable and surveyed/controlled by managers.

But even in the current McDonaldized, post-Fordist working environment social workers working as care managers still mediate between service users and their organizations, work to integrate service users in the community, represent those with power to those without power. Lastly, they perform a surveillance role in society, 'surveying' the community for the purpose of protecting the most vulnerable members of society. Care management can therefore be interpreted as having some continuity with a casework role, but it is now a specialist instrumental role in the McDonaldized post-Fordist welfare state.

Chapter 7 attempts to bring together social theory and issues related to practice in the current late capitalist era. The introduction of quasi-markets, the commodification of social care and the changed role of social workers has shifted the foundations upon which social work is practised and these changes present tremendous challenges to social workers. Social workers practising as care managers need to consider their ethics and values in the McDonaldized market of care.

Chapter 7

Social Work Practice in the Specialist Field of Care Management

Introduction

Social workers work with the most vulnerable marginalized members of society. The work is carried out in social contexts which differ across time and place. What is considered a social problem in a developed country will be different from what is considered a social problem in a developing country. The factor that draws social work activities together is the work with vulnerable people. It has been argued here that developed societies are cutting back on their welfare provision in order to be more competitive in the global market place.

Social workers find themselves in an era of material postmodernity or late capitalism with an increased emphasis on the value of tangible goods. Care management is part of this move toward the value of tangible products with a de-emphasis on intangibles, that is, social relationships and the meaning of what is produced and consumed. Care management is about rationing goods and services to the most vulnerable. Social workers working in care-management systems could easily lose sight of broader issues related to social justice and anti-oppressive practice. This chapter is a reflection on social theory in relation to social work practice within care management.

Human rights are presented as an 'ultimate' unassailable basis upon which to ground social workers in their work with service users. Social work as 'science' versus social work as 'art' is discussed in relation to Habermas's systems and lifeworlds (Lorenz 2004, 146–7). Social workers are being positioned closer to 'science', that is, rationality, efficiency, predictability in rational bureaucratic systems. They are simultaneously less able to apply 'art', that is, the intangibles of personal relationships, intuition and the valuing of the lifeworld perspectives of the people they work with. Social workers are positioned between different kinds of rationality and must balance these competing discourses in their practice.

Issues about what is 'true' in the assessment of needs and the importance of dialogue are discussed. Hermeneutics or 'truth in context' concerns balancing science/systems with art/lifeworlds. This is presented as an important concept to describe the local factors involved in defining and meeting need. Some of the ironies and irrationalities of McDonaldized systems are discussed. Finally, perspectives on resisting the unintended effects of McDonaldized systems are reviewed. Social workers are in a key position to defend service users against the irrational aspects of rational bureaucracies and they must be mindful of their power, albeit limited power, to enhance outcomes for service users.

Implications for Social Workers Working in Care Management Bureaucracies

In this chapter, the relevance of social theory for social work is revisited. Social workers always work in a changing landscape of care, in whatever national context they find themselves. They work in service organizations that struggle for resources, and by definition do not produce a profit, in market economies where profit maximization is the goal. They work with vulnerable people who are often poor themselves in societies where poverty is a stigmatizing experience.

Like the barefoot doctors of China who had basic skills to deal with immediate medical problems, social workers are the barefoot doctors of the welfare state. They work 'on the ground' or 'at the front line' helping where they can, but recognizing that there are social problems which they are not capable of resolving. They are often unprepared and ill trained for the enormity of the roles that they are asked to fill. Capitalism by its very nature creates winners and losers. It is more cost effective (in the short term) for the state to employ social workers to patch up individual problems than it is to organize a society that would minimize individual problems through strong (but expensive) health, education and housing programmes. It may be unfair to expect government bodies to solve or minimize social problems because there will always be individuals with personal and social problems. Even Beveridge himself, designer of the British Keynesian Welfare State, could not design a society that did away with the need for social workers. So social workers work with individuals whatever their circumstances and 'patch up' situations as they can.

Although social workers are aware of 'macro' structural issues that produce social problems, they usually work from a 'micro' perspective. They believe that it is not their role to address wider social problems that lead to individual distress or malfunction in their social circumstances. Their role is to help individuals adjust, adapt and make the most of the resources available to them. However, social workers need to consider the 'bigger picture', that is, how service users arrive at the state they are in, how social forces conspire to make life difficult for them and how society has organized whatever services exist. In a study by Keating and Robertson (2003), analysing the problems that black women have in the mental health system in the UK, they suggested that professionals often ask 'what is wrong with this woman' instead of 'what has happened to this woman'. This is a powerful way of expressing the need for social workers to consider the impact of structural, sexual and racial factors that impact upon service users, and for social workers not to assume that something is simply 'wrong' with an individual.

A postmodern social theory perspective ends the modernist 'either/or' perspective, instead facilitating an 'and/both' perspective that 'strives to maintain a broad vision while focusing on the personal detail of people's troubled lives and encourages self-reflection on the pain and contradictions deep within us all (Walker 2001, 37). It benefits social workers to lift their eyes to the wider picture when they can, using social theory to put individual problems into social and organizational contexts. At the very least this can ameliorate the process of 'blaming the victim'.

Practice in a Modern (McDonaldized) Yet Postmodern Context

Social workers work with people from different cultures; they also operate in a social climate wherein the power and knowledge of experts are sometimes distrusted. One set of values does not fit all service users and all cultural values are not defensible from a human rights perspective. Into this postmodern maelstrom has come care management as a McDonaldized form of social work, which imposes fixed criteria of need and rigid budgets. The issue for social workers is how to reconcile the competing demands and oppositional pulls in their work; for instance, when personal ethics differ from the ethics of the organization, moral dilemmas arise. 'This problem may be particularly acute when a feminist ethics-oriented case manager works in a regulatory system-oriented agency … and may regard themselves as a double agent constantly distressed by trying to serve both the client and the agency' (McAuley et al., 1999, 9). In Britain, Evidence Based Practice (EBP) has been proposed to provide a modern scientific, research-based, empirically tested rationale for social work practice. Parton has suggested that this emphasis on empirically 'proven' methods of work is a result of increasing postmodern uncertainty and loss of faith in social work ability to proscribe (Parton 2004, 35). It represents a loss of trust in social workers and requires social workers to base their actions and decisions on research evidence.

The problem in relation to implementing EBP in social work is that no two situations are the same. Each situation, each individual and each assessment are different (Lorenz 2004, 149). Once social work 'surrenders to the rationalistic requirement of the system and therefore adopts the dogma of positivism, it becomes set on an instrumental perspective on action and its identity becomes negatively constructed' as the differences emerge between its claims to efficiency and its actual achievements (Lorenz 2004, 151). Social workers need to be aware of evidence from research and use such evidence as guidance for their work, but such research needs to be thought through and applied carefully in each particular instance of practice. Results of research need to be interpreted and adapted to practice situations, consistent with a hermeneutic approach to interpretation of meaning. EBP can inform practice, but it cannot dictate practice. The original pilot projects in England discussed above are an example of the difficulties of applying research to policy development. The original projects were successful, but the outcomes of these projects have not been applied successfully in all situations. This demonstrates the 'margin to mainstream' issue in application of research. Individual studies do not necessarily translate into mainstream solutions. Findings of research must be interpreted and applied in a nuanced way for each situation a social worker encounters.

Adding McDonaldized care management into the practice equation, social workers are required to work in prescribed ways with reference to limited budgets. Social workers may experience conflict reconciling the demands of care management and EBP. Research could suggest one course of action and procedures require another course of action. Social workers must interpret the best outcome in every situation. It is axiomatic that social workers work in situations where there are competing demands. Social workers intervene 'in conditions and circumstances that require action, often as a matter of urgency and where there may be conflicting interests' (Tompsett 2005, 11).

Knowing 'How to Go On' – Social Work Practice as Science or Art

Social workers, wherever in the world they find themselves, need to think about 'how to go on' (Kearney 2004), that is, how to maintain their historical concern for the disadvantaged while at the same time adapting to current demands of late capitalism. Social workers usually work in bureaucratic structures that both constrain and enable them (Miles 2001, 11). It has been argued that care management is a McDonaldized form of social work and an added constraint to their work. Social workers are limited in what they can do by the structures of their working environments, but conversely, these environments form the basis from which they can work with vulnerable people. They rely on organizations to facilitate their work. They need to use their own initiative, discretion and creativity to ameliorate the worst excesses of the rational bureaucracies that they work in. Social workers who work as care managers need to consider how to maintain a professional, ethical, rights-based practice in the face of 'rational' bureaucratic procedures.

There is an ongoing debate about whether social work is science (Sheldon 1978) or art (Jordan 1978, England 1986, Lorenz 2004, 148). 'The history of the debate surrounding the role of research in social work practice reflects the profession's continued attempt to negotiate the elements of both 'art' and 'science' in clinical intervention' (Magill 2006, 101). This issue can be returned to in the context of modernity/postmodernity as discussed in Chapter 1. Social work as science is a modern concept. The introduction of care management and EBP seem to be an attempt to make social work more modern and scientific. Social work as art is out of date from this perspective. However, the seemingly old fashioned concept of 'use of self' could be perhaps now be reintroduced or resurrected as a postmodern idea, one that supports social work as art (Irving 1999, 46). The problem with care management is that it is neither art nor science. It is a bureaucratic accountability exercise, fitting people into predetermined categories (even though it claims to be needs-led) and assigning monetary value to service provision. Various models of social work have been proposed and can be conceptualized as either science or art (see Table 7.1).

The dichotomy between science and art is parallel to Habermas's distinction between systems and lifeworlds (Lorenz 2004, 146–7). Systems are about organizations. Lifeworlds are about the personal lives of individuals. Instrumental rationality is appropriate to modern organizational life; communicative rationality is constructed and relativistic and important in the interactions between individuals in society. Instrumental rationality equates to social work as science. Communicative rationality equates to the art of social work, that is, the use of self.

Systems operate on the basis of instrumental rationality. Lifeworlds operate on the basis of communicative rationality (Habermas 1987, 119). Social workers operate between the instrumental/systems paradigm appropriate to organizations, and the communicative/lifeworlds paradigm, which is more relevant to interactions between individuals. Social workers therefore mediate between two kinds of rationality, which is, by its very nature, a difficult task.

Table 7.1   Conceptualizations of social work as a 'modern' scientific enterprise versus social work as a 'postmodern' art, including the application of intangible qualities of reflection and engagement

	Modernity	Postmodernity
Conceptualization of social work	Social work as science	Social work as art
Ideal practice	Evidence Based Practice	Use of self
Toren (1972)	Instrumental role	Normative role
Schon (1983)	Professionalism as 'technical rationality'	Professionalism as 'reflection-in-action'
Habermas (1984)	Instrumental rationality applied	Communicative rationality applied
Habermas (1987)	Systems perspective	Lifeworlds perspective
Payne (1997)	Individualistic-reformist model of practice	Reflexive-therapeutic model of practice
Parton and O'Bryne (2000)	Rational/technical approach to practice	Moral/practical approach to practice
Parton (2004)	Determinant judgement applied	Reflexive judgement applied

Payne's individualist-reformist version of social work addresses practical need within the welfare system efficiently. It is not bringing about change within individuals or society (Payne 2005, 9). This version of social work has been placed above in the 'social work as science' typology above. Harlow has added position to this debate, which is even more science and less art than Payne's individualistic-reform position, that is, the managerial-techniques position (Harlow 2003, 33). This reflects the increasingly managerial role of social workers and is a refinement of Payne's individualist-reformist role. There is no equivalent to Harlow's position because it has been put forward to conceptualize the realities of work as a care manager, a recent phenomenon and one that has emerged subsequent to most other paradigms of social work practice.

In Parton's discussion of the relevance of 'post-theories' for social work, relevant to the above typology of social work approaches, emphasis is on process, relationships and the interaction of knowledge, language and 'voice'. This is consistent with the core values and traditions of social work, and proceeds on an assumption that service users, no matter what their circumstances, have significant resources within and around them in order to bring about positive change. This argues that social work is as much, if not more, an art than a science. Social work practice should be understood as much a practical-moral activity as a rational-technical activity. The 'social work as art' positions in the chart above emphasize social work's affirmative and reflexive attributes and focus on dialogue, listening to and talking with the Other. An ability to work with ambiguity and uncertainty, both in terms of process and outcome, are seen as key skills. The principle if indeterminacy suggests 'the fluid, recursive and non-determined way that social situations unfold' (Parton 2004, 41). Reflexive judgement involves 'imaginative and inter-subjective approaches to uncertain or contested areas of knowledge – with interpretation and negotiation replacing calculation and prediction' (Parton 2004, 42). Social work as art rests on the assumption that social reality is not fixed or immutable. It is sometimes difficult to fit service users into care-management assessment criteria, but this is the task that faces care managers.

Social work is both art and science, consistent with a postmodern 'and/both' perspective (Walker 2001, 37). It would be dangerous for social work to set itself up as strictly an art based on intuition, with no basis in knowledge or research, but modern scientific positivism has its limits in social work practice (Smith 1987, Lorenz 2004). Social workers must be aware of the need for instrumental rationality/ science. They must also be able to exercise communicative rationality/art.

Social workers, especially those working as care managers, have to mediate and reconcile contradictory kinds of rationality, because their work is situated between organizations (instrumentality rationality) and service users (lifeworlds rationality). This balancing act is one of the reasons that the social work role has always been challenging.

Dialogue and Human Rights

When care managers meet with service users a dialogue should take place about their needs. Care managers represent their 'system's' organizational rationality and service users with their 'lifeworld' perspective. Their two 'truths' are brought together. It is possible to reconcile different truths and arrive at a consensus if those involved participate in a reciprocal dialogue. Dialogue requires 'a preparedness on the part of each of those involved to be influenced by the other' (Lovelock and Powell 2004, 212). The Truth and Reconciliation exercise in South Africa carried out after the end of apartheid could be considered such a dialogue. Dialogue is enhanced if actors have equal power. 'It is only the equal chance to participate in the discourse which can, at least potentially, prevent a consensus being based on deception' (Bauman 1978, 242). But all actors are rarely equal, the most powerful actor in a discourse, or discussion for social work purposes, will define the 'truth'.

The most obvious problem in any given social work situation is that social workers and services users rarely have equal power. Social workers' struggle with the issue of how much power they themselves have. Almost by definition, social workers also mediate between other actors who are unequal, between those with power and those without power. In their role as mediators, therefore, social workers need to equalize power as much as possible in order to have any hope of arriving at consensus, that is, by empowering service users, by allowing service users to be aware of the power they have. In social work, this would include a strengths' model (Saleebey 1990). The work of Paulo Freire (1992) is useful as a model of empowerment and consciousness raising. However, dialogue might not lead to agreement, in which case the dominant actor or the actor with more power may exercise their power to define the outcome of the dialogue on their terms. But at least each party should listen to the other and understand their relative positions. If power is imposed on a service user, at least they will understand why, which is preferable to having power imposed without understanding why.

These are murky issues of truth, power and postmodern relativism. The question is, what is the ultimate, final 'bottom line' in these considerations? McDonaldized care management would dictate cost as the 'bottom line'. For the social worker, where there is a conflict between cost, values and evidence from research, the resolution of the conflict should be grounded in ethics, social justice and human rights (Williams 2001). However, in the current era of late capitalism, the reality is that decisions are often dictated by cost.

The promotion of human rights has arisen concurrently with the rise of globalization, capitalism and mass culture. The importance of the movement toward a conceptualization of human rights in general and the Human Rights Act (1998) in particular was raised early in this discussion. Attention to human rights has risen with globalization and has been stronger in conditions of late capitalism than ever before. At the 2005 Forum of the Social Care and Social Work Assembly of the British Association of Social Work, key features applicable to the whole of the social work and social care workforce were identified. The first was 'respecting and championing human rights across a range of situations and people in adult social care and children's services' (Tompsett 2005, 11). Arguing a solution to a problem on the grounds of human rights can cut through issues of cost and cultural values. However, even human rights still need to be interpreted and supported (Dustin and Davies 2007). Human rights' arguments can be used spuriously (Becky's Story 2006). However, if human rights are the ultimate goal or the 'bottom line' then issues of cost and cultural relativity are subsumed in the higher level standards of human rights. Human rights provide an unassailable position as the foundation of social work practice. It is a position that should be central to all social work decision making.

Rights are still not absolute and must be argued on a case by case basis. In the UK, where the European Convention on Human Rights (1998) has been incorporated as part of domestic legislation, it is possible to refer to this legislation to justify good practice. In countries that do not have similar legislation, this will be more difficult. However, even where specific human rights legislation is not in place, moral grounds for human rights can be argued on the basis of the United Nations Universal Declaration of Human Rights (1948) and on the United Nations Convention on the Rights of the Child (1989).

Truth in Context

Social workers usually work with 'the most constrained and marginalised of those in our society' (Parton 2004, 41) who do not 'fit' the profile of the ideal citizen; they work with those who have fallen foul of cultural values or norms, or who have been oppressed by cultural values or national policies that allow ageism, disablism, racism or sexism. Social workers work with disadvantaged people (Cree 2005, 208), with the socially excluded who suffer inequality and disadvantage (Sheppard 2006, 1).

Social workers usually work with the Other, people who not white, not heterosexual, not able bodied, not adult or not men (Bartens 1995, 8).

No matter where a social worker is employed, they will need to reconcile the values of the local culture, national policies, procedures and guidelines and the demands of the organization that employs them. '… knowledge is socially generated – it arises in a particular context' (Sheppard 2006). It is accurate, and indeed helpful, to use a social theory concept which describes 'truth in context'. Habermas's (1987, 119) concept of 'hermeneutics' or 'truth in context' avoids the modern perspective that there is one truth that everyone must aspire to. It also avoids extreme relativism.

'Hermeneutics is concerned with interpretation as an *exceptional accomplishment* (italics in original), which becomes necessary only when relevant segments of the lifeworld become problematic, when the certainties of a culturally stable background break down and normal means of reaching understanding fail …' (Habermas 1984, 131). A hermeneutics approach assists '… the practice of communication and the effort of reaching agreement' (Bauman 1978, 241). Any social work situation brings together the service user, the social worker, the national/political climate they find themselves in, the resources available, the social/cultural context and the times they live in. If any of these variables change, then the 'truth' for those in the situation will be altered.

Social workers work hermeneutically in small local situations interpreting various meanings and interpretations of what constitutes a problem and how the problem should be resolved. Hermeneutics at its simplest implies interpretation of meaning. Some argue that it is never possible to arrive at a 'true' interpretation or conclusion because objective truth in the interaction between individuals is ultimately unknowable (Sampaio 2006). An example of this is the phenomenon of hearing voices associated with schizophrenia. In traditional societies, hearing voices may be a sign of special privilege or status. From a modern scientific perspective, hearing voices is a highly stigmatized condition which is considered a bio-chemical problem which should be treated by medication. From a postmodern interpretivist perspective, hearing voices may be a result of social trauma or oppression, which is best worked with through understanding the meaning of the voices in the context of service user-led support groups (Hearing Voices Network, accessed 28 June 2007).

Hermeneutics is related to the concept of social construction of reality. Social workers are context dependent. They work hermeneutically in social contexts, mediating conflicting interpretations of a situation from the different perspectives of the actors in that situation. They can debate relative truths, but unlike philosophers or sociologists, they must take action and try to come to a resolution of a problem, reconciling different values and truths, for example, those of their agencies, their own truths in the context of local and national legislation and those of the service user. Social workers must intervene and take action '… often as a matter of urgency in complex and sometimes high risk situations' (Tompsett 2005, 11). A 'skeptical' postmodernist position (Rosenau 1992, 53) of extreme nihilistic relativism would paralyse a social worker. There would be no grounds to take any action to help anyone. Healthy scepticism is a valuable asset for social workers, but doubt for its own sake is not helpful (Sardar, 2007, 21, Sim 2006). Social workers need to adopt an 'affirmative' postmodernist position that rejects absolutes and recognizes uncertainty but allows a concern for 'the daily life at the margin' (Rosenau 1992, 57) and retains the incentive to take action from a humanist perspective. Social workers need to practice from a concept of professional ethics based on human rights as grounds for decision making. This demands a higher moral requirement than that represented by the cost containment ethos of care management. While it would be unethical to waste money, it may also be unethical to conserve money for its own sake and not use it to better conditions for vulnerable individuals where this is possible.

Ethics

Ethics are the point at which 'systems' and 'lifeworlds' intersect. Ethics must determine the application of bureaucratic principles to personal and social problems. Ethics that direct social work practice must rest on human rights, professional codes of practice and communicative rationality, not just on McDonaldized procedures based on 'systems' instrumental rationality. Ultimately, it is intangible values that determine action. Efficiency is a technique to achieve goals. Values determine goals and rational efficiency is used to achieve these goals. Social workers need to think about ethics, social justice and Human Rights, not just assessment criteria. McDonaldization is an example of an almost 'pure' rational bureaucracy. A pure rational bureaucracy without the need for human interpretation of rational procedures is difficult to achieve, but the McDonald's organization attempts to approximate that goal. Viewing McDonaldized social service organizations as 'systems' based on instrumental rationality makes sense, that is, it is rational to manage organizations so that they achieve their goals in an efficient manner. However, 'systems' and 'lifeworlds' are governed by different principles. The application of instrumental rationality to life worlds is awkward at the very least. In the extreme, applying instrumental rationality to situations which require communicative rationality is inhuman. One of the reasons that the killing of Jewish people, homosexuals and disabled children and adults during the Holocaust was so abhorrent was because it was based completely on instrumental rationality (Bauman 1989). It was carried out with factory assembly line precision and was utterly calculated and efficient.

The purpose of rational bureaucracies is to apply instrumental rationality to goal achievement, which can be applied to any project, whether it is ethical or unethical. Ultimately, the agents of organizations must face 'point-blank the consequences of their actions and ... need to justify argumentatively the values that inform their activities' (Beilharz 2001, 186). The problem for social workers is that rational bureaucracies have no ethics. Bureaucracies are by definition 'impersonal', applying rules impersonally. At one time in the UK, the social services were called the Personal Social Services. There is some irony in placing 'personal' social services in 'impersonal' bureaucracies. 'Along this borderline [between institutional procedures and professional ethics] new issues arise which can be settled only through ethical debate' (Beilharz 2001, 187). Social workers must still reconcile professional ethics with bureaucratic procedures.

Social workers may have some difficulty implementing managerial dictates in care-management situations. In resisting a manager's instruction, they could lose their job. But social workers have a higher responsibility to their professional code of ethics than to their employers. '... social work has to be defined not only by its function for the state but by its value base' (Jones et al., 2007, 201). Social workers who identified disabled children for extermination in Nazi Germany were carrying out their role, no doubt scientifically and efficiently. They were doing what their organization required of them (Lorenz 2004, 156). However, they were violating professional ethics. They had a choice. They could have resigned from the organization that asked them to carry out practices that contravened professional ethics, even though such a decision would have carried great personal risk, but those who stayed chose to participate in efficient but unethical practice.

Social workers must take individual professional decisions about what they believe is ethical and right in their work with service users Therefore social workers need to be aware of the purposes to which efficiency is put. They should not blindly follow procedure when procedure may disadvantage a vulnerable service user who needs help. A social worker must think about the intention of procedures and whether they are rights-based and ethical or whether their main goal is to contain cost.

Social workers have choices regarding how to where they are employed, how they use their skills and how to relate to service users. Social workers need jobs, but there are enough jobs available in most Western countries for social workers to be selective about where they work. They can choose to apply for employment in organizations that are rights-based. In the UK, this does not necessarily mean that they should apply to the SSD in the public sector which has the highest ranking in the league tables of performance. League tables are based on instrumental efficiency. The important point is the purpose to which efficiency is applied. An organization may be ranked highly because it is getting the most services to the most people in the quickest time. However, these criteria are often based solely on tangible, measurable criteria such as how many services were provided and how quickly responses were made. These are important elements of good service. But good service also implies an intangible valuing of the human beings to whom these tangible services are delivered. Social workers should ask how the service users, the recipients of services, rate the organization. This would mean favouring organizations that support active, effective service user advisory groups. This information can then be balanced against the other factors that an organization puts forward to recruit social work staff.

Ironies and Irrationalities within McDonaldized Care-managed Services

The most obvious negative aspect of McDonaldization is the 'irrationality of rationality', introduced through a highly managerialized approach to social service delivery. Social workers need to take a critical reflexive stance, based on professional ethics, social justice and human rights to ensure that the needs of service users and carers remain at the forefront of practice and to avoid being overwhelmed by narrowly conceived bureaucratic measures instituted to ensure efficiency and cost containment.

Ritzer has been criticized for having no real strategy for resisting McDonaldization (Miles 2001) and not going far enough in suggesting how to counter the influence of McDonalds. Becoming a vegetarian could be a form of protest against McDonalds

(Tester 1999). We can refuse to eat McDonaldized food as a form of protest (Kellner 1999, 203). Consumers can boycott McDonald's restaurants if they believe they are cutting down the rainforest to produce beef for Big Macs. However, people who need the services of a care manager do not have the luxury of boycotting social services. Advising service users to boycott social services would be wrong unless there is an alternative. The McDonaldization process is not going to go away. We need to consider 'which forms of McDonaldization are positive and beneficial and which are harmful and destructive' (Kellner 1999, 203).

Comparisons have been made between social work as care management and McDonald's restaurants. The analogy has been drawn in the context that social work has lost its way, 'that we are in danger of losing our critical edge in terms of understanding the meaning of quality in social work and have substituted fast food for *haute cuisine*, or at least for individually prepared and served meals' (James 2004, 37).

Social workers working as care managers are aware of what Ritzer (2004, 134) and Smart (1999, 15) have called the unintended irrational consequences of rational bureaucracies. Some of the 'ironies' that these unintended consequences produce have been raised in Chapter 3. These ironies and irrationalities are discussed below as the irony of 'caring' services located in impersonal bureaucracies, of mindlessness in rational bureaucracies, of promoting choice when choice is limited, of predetermining and limiting needs based on assessment protocols when rhetoric promotes needs-led services, of improved services in the context of widening social differences, the irrationality of 'false economy' and the irrationality of applying cost criteria to ethical dilemmas and the inefficiency of efficiency.

The irony of 'caring' services located in impersonal bureaucracies

McDonaldization can bring 'unintended irrational consequences' to rational bureaucracies (Smart 1999, 15). Ritzer (1996) introduced the term 'McDonaldization' to describe the application of Fordist techniques to service industries to promote efficiency. In care management, the process of care has been transformed into a system that is essentially uncaring as care managers cannot assume the role of 'one who engages with the client in a supportive, nurturing encounter' (Davies and Leonard 2004, x). McDonaldized organizations are characterized by hierarchy, procedures and rules where creativity and genuine emotion are not valued (Ritzer 1996, 130, Ritzer 2004, 197). For care managers, this can be related to their perception that they have lost a degree of professional discretion and the ability to engage in a caring dialogue with service users.

Care management is a simulacrum (Baudrillard 1983) of care or an imitation of care in the same way that McDonald's food is a simulacrum of food. McDonald's food is highly processed and the relationship between the food served in McDonald's and 'real' or natural food is tenuous. Care management is not 'natural' in the sense that it is not care expressed in naturally occurring groups such as family or communities of identity. It is highly processed and bureaucratized and serviced by people who do not 'care' in the sense that they must maintain professional boundaries between themselves and those they 'care for'. At the end of the working day, they must cease to 'care' for their own wellbeing, that is, to avoid burnout.

Care management purports to 'care', but delivering impersonal bureaucratized services is not 'real' caring. We think of 'real' care as being delivered to family members in the home by family members, people who not only 'care for', that is, carry out acts of care, but also 'care about' or have an emotional investment in their elderly or disabled family member. Care provided by families or community groups based on a shared identity (Barnes 1999) is more likely to be 'real' care. Care management is a far cry from this concept of care and could therefore be regarded as a simulacra of care. It is a copy of caring. It is not the 'real thing'. It is organized as a bureaucratic, faceless exercise in a standardized, routinized manner. People who deliver care in these circumstances must appear to care, when in fact they hardly know the people they are 'caring' for. Carers in this system who do 'care about' the people they look after are barely able to communicate their human concern because of the 'fast food' factory orientation to task and the pressures towards performativity (Rosenau 1992, xiii). It takes time to communicate meaningfully, but these systems are now geared to efficiency rather than human caring in a traditional sense.

The irony of mindlessness in rational bureaucracies

One of the ironies of McDonaldization is that it is a modern approach to organization of service delivery based on rationality. However McDonalds encourages mindlessness among its workers (Miles 2001, 113), for example the emphasis on procedures which must be followed even if they do not make sense in some circumstances. Managers sometimes seem to assume that their employees do not have the capacity to think about what they are doing; workers are not encouraged to think creatively, whether it is a worker at a McDonald's restaurant or in a more traditional factory. Workers are merely expected to perform. Performativity is valued over creativity. Although care managers are not fast-food workers, analogies can be drawn. The focus on efficiency, defined as saving money, the routinized procedures to be followed, the lack of discretion, the difficulty in thinking outside the requirements dictated by procedures, and the immediate accountable to managers are all relevant to both McDonald's workers and care managers. It is ironic that the Enlightenment project that was based on rational thought has spawned rational organizations where employees are not encouraged to think.

The irony of promoting choice when choice is limited

The issue of choice in care-managed services is contentious. One of the rationales for care management was that it would increase service user choice. It was anticipated that creating a market of services would increase choice. SSDs were intended to assess need in the community and commission community-based private/voluntary organizations located in the community to provide services, thereby increasing choice. It is debatable how far this has been achieved, but that aside, choice is still restricted to what is available on the menu of services available. It is not altogether correct to claim that care management is needs-led, when care management is, and indeed must be, service-led. The economies of scale provided by block contracts cannot be dismissed by large bureaucracies, but block contracts restrict choice.

Service users only have choice among the options on the menu of available services. Block contracts allow limited choice, contrary to the early intentions of policy makers.

People have a choice as to whether to patronize McDonald's or not. Once they enter the restaurant they have choice as long as what they want is on the menu. Even at McDonald's restaurants, choice is an anomaly. 'Customers' of care-managed services often have little choice about whether to use care-managed services. Most people who use care-managed services, unlike McDonald's customers, do not have a choice about whether or not to use them.

Care managers make decisions that can fundamentally affect people's lives, with or without their agreement. If service users had enough money, they would probably exercise their choice to purchase services privately (hence the introduction of Direct Payments in the UK with the Community Care [Direct Payment] Act 1996) so they could exercise choice and control over the service they got.

The irony of predetermining needs based on assessment protocols when rhetoric promotes needs-led services

For example, limiting the definition of need to what is outlined in a needs-assessments' protocol can work against the best interest of service users. If a service user presents a need that is not defined by the organization as part of its 'core business' and for which the government has established performance measures, then care managers struggle to meet that need. It can be argued that by not meeting needs identified by service users, problems are being 'stored up' that will cost the organization more to address later and about which it will have to take a more invasive action in the future, 'to say nothing of the distress that it might cause the service user or indeed the social consequences to society of that need not being met' (Chappell 2007). It is therefore irrational to restrict needs assessments to needs protocols.

To the degree that care-management decisions are made strictly on mechanistic, prescribed, rigid assessment criteria, need is not considered in its human context. In McDonaldized care management, it is possible that the meaning of the process for the service users and carers involved is not taken into account. The need to 'provide' tangible services efficiently can pressure care managers into a rote 'questioning' procedure (Smale and Tuson 1993) that discourages partnership and exchange, sets up the care manager as the expert, disempowers the service user and does not acknowledge the strength of the service user.

The irony of improved services in the context of widening social differences

The rhetoric of choice and needs-led services conceals the overriding purpose of the introduction of care management, which was cost containment. The rhetoric of care management masks the rationing of public monies devoted to social services. Residualized, targeted services serve a small number of people better, but historically, this process results in the stigmatization of those who receive these residualized services. Care management is delivering better services, but to fewer people, which is entirely consistent with a targeted, selective model of service delivery. Changes have benefited the wider population, especially among older people and people with disabilities (Levin and Webb 1997, ix). Care management, a residualized service, can contribute to divisions in society. '... when consideration is given to some of the consequences of an extension of "McDonaldized" processes of rationalization, particularly economic rationalization, to public services and institutions, notably the extension of what are called "free-market" principles to education health and welfare, it is clear that the outcome has been not a reduction in differences in treatment, but rather a pronounced widening of the quality gap between those dependent on public provision and those able to afford private provision' (Smart 1999, 15). The question must be asked as to whether it is rational for governments to exacerbate social divisions.

The irrationality of 'false economy'

It is irrational to tell a disabled or an older person that they are not disabled enough to get help according to eligibility criteria and that they should come back when their condition worsens; 'lack of support can accelerate their deterioration' (Jones 2001, 558). It is irrational because when they come back with higher levels of need, the cost of their care may be greater than it would have been if their condition had been dealt with preventively. This approach is also unethical because the bureaucracy is condemning the person to endure suffering without help when help is available. But the problem with rationality is that it has no ethics. It is up to the people operating the bureaucracy to apply ethics to rationality. It is up to social workers to do this if no one else does (James 2004, 51). Balancing ethics and cost is difficult in a bureaucracy. In terms of rational economics, it would be rational to tell the person to go away and die, because that would save the bureaucracy a great deal of money. It would be very cost effective not to provide any help at all. But this would not be ethical. So social services located in welfare bureaucracies must balance rationality and ethics.

The irrationality of applying cost criteria to ethical dilemmas and the inefficiency of efficiency

An example raised in the chapter on empowerment raised the conflict between cost containment and ethics. A manager wanted to give a young girl who was in care of the local government a one-way ticket from the UK to her father's funeral in another country. In terms of economics, this was a rational position. This would have saved the SSD both the cost of a return ticket and the cost of her ongoing care. The social worker in this situation was able to use her discretion and convince the manager that the girl's welfare would be damaged if they sent her away and the manager relented. If the social worker had not intervened, the manager would have made a perfectly valid rational decision to save money, but it would have been unethical because the social and emotional consequences for the young girl would have been devastating.

It also seems irrational to carry out an assessment of need for a service user even when it is known that the budget is exhausted and the service user will not be getting any services. Procedures dictate that an assessment be carried out so it must be done, but the service user's expectations may be raised only to be told nothing can be done.

A related concept is the inefficiency of efficiency. There is some irony in the fact that care management was introduced to create efficiency and yet the staff turnover levels created by managerialism and bureaucracy are 'grossly inefficient' (Foster 2002). The inefficiency of efficiency can be added to the irrationality of rationality in this case.

Countering the Unintended Effects of McDonaldized Care Management

Social workers working as care managers must bring honesty, genuineness, integrity, engagement and transparency to their work with service users. Social workers can minimize the unintended effects of care management by considering the following.

Be authentic

Authenticity requires that uncertainty is acknowledged. Subjectivity is accepted and valued and reflected upon in terms of universal aspirations to social justice. Social workers should not claim to be experts who can dictate solutions. They need to bring their expertise to the solution of problems in partnership with service users and other professionals. Authenticity in practice is defined as 'discarding the bad faith which denies uncertainty and seeks false comfort in rationality and positivism … consistency of thoughts, feelings and actions, a genuine integration of theory and practice' (Walker 2001, 36). For some, authentic social work was possible in the post-Barclay era when social workers were actively engaged in prevention and social change-oriented community-based work (Davies 2005). The change agent role is no longer possible for care managers working within local government, at least in the UK. This kind of authentic social work may only be possible in voluntary organizations. Even though the autonomy of voluntary organizations has been reduced through contractual funding by local government, voluntary organizations 'may eventually become the only agencies engaged in delivering earlier versions of social work practice' (Harlow 2003, 40). 'It takes courage to be an authentic social worker, pursuing a firm commitment to social work ethics and values and realising the importance of the profession over and above the employment context' (Davies 2005, 13). Social workers need to think about where they can practice authentically, where they can practice in such a way that there is consistency between their own values, professional values and the values of the organization that they work for.

Maintain personal/professional integrity

Integrity involves honesty with oneself and others and being true to professional values. Social workers need to be 'affirmative' postmodernists. Social workers cannot afford to be 'skeptical' postmodernists (Rosenau 1992, 110) who deny that there is any reality and believe that we are all living an illusion. Social workers cannot be the kind of relativists who make no judgements. Social workers must make decisions and recommendations. They need to make a positive contribution to the social construction of the lives of their service users. Therefore social workers need to be the kind of relativists who know that when they are making judgements, they are standing on the shifting ground of their own socially-constructed cultural worldview, but that judgements need to be made and actions need to be taken. Social workers need to be reflective and honest with themselves and their service users about how their own worldview is constructed. From this perspective, global concepts of human liberation and social justice become the guiding moral and ethical principals by which social work actions should be judged.

Engage with service users at an individual and a collective level

Engagement at the individual level is consistent with Payne's reflexive-therapeutic social work position. Care managers may feel they are required to go through assessment protocols in scripted interactions with service users (Ritzer 2004, 149, Hensher 2007, 27). These protocols can act as a barrier to communication and engagement and can lead to a level of superficiality in communication between care managers and service users (Harris 2003, 2). Social workers need to 'get past' the obstacle of scripted interactions to actually engage with service users as valued people. Social workers are part of the process of socially constructing service users and their problems (Schweppe 2007, 96) and can therefore contribute to their feeling valued, or conversely, not valued. In spite of the fact that social workers often have limited time to assess service-user need, they need to maintain their skills to engage service users. Engagement means truly listening to service users and is consistent with person-centred therapies (Rogers 1951 and 1961) and narrative therapy (White and Epson 1990). It can be incredibly empowering to be able to tell one's story and be fully listened to because it means that the listener values the speaker. It can be difficult for care managers to genuinely listen when there are time limits on carrying out assessments, but social workers need to find a way for service users to talk and be listened to. In practical terms for care managers, this may mean discussing issues before going through the assessment forms and going back through the forms if something was missed in the initial discussion. Social workers who work as care managers need to actively engage with service users from the moment they meet them. They should not give up good practice because of the superficiality of McDonaldized assessment forms.

   Engagement at a collective level goes back to a radical social work position, of which there was evidence in the late 1960s and the 1970s. Payne (2005, 9) refers to this as the socialist-collectivist position. Involvement in collective action to promote justice is a time-honoured social work activity, but one which has fallen into disrepute as social workers have been submerged in the neo-liberal tide of individualism. In the UK, a group of social work academics and practitioners have written a Social Work Manifesto which puts social justice at the centre of social work. This represents an attempt to address the loss of direction that social workers have experienced as a result of the imposition of managerialism. This loss of direction is caused 'by the fragmentation of services, by financial restrictions and lack of resources, by increased bureaucracy and work-loads, by the domination of care-management approaches with their associated performance indicators and by the increased use of the private sector which increase the distance between social worker and service user'. The manifesto goes on to say '… The need for a social work committed to social justice and challenging poverty and discrimination is greater than ever. Too often today social workers are doing little more than supervising the deterioration of people's lives' (Jones et al. accessed 16 March 2007). The Manifesto, also available in hard copy (Jones et al., 2007, 197–202), promotes the perspective that social workers still need to engage in collective action in whatever way they can to address the problems of service users and not give up the struggle at a collective level to improve conditions in society.

Be reflective and reflexive

Social workers are caught up in government efforts to modernize, that is, to be ever more efficient, effective and economical with tax-generated resources. It is difficult to find fault with that. However 'false economy' can lead to greater problems and more expensive problems. Case management is a false economy in that it uses the skills of expensively trained qualified social workers to manage the use of care resources when their interpersonal skills could be used in community-based preventive work. Social workers are not in a position of power to change existing systems. They have to be aware of and work with what exists. But they can use their ability to critically reflect about situations and systems that affect service users and to think about their own position in the welfare system in which they work. They need to find ways to value the individual they are working with even if s/he is not valued by the system set up to help them.

Promote empowerment

Empowerment (Bray and Preston-Shoot 2003) is the process of 'advocating for, facilitating, enabling and empowering socially excluded individuals, groups and communities to take control of their lives' (Tompsett 2005, 11) and is central to the social work role wherever they practice. Empowerment is part of anti-oppressive practice, which itself is located in a critical social theory perspective (Dalrymple and Burke 2007, 10). Critical theories highlight that through conscious and collective action people are able to achieve a society that is non-exploitative and free from domination (Healy 2000). Adopting a human rights/social justice stance leads to empowering practice. The problem for care managers is that they have lost their normative case role through which social workers helped service users develop strength and coping strategies. Therefore care managers need to think laterally and creatively about empowerment and partnership within the care-management role.

Empowerment is not a single way of practising (Askheim 2003). Social workers practising as care managers may not be able to empower service users through an ongoing casework relationship because they have lost their normative role. However, because of the rise of the service-user movement, care managers can make service users aware of service-user-based services, which are empowering by their very nature (see below).

Some requirements associated with care management can be regarded as empowering. These elements of care management need to be promoted and used to their maximum effect. Policies to ensure that race and culture of service users are addressed and to ensure that service users sign their care-plan agreements, indicating their agreement with their care plans, are empowering for service users because these agreements form a contract that the service user can use to hold the service provider accountable. In addition, the requirement that service users should be given copies of their written care plans with the summary of the assessment of their needs in language they can understand is empowering. A positive outcome of a thorough assessment and a discussion of their needs and a care plan shared with service users can bring them an awareness of their situation and empower them to get the service they need.

SSD local government consultations with service-user groups to ask them what services they want to have commissioned are empowering to service users. Direct payments to service users are empowering. These payments can be made directly to disabled service users and are empowering because this allows service users to purchase their own services in the capacity of a genuine consumer. This is more empowering than having services purchased by care managers on their behalf.

Where care managers have a role in reviewing the provision of services that have been purchased for them, they can require providers to meet their contractual obligations. Exposing poor providers and requiring organizations to live up to their own hyperbole in terms of efficiency requires them to provide good service to service users, which is what, at the very minimum, care management should be about.

Promote service users' rights

Know service user's rights and tell service users what their rights are. Although social workers do not have as much power as other professionals, such as doctors and lawyers, they have some degree of discretion within organizations. How they use it and whether they use it in service users' interest varies from worker to worker. As organizations become more 'rational' bureaucratically, social workers need to draw on human rights' principles in order to advocate for service users. This involves informing service users of their rights and encouraging them to get support outside the process of assessment.

In this study, discussed in Part II, the rights of care-managed service users were limited and contingent upon the interpretation of team managers within the policies and resources of individual SSDs. Care managers' own ideas about service users' rights needed to be negotiated within the context of SSD policies, procedures and resources. Care managers' comments about service users' rights were related to rights within their organizations rather than more abstract rights such as social rights (Marshall 1950, Plant 1992) or human rights (Croft and Beresford 2002, 391). Expanding the conceptualization of rights to include human rights will expand the horizons of care managers and take their frame of reference outside the confines of the own organization.

Informing service users of their rights can be a subversive strategy. For example in the US in the 1970s, it was suggested that if social workers ensured that all service users received the services they were entitled to, so much pressure would be put on the benefit systems that national reforms would be required, re-opening the debate about the introduction of national guaranteed minimum income (Piven and Cloward 1993 [1971], 321, n27). Making sure that service users know about their entitlement to services and what resources are available to them is good practice, but it is also a way to resist McDonaldized social service organizations where cost containment is paramount. Every organization should have a complaints procedure and service users should be informed about grounds and procedures for appeals so that they get what they are entitled to.

Support and encourage the service user movement

It is desirable to have alternatives based on local helping networks among like-minded service users. This was the aim underlying SSDs efforts to commission and fund community services in the private and voluntary sectors. This aim has been thwarted by the tendency for SSDs to want to work with large organizations through block contracts. It is possible that the service-user movement could contribute alternative services, but these are difficult to set up without support to these potential service providers.

Social workers should be aware of and work in harmony with the growing service-user movement in an empowering partnership ethos to improve the lives of service users (Beresford and Croft 1993 and 1995, Croft and Beresford 2002). Over the last two decades the growth of service user movements (like the disability movement and the mental health users' movement) has brought innovation and insight to our ways of seeing social and individual problems. 'These movements have developed many relevant and interesting approaches to dealing with service users' needs – collective advocacy, for example, or (in the mental health field) the Hearing Voices Network' (Hearing Voices Network, accessed 28 June 2007), or user-led approaches such as the Clubhouse model. 'The fact that these models have come, not from professional social work, but from service users themselves, emphasizes that social work needs to engage with, and learn from, these movements in ways that will allow partnerships to form and new knowledge bases and curricula to develop' (Jones et al. accessed 16 March 2007). Other examples of user-led movements include the Voice of the Child in Care (Voice of the Child in Care, accessed 20 March 2007) and Karma Nirvana, a charity for aiding and campaigning on Asian women's issues such as honour killings (Community Care 2006, Sanghera 2007).

The service-user movement is a postmodern development in the sense that in a modernist context service users are not considered to be 'experts' or professionals. Therefore they are often not consulted about how they define their own problems and solutions. With the devaluing of the idea of professional expertise and the loss of trust in professionals has come the increased influence of service users. Social workers can refer service uses to organizations run by service users. One positive aspect of the care-management model in the UK is that it is about promoting care by the community. State run facilities in the community, such as small homes for learning disabled people or people discharged into the community from mental health facilities, are not care by the community. Care by the community means relevant people and organizations caring for people for whom they have a genuine concern. These could be faith-based organizations or service-user groups looking after each other's interests. The problem is that this has not happened to the degree that was expected. For example, carers may be given direct payments to purchase services for the person they care for, but there may be no services in the community from which to purchase this service, especially in rural areas.

Maximize the constructive aspects of the instrumental role

Most care managers interviewed for the study reported in Part II thought they could empower service users through their knowledge of resources. They felt they could help service users make informed choices from available options. This conceptualization of 'empowerment' is consistent with an instrumental (Toren 1972), individualistic-reformist (Payne 2005), managerial technicist (Harlow 2003) social work role. They could not empower service users by spending time with them, enhancing their coping skills or raising their consciousness about their situation. They could no longer take a reflective (Payne 2005, 32), normative (Toren 1972) social work role. However, care managers should at least maximize the benefits of their instrumental care-management role in their work with service users.

Knowledge is power. If knowledge of the systems of care is the only power social workers have, they should use it to the advantage of service users. Care management is an instrumental role and there are limits to what social workers can do in their role. Care managers should maximize the help that a service user can get, but if a care manager cannot help a service user because of constraints on their role, then they need to know who can help and refer the service user to the appropriate service.

Maximize financial benefits for service users

In a market economy, money solves many problems. Sometimes service users do not know the benefit system well enough to receive what is rightfully theirs or stigma prevents them from applying for benefits that they are entitled to. For example, older people in the UK are entitled to Income Support if their income is below a certain level, but many older people are either not aware of entitlement or do not want to avail themselves of what they consider a stigmatized benefit. They therefore struggle with basic needs such as heating and food, which affects their health and their ability to engage in social interaction.

Direct payments are empowering when they can be arranged for service users. They allow service users to purchase their own services privately. They offer a way for service users to sidestep the bureaucracies of SSDs. This does allow more choice to service users, provided the services are available to be purchased. The irony is that in order to be eligible for Direct Payments, service users in the UK must get through the bureaucracy set up to decide who is eligible for Direct Payments, although this differs from country to country (Ungerson 2003). It is interesting that more choice is not available to service users within SSDs and that choice can only be facilitated in the market place. Perhaps it is the case that the ideal of buying and selling in the market place is so deeply embedded in the market discourse of the Western world that choice is only available to those who have money to pay for what they want.

Support professional registration

There may be social workers who resist professional registration because it runs counter to the tradition of setting the interests of service users above professional interests (Lorenz 2004, 145–6). Prior to the establishment of a professional register in the UK, social workers protected themselves from management and worked toward better working conditions through unionization. However, the problem with unions from a professional perspective is that unions defend the worker against accusations of misconduct even when the worker may have been responsible for bad practice. Unions operate to protect workers, not necessarily consumers of professional services. In the extreme, this could mean that paedophiles working as social workers with children would be protected from dismissal by their union. It may be that social workers should be both registered by professional bodies and members of unions because the purposes of the two systems are different.

The advantage of professional registration is that social workers who are registered are required to uphold professional ethics and there are mechanisms in place to hold individual social workers accountable to these ethics. Social workers acting as care managers could use professional registration to offset the negative effects of managerialism. Registration could form the basis of resistance to the 'irrationality of rationality' (Ritzer 996, 121) inherent in the McDonaldization of social care. Irrationality in this sense means that 'rational systems are unreasonable systems that deny the humanity, the human reason, of the people who work within them or are served by them' (Ritzer 1996, 121). McDonaldization, New Public Management (NPM) and managerialism all represent efforts to bring certainty and rational procedures to human interaction. However, they tend to deny the exercise of individual human reason or discretion within these systems. Professional registration could be influential in keeping social workers oriented to professional knowledge, skills and values in the face of NPM pressures in SSDs, pressures to conform unreflectively to procedures in the 'individualistic-reformist' (Payne 2005, 9) model of practice, which is a technical rational model of practice and hence does not facilitate reflection-in-practice (Schon 1983).

In spite of the social worker's complaints about the deskilling aspects of care management, it is better to have trained and qualified social workers acting as care managers in social services organizations than untrained workers. At least trained social workers try to maintain a sensitive, empathetic approach to their work in spite of the McDonaldizing pressures of bureaucratization. Untrained workers could easily become mechanistic and uncaring if they are not supported by ethical requirements beyond the organization they work for. Where professional registration exists, the social worker is individually responsible for their work and can face disciplinary procedures if they do not adhere to requirements for professional behaviour. This provides some balance to the demands of organizations to cut corners and cut costs.

Conclusion

To return to the analogy of care managers as poachers turned gamekeepers, if social workers are indeed now gamekeepers in the care-managed systems of service delivery, working within the system to protect resources and using their skills and knowledge developed as poachers, then hopefully they will at least retain a sensitivity to the people that they previously 'poached' for.

It is hoped that both managers and practitioners can use the material presented here, both theoretical and practical, to think more broadly about practice issues, that is, the social, political and economic contexts within which they work. Social workers are always encouraged to take an empowering approach to service users, which includes valuing service-user's experiences, learning from them and working in partnership with them. Ultimately, this broad approach could lead to consciousness raising (Freire 2000) with service users so that they can be helped to understand their own social contexts, how they fit within these contexts and how they want to manage their own lives. Links with the emerging service user and carer movement are critical to these considerations. Social workers need to think about the way that the organizations that they work in shape them as workers and their service users variously as employers, clients, consumers and citizens, and how they want to respond to these forces.

Social work has experienced significant change in the context of its work with the introduction of quasi-markets, managerialism and the McDonaldization of the social care sector. However, in spite of the differences between casework and care management, social workers working as care managers retain the basic elements of the social work role. They still mediate between the individual service user and their society, but they must now be more closely attuned to the market, which is not surprising in the current era of late capitalism. Care management forces social workers to mediate between the individual and the market. They continue to integrate individuals into society, represent those without power to those with power, and assess service users for the purpose of matching needs to resources. It is suggested that care management is a new specialism within social work, one that is consistent with and necessary for practice within the culture of late capitalism, even though it is often not a valued area of work among qualified social workers.

Social work is practised in different ways in different socio-economic eras. Postmodernity as late capitalism brings new challenges to social workers. Social workers who work in McDonaldized care-management roles need to be aware of ways to resist the irrationality of rationality in order to empower and promote the welfare of the service users with whom they work. Adherence to professional values, supported by professional registration, and an awareness of power, both instrumental and normative, can promote good practice in spite of the McDonaldization of the social care sector.

While this book has focused on the development of the care-manager role in the UK, it is clear that this role is spreading to other Western industrial countries as a way of containing the cost of social care. It is hoped that the experiences of social workers in the UK can shed light on the issues for managers and social workers in other national contexts and can serve as a case study for the application of social theory to the lived reality of those experiencing care management.

Bibliography

Adams, A. and Shardlow, S. (2000) 'Social work practice in the United Kingdom' in A. Adams, P. Erath and S. Shardlow (eds) *Fundamentals of Social Work in Selected European Countries*. Lyme Regis: Russell House Publishing.

Adams, R. (1996a) *The Personal Social Services: Clients, Consumers or Citizens*. London: Longman.

—— (1996b) *Social Work and Empowerment*. London: Macmillan.

—— (2002) *Social Policy for Social Work*. Basingstoke: Palgrave.

Adcock, M. (1985) *Good Enough Parenting: A Framework for Assessing*. London: British Agencies for Adoption and Fostering.

Ahmad, B. (1990) *Black Perspectives in Social Work*. Birmingham: Venture.

Alaszewski, A. (1995) 'Restructuring health and welfare professionals in the United Kingdom: the impact of internal markets in the medical, nursing and social work professions' in T. Johnson, G. Larkin and M. Saks (eds) *Health Professionals and the State in Europe*. London: Routledge.

Alaszewski, A. and Manthorpe, J. (1990) 'Literature review: the new right and the professions' *British Journal of Social Work*, 20, 237–51.

Askheim, O. P. (2003) 'Empowerment as guidance for professional social work: an act of balancing on a slack rope' *European Journal of Social Work*, 6(4), 229–40.

Audit Commission (2002) *Tracking the Changes in Social Services in England*. London: Audit Commission.

Austin, C. D. (1992 'Have we oversold case management as a "quick fix" for our long-term care system? *Journal of Case Management*, 1, pp. 61–5.

Bailey, R. and Brake M. (eds) (1977) *Radical Social Work*. London: Edward Arnold.

Baldock, J. (1999) 'Economics and social policy' in J. Baldock, N. Manning, S. Miller and S. Vickerstaff (eds) *Social Policy*. Oxford: Oxford University Press.

Baldwin, M. (2000) *Care Management and Community Care – Social Work Discretion and the Construction of Policy*. Aldershot: Ashgate.

Bambauer, K. (2005) 'Proposition 63: Should Other States Follow California's Lead?' *Psychiatric Services*, 56(6), pp. 642–4.

Barclay Committee Report (1982) *Social Workers: Their Roles and Tasks*. London: Bedford Square Press.

Barnes, M. (1999) 'Users as citizens: collective Action and the local governance of welfare' *Social Policy and Administration*, 33(1), pp. 75–90.

Bartens, H. (1995) *The Idea of the Postmodern: A History*. London: Routledge.

Baudrillard, J. (1983) *Simulations*. New York: Semiotext (e).

Bauman, Z. (1978) *Hermeneutics and the Social Science – Approaches to Understanding*. London: Hutchinson and Co.

—— (1987) *Legislators and Interpreters.* Cambridge: Polity Press.

—— (1989) *Modernity and the Holocaust.* Oxford: Polity Press.

—— (1997 [1992]) *Intimations of Postmodernity.* Cambridge: Polity Press.

Beardshaw, V. (1990) 'Squaring the Circle: The Implementation of Caring for People' *King's Fund News*, 13(1), 1.

Becky's Story (2006) 'Care Home Girl Abused by 25 Men in 2 years', http://www.thisislondon.co.uk/news/article-23364779-details/Care+home+girl+abused+by+25+men+in+2+years/article.do (accessed 16 March 2006).

Beilharz, P. (2001) (ed.) *The Bauman Reader.* Oxford: Blackwell Publishing.

Beistek, F. (1957) *The Casework Relationship.* Chicago: Loyola University Press.

Beresford, P. and Croft, S. (1993) *Citizen Involvement.* London: Macmillan.

—— (1995) 'Whose empowerment? Equalising the competing discourses in community care' in R. Jack (ed.) *Empowerment in Community Care.* London: Chapman and Hall.

Bernabie, R., Landi, L., Bambassi, G., Sgadari, A., Zuccala, G., Mor, V., Rubenstein, L. and Carbonin P. (1998) 'Randomised trial of impact of model of integrated care and case management for older people living in the community' *British Medical Journal*, 2 May; 361 (7141, 1348–56).

Best, S. (1994) 'Foucault, postmodernism and social theory' in D. Dickens and A. Fontana, *Postmodernism and Social Inquiry.* London: UCL Press.

Best, S. and Kellner, D. (1991) *Postmodern Theory – Critical Interrogations.* Hampshire.

—— (1997) *The Postmodern Turn.* New York: Guilford Press.

Beveridge, W. H. (1942) *Social Insurance and Allied Services*, Cmnd 6404 (London: HMSO).

Bilson, A. and Ross, S. (1999) (2nd Edition) 'A systems approach to social work management' in *Social Work Managers and Practice – Systems Principles.* London: Jessica Kingsley Publishers, Ltd.

Bobbitt, P. (2003) 'If the US faced a Europe surrounded by trade barriers, the 21st century could again see armed violence between great powers' *New Statesman*, 13 January 2003, 29.

Bradley, G. (2005) 'Movers and stayers in care management in adult services' *British Journal of Social Work*, 35: 511–30.

Braverman, H. (1998 [1974]) (25th Anniversary Edition) *Labor and Monopoly Capital – The Degradation of Work in the Twentieth Century.* New York: Monthly Review Press.

Bray, S. and Preston-Shoot, M. (2003) *Empowering Practice in Social Care.* Maidenhead: Open University Press.

Brewer, C. and Lait, J. (1980) *Can Social Work Survive?* London: Temple Smith.

Brindle, D. (2007) 'Families told elderly care crisis looming – Relatives to get little help from state' *Guardian*, 10 January 2007.

Brown, P. and Lauder, H. (2001) *Capitalism and Social Progress – The Future of Society in a Global Society.* Basingstoke: Palgrave.

Brynon, H. (1984) *Working for Ford.* Harmondsworth: Penguin

Burr, V. (1995) *An Introduction to Social Constructionism.* London: Routledge.

Butcher, T. (1995) *Delivering Welfare – The Governance of the Social Services in the 1990s.* Buckingham: Open University Press.

Campbell, B. (1997) *Unofficial Secrets – Child Sexual Abuse: The Cleveland Case.* London: Virago.

Capitman, J. (1985) *Evaluation of Coordinated Community-Oriented Long-Term Demonstration Programs.* Berkeley, California: Berkeley Planning Associates.

Carey, M. (2003) 'Anatomy of a care manager' *Work, Employment and Society,* 17(1), 121–35.

Carey, M. (2007) 'White-Collar proletariat? Braverman, the deskilling/upskilling of social work and the paradoxical life of the agency care manager' *Journal of Social Work,* 7(1), pp. 93–114.

Caring for People (1989) The Secretaries of State for Health, Social Security, Wales and Scotland, Care Manager 849. London: The Stationery Office.

Carter, J. (1998) *Postmodernity and the Fragmentation of the Welfare State.* London: Routledge.

Carter, J. and Rayner, M. (1996) 'The curious case of post-Fordism and welfare' *Journal of Social Policy,* 25(3), 347–67.

Challis, D. and Davies, B. (1980) 'A new approach to community care for the elderly' *British Journal of Social Work,* 10: 1–18.

—— (1985) 'Long term care for the elderly – The community care scheme' *British Journal of Social Work,* 15: 563–79.

—— (1986) *Case Management in Community Care.* Aldershot: Gower Publishing Company.

Challis, D., Darton, R., Hughes, J., Stewart, K. and Weiner, K. (2001) 'Intensive care-management at home: an alternative to institutional care?' *Age and Ageing,* 30(5), 409–13.

Challis, D., Chessum, R., Chesterman, J., Luckett, R. and Woods, R. (1988) 'Community care for the frail elderly: an urban experiment' *British Journal of Social Work* 18: 13–42 (supplement).

Chappell, Y. (2007) 'Evaluating whether the performance indicators set by Central Government are measuring the right processes from the perspectives of field social workers' Unpublished MBA Dissertation. London Metropolitan University.

Cheetham, J. (1993) 'Social work and community care in the 1990s: pitfalls and potential' in R. Page and J. Baldock, *Social Policy Review 5 – 1993.* Cambridge: Social Policy Association.

Children Act (1989) London: The Stationery Office.

Clarke, J. (1993) 'The comfort of strangers: Social work in context' in J. Clarke (ed.) *A Crisis in Care? Challenges to Social Work.* London: Sage.

—— (1998) 'Thriving on chaos? Managerialism and social welfare' in J. Carter. (ed.) *Postmodernity and the Fragmentation of Welfare.* London: Routledge.

Clarke, J., Cochran, A. and McLaughlin, E. (1995) (eds) *Managing Social Policy.* London: Sage.

Clarke, J., Gewirtz, S. and McLaughlin, E. (2000) 'Reinventing the welfare state' in J. Clarke, S. Gewirtz, and E. McLaughlin (eds) *New Managerialism – New Welfare.* Buckingham: Open University Press.

Clarke, J., Gewirtz, S., Hughes, G. and Humphrey, J. (2001) 'Guarding the public interest? Auditing public services' in J. Clarke, S. Gewirtz, and E. McLaughlin (eds) *New Managerialism – New Welfare*. Buckingham: Open University Press.

Community Care (2006) 'My best friend was killed by her dad' 16 November 2006, http://www.communitycare.co.uk/Articles/2006/11/16/102242/my-best-friend-was-killed-by-her-dad.html (accessed 31 March 2007).

Corby, B. (2006) *Applying Research in Social Work Practice*. Maidenhead, Berkshire: Open University Press.

Coulshed, V. and Mullender, A. (2001) (2nd Edition) *Management in Social Work*. Basingstoke: Palgrave.

Cowan, H. (1999) *Community Care, Ideology and Social Policy*. Hertfordshire: Prentice Hall Europe.

Cree, V. (2005) *Sociology for Social Workers and Probation Officers*. Harrow: Routledge.

Croft, S. and Beresford, P. (2002) 'Service Users' Perspectives' in M. Davies (2002) (ed.) (2nd Edition) *The Blackwell Companion to Social Work*. Oxford: Blackwell Publishing.

Crook, S. and Pakulski, J. (1994) *Postmodernization: Change in Advanced Society.* London: Sage.

Cutler, T. and Waine, B. (1994) *Managing the Welfare State: The Politics of Public Sector Management*. Oxford: Berg.

Dalrymple, J. and Burke, B. (2007) *Anti-Oppressive Practice and the Law*. Maidenhead: McGraw Hill/Open University Press.

Davies, B. (1987) 'Equity and efficiency in community care: Supply and financing in an age of fiscal austerity' *Ageing and Society*, 7: 161–74.

Davies, B. and Challis, D. (1986) *Matching Resources to Needs in Community Care: An Evaluated Demonstration of a Long-term Care Model*. Aldershot: Gower Publishing Company.

Davies, L. (2005) 'Authentic Practice Works' *Professional Social Work*. December, 2005.

—— (2007 forthcoming) 'Reclaiming the language of child protection' in M. Calder (ed.) *Contemporary Risk Assessment*. Dorset: Russell House Publishing.

—— (2007) 'Our children have less protection now than did Victoria Climbie' *Guardian*. 28 February 2007.

Davies, L. and Leonard, P. (2004) *Social Work in a Corporate Era*. Aldershot: Ashgate.

de Schweinitz, K. (1975) (7th Edition) *England's Road to Social Security.* New York: A. S. Barnes.

Denny, D. (1998) *Social Policy and Social Work*. Oxford: Oxford University Press.

Department for Education and Skills (accessed 27 June 2007), http://www.dfes.gov.uk/.

Department of Health (1989) *Caring for People: Community Care in the Next Decade and Beyond.* London: The Stationery Office.

—— (1991b) *Purchase of Service*. London: The Stationery Office.

—— (1996) *Community Care Act (Direct Payments)*. London: The Stationery Office.

—— (1998*) A Third of a Million: the Social Services Workforce in the 90s*. NISW 1998 Research Summary 13, http://www.nisw.org.uk/publications/research summary 13.html.

—— (2000) *Community Care Act (Direct Payments) 1996: Policy and Practice Guidelines*. London. The Stationery Office.

Department of Health, Department for Education and Employment, Home Office (2000) *Framework for the Assessment of Children in Need and their Families*. London: The Stationery Office.

Dickens, D. and Fontana, A. (1994) *Postmodernism and Social Inquiry*. London: UCL Press.

Dill, A. (1993) 'Defining needs, defining systems: A critical analysis' *The Gerontologist*: 33, 453–60 in W. McAuley, P. Teaster and M. Safewright (1999) (eds) 'Incorporating feminist ethics into case management programs' *The Journal of Applied Gerontology*, 18(1), March 2–24.

Dinsdale, P. (2003) 'On the Move' *Guardian Society.* 29 January, 136.

Dominelli, L. (1996) 'Deprofessionalizing social work: anti-oppressive practice, competencies and postmodernism' *British Journal of Social Work*, 26: 151–75.

Dominelli, L. and Hoogvelt, A. (1996) 'Globalization and the technocratization of social work' *Critical Social Policy*, 47: 45–62.

Douglas, A. and Philpot, T. (1998) *Coping and Caring – A Guide to Social Services*. London: Routledge.

Downes, C., Ernst, S. and Smithers, M. (1996) 'Maintaining the capacity for concern during organisational restructuring for community care' *Journal of Social Work Practice*, 10(1), 25–40.

Drakeford, M. (1998) 'Poverty and community care' in A. Symonds and A. Kelly (eds) *The Social Construction of Community Care*. London: Macmillan.

Dustin, D. (2000) 'Managers and Professionals: New Perspectives on Partnership', *Managing Community Care*, 8(5), 14–20.

—— (2004) 'The Impact of Care Management upon Social Work' (Unpublished PhD Dissertation) London: London Metropolitan University.

—— (2006) 'Skills and Knowledge needed to practice as a care manager – Continuity and Change' *Journal of Social Work*, 6(3), 293–313.

Dustin, D. and Davies, L. (2007) 'Female genital cutting and children's rights: implications for social work practice' *Child Care in Practice* 13(1) pp. 3–16.

Eagleton, T. (2003) *After Theory*. New York: Basic Books in A. Harrington (2005) (ed.) *Modern Social Theory – An Introduction*. Oxford: Oxford University Press.

Editorial (2001) 'Righting wrongs' *The Economist*, 8235: 19–21.

Ellis, K., Davis, A. and Rummery, K. (1999) 'Needs assessment, street-level bureaucracy and the new community care' *Social Policy and Administration*, 33(3), 262–80.

Ellison, N. and Pierson, C. (1998) *Developments in British Social Policy*. Houndmills: Macmillan.

England, H. (1986) *Social Work as Art.* London: Allen and Unwin.

Every Child Matters: Change for Children (2004) London: Stationery Office.

Exworthy, M. and Halford, S. (1999) 'Professionals and managers in a changing public sector: conflict, compromise and collaboration?' in M. Exworthy and S.

Halford (eds) *Professionals and the New Managerialism in the Public Sector*. Birmingham: Open University Press.

Fawcett, B. and Featherstone, B. (1998) 'Quality assurance and evaluation in social work in the postmodern era' in J. Carter (ed.) *Postmodernity and the Fragmentation of Welfare*. London: Routledge.

Fererra, M. (1996) 'The "southern model" of welfare in Europe' *Journal of European Social Policy*, 6(1).

—— (1998) 'The four social Europes' in M. Rhodes, and Y. Meny (eds) *The Future of European Welfare*. Basingstoke: Macmillan.

Fischer, J. (1973) 'Is casework effective? A review' *Social Work*, 18(1), 5–20.

—— (1978) *Effective Casework Practice: An Eclectic Approach*. New York: McGraw-Hill.

Fitzpatrick, T. (1999) 'Cash transfers' in J. Baldock, N. Manning, S. Miller and S. Vickerstaff (eds) *Social Policy*. Oxford: Oxford University Press.

Fook, J. (2004) 'Critical reflection and transformative possibilities' in L. Davies and P. Leonard (eds) *Social Work in a Corporate Era*. Aldershot: Ashgate.

Foster, A. (2002) in Russell, B. (2002) (ed.) 'Watchdog warns of crisis as workers quit public sector' *Guardian*, 3 September 2002.

Foucault, M. (1979) *Discipline and Punishment: The Birth of the Prison*. Translated by Alan Sheridan. New York: Vintage.

Franklin, B. (1999) 'Hard pressed – national newspaper reporting of social work and social services' *Community Care*. London.

Franklin, B. and Parton, N. (1991) *Social Work, the Media and Public Relations*. London: Routledge.

Freire, P. (2000) (30th Anniversary Edition) *Pedagogy of the Oppressed*. New York: Continuum International Publishing Group Ltd.

Garrett, P. M. (2003) 'Swimming with dolphins: The assessment framework, New Labour and new tools for social work with children and families' *British Journal of Social Work*, 33, pp. 441–63.

George, V. (1998) 'Political, ideology, globalisation and welfare futures in Europe' *Journal of Social Policy*, 27, pp. 17–36.

Germaine, C. (1979) 'Introduction: ecology and social work' in C. Germaine (ed.) (1979) *Social Work Practice: People and Environments – an Ecological Approach*. New York: Columbia University Press.

Giddens, A. (1990) *The Consequences of Modernity*. Cambridge: Polity Press.

Ginsburg, N. (1998) 'Postmodernity and Social Europe' in J. Carter (ed.), *Postmodernity and the Fragmentation of Welfare*. London: Routledge.

Gray, A. and Jenkins, B. (1999) 'Professionals, bureaucracy and social welfare' in J. Baldock, N. Manning, S. Miller and S. Vickerstaff (eds) *Social Policy*. Oxford: Oxford University Press.

Green, D. (1988) *The New Right: The Counter-revolution in Political, Economic and Social Thought*. London: Harvester Wheatsheaf.

Green, L. C. (2006) 'Pariah profession, debased discipline? An analysis of social work's low academic status and the possibilities for change' *Social Work Education*, 25(3), April 2006, pp. 245–64.

Griffiths, Sir Roy (1988) *Community Care: Agenda for Action*. London: The Stationery Office.

Grover, C. and Stewart, J. (1999) '"Market workfare": social security, social regulation and competitiveness in the 1990s' *Journal of Social Policy*, 28(1), 73–96.

Habermas, J. (1984) *The Theory of Communicative Action Volume One – Reason and the Rationalization of Society.* Translated by Thomas McCarthy. London: Heinemann.

—— (1987) *The Theory of Communicative Action, Volume Two – Lifeworld and System – A Critique of Functionalist Reason*. Translated by Thomas. McCarthy. Cambridge: Polity.

Haney, L. (2002) *Inventing the Needy – Gender and the Politics of Welfare in Hungary.* London: University of California Press.

Harlow, E. (2003) 'New managerialism, social service departments and social work practice today' *Practice*, 15(2), 29–44.

Harrington, A. (2005) *Modern Social Theory – An Introduction.* Oxford: Oxford University Press.

Harris, J. (1998) 'Scientific management, bureau-professionalism, new managerialism: the labour process of state social work' *British Journal of Social Work*, 28, 389–862.

—— (2003) *The Social Work Business*. London: Routledge.

Harris, J. and McDonald, C. (2000) 'Post-Fordism, the welfare state and the personal social services: A comparison of Australia and Britain' *British Journal of Social Work*, 30, 51–70.

Harvey, D. (1989) *The Conditions of Postmodernity: an Enquiry into the Origins of Cultural Change.* Oxford: Basil Blackwell in G. Ritzer (1996) (ed.) *The McDonaldization of Society – An Investigation into the Changing Character of contemporary Social Life*. Thousand Oaks, California: Pine Forge Press.

Healy, K. (2000) *Social Work Practices: Contemporary Perspectives on Change.* London: Sage.

Hearing Voices Network, http://www.hearing-voices.org. (accessed 28 June 2007).

Henkle (2000) 'Social work practice in the United Kingdom' in A. Adams, P. Erath and S. Shardlow (eds) *Fundamentals of Social Work in Selected European Countries.* Lyme Regis: Russell House Publishing.

Hensher, P. (2007) 'A cautionary tale of today's customer service' *The Independent*, Editorial and Opinion, 2 January 2007.

Hollis, F. (1972) (2nd Edition) *Psychosocial Therapy*. New York. Random House.

Holme, A. and Maizels, J. (1978) *Social Workers and Volunteers*. London: George Allen and Unwin, in D. Howe (1986) (ed.) *Social Workers and Their Practice in Welfare Bureaucracies*. Aldershot: Gower Publishing Company.

Hood, C. (1991a) 'Contemporary public management: A new global paradigm' *Public Policy and Administration*, 10(2), 104–17 in J. Harris (ed.) (2003) *The Social Work Business*. London: Routledge.

Hopkins, J. (1996) 'Social work through the looking glass' in N. Parton (ed.) (1996) *Social Theory, Social Change and Social Work*. London: Routledge.

Horder, W. (2002) 'Care management' in M. Davies (ed.) (2nd edn) (2002) *The Blackwell Companion to Social Work*. Oxford: Blackwell Publishers.

Horner, N. (2003) *What is Professional Social Work?* Exeter: Learning Matters Ltd.

Howe, D. (1986) *Social Workers and Their Practice in Welfare Bureaucracies.* Aldershot: Gower Publishing Company.

—— (1994) 'Modernity, postmodernity and social work' *British Journal of Social Work*, 24, 513–32.

—— (1996) 'Surface and depth in social work practice' in N. Parton (ed.) *Social Theory, Social Change and Social Work*. London: Routledge.

Hoyes, L., Lart, R., Means, R. and Taylor, J. (1994) *Community Care in Transition.* York: Joseph Rowntree Foundation and London: Community Care.

Hoyle, E, and Wallace, M. (2005) *Educational Leadership – Ambiguity, Professionals and Managerialism.* Sage: London.

Hughes, J. (1995) *Older People and Community Care – Critical Theory and Practice.* Buckingham: Open University Press.

Human Rights Act (1998), http://www.opsi.gov.uk/acts/acts1998/80042--d.htm (accessed 13 March 2007).

Humphries, J. (2003) 'New Labour and the Regulatory Reform of Social Care' *Critical Social Policy*, 23(1), 5–24.

Irving, A. (1999) 'Waiting for Foucault' in A. Chambon, A. Irving, L. Epstein (eds) *Reading Foucault for Social Work*. New York: Columbia University Press.

Jacobs, K. and Manzi, T. (2000) 'Performance indicators and social constructivism: Conflict and control in housing management' *Critical Social Policy*, 20(1), 85–104.

James, A. (2004) 'The McDonaldization of Social Work – or "come back Florence Hollis, all is (or should be) forgiven"' in R. Lovelock, K. Lyons, and J. Powell (eds) *Reflecting on Social Work – Discipline and Profession.* Aldershot: Ashgate.

Jameson, F. (1984b) 'Postmodernism, or the Cultural Logic of Late Capitalism' *New Left Review*, 146, 53–92.

Jessop, B. (1994) 'The transition to post-Fordism and the Schumpeterian workfare state' in R. Borrows and B. Loader (eds) *Towards a Post-Fordist Welfare State?* London: Routledge.

Johnson, N. (1995) (ed.) *Private Markets in Health and Welfare: An International Perspective.* Oxford: Berg.

Jones, A. (1992) 'Civil Rights, Citizenship and the Welfare Agenda for the 1990s in *Who Owns Welfare? Questions on the Social Services Agenda.*' NISW/Social Services Policy Forum.

Jones, C. (1996) 'Anti-intellectualism and social work education' in N. Parton (ed.) *Social Theory, Social Change and Social Work*. London: Routledge.

—— (1999) 'Social work: regulation and managerialism' in M. Exworthy and S. Halford (eds) *Professionals and the New Managerialism in the Public Sector.* Birmingham: Open University Press.

—— (2001) 'Voices from the front line: State social workers and New Labour' *British Journal of Social Work*, 31, pp. 547–62.

Jones, C., Ferguson, I., Lavalette, M. and Penketh, L. (2007) 'Social work and social justice: A manifesto for a new engaged practice' in M. Lavalette and I. Ferguson (eds) *International Social Work and the Radical Tradition.* Birmingham: Venture Press.

—— (2007) *'Social work and social justice: a manifesto for a new engaged practice'*, http://www.liv.ac.uk/sspsw/Social_Work_Manifesto.html (accessed 16 March 2007).

Jordan, B. (1978) 'A comment on "Theory and practice in social work"' *British Journal of Social Work*, 8, pp. 23–5.

Jordan, B. and Jordan, C. (2000) *Social Work and the Third Way: Tough Love as Social Policy*. London: Sage.

Katz, I. (1996) *The Construction of Racial Identity in Children of Mixed Parentage*. London: Jessica Kingsley Press.

Kearney, J. (2004) '"Knowing how to go on": Towards situated practice and emergent theory in social work' in R. Lovelock, K. Lyons and J. Powell (eds) (2004) *Reflecting on Social Work – Discipline and Profession*. Aldershot: Ashgate.

Keating, F. and Robertson, F. (2003) *Ethnic diversity and mental health in London – recent developments*. London: Kings Fund Working Paper.

Kellner, D. (1999) 'Theorizing/Resisting McDonaldization: A Multiperspectivist Approach' in B. Smart (ed.) *Resisting McDonaldization*. London: Sage.

—— (2007) 'The Frankfurt School and British Cultural Studies: The Missed Articulation', http://www.uta.edu/huma/illuminations/kell16.htm (accessed 27 June 2007).

Kessler, S. (1998) *Lessons From the Intersexed*. New Brunswick, New Jersey and London: Rutgers University Press.

Kirkpatrick, I., Kitchener, M., Owen, D. and Whipp, R. (1999) 'Un-charted Territory? Experiences of the Purchaser/Provider Split in Local Authority Children's Services' *British Journal of Social Work*, 29, 707–26.

Lane, J. (2000) *New Public Management*. London: Routledge.

Langan, M. (1993) 'The rise and fall of social work' in J. Clarke (ed.) *A Crisis in Care? Challenges to Social Work*. London: Sage.

—— (1998) 'The personal social services' in N. Ellison and C. Pierson (eds), *Developments in British Social Policy*. London: Macmillan.

Lash, S. and Urry, J. (1994) *Economies of Signs and Space*. London: Sage.

Lavalette, M. and Ferguson, I. (2007) *International Social Work and the Radical Tradition*. Birmingham: Venture Press.

Lawrence, S., Dustin, D., Kasiram, M. and Partab, R. (2003) 'Exploring Partnership: Student Evaluations of International Exchanges in London and Durban' in L. Dominelli and W. Bernard (eds) *Broadening Horizons – International Exchanges in Social Work*. London: Ashgate.

LeGrand, J. (1991) 'Quasi-markets and social policy' *Economic Journal*, 101, 1256–67 in T. Butcher (ed.) *Delivering Welfare: The Governance of the Social Services in the 1990s*. Buckingham: Open University Press.

Leuchtenburg, W. E. (1963) *Franklin D. Roosevelt and the New Deal 1932–1940*. New York: Harper and Row.

Levin, E. and Webb, S. (1997) *Social Work and Community Care: Changing Roles and Tasks*. London: National Institute for Social Work Research Unit.

Lewis, J. and H. Glennerster (1996) *Implementing the New Community Care*. Buckingham: Open University Press.

Liddiard, M. (1999) 'Social need and patterns of inequality and difference' in J. Baldock, N. Manning, S. Miller and S. Vickerstaff (eds) *Social Policy*. Oxford: Oxford University Press.

Link, A. (1997) *Group Work With Elders: 50 Therapeutic Exercises for Reminiscence, Validation, and Remotivation*. Sarasota, Florida: Professional Resource Press.

Lipsky, M. (1980) *Street Level Bureaucracy*. New York: Russell Sage Foundation.

Little, M. (1995) 'Summarising Child Protection: Messages from Research' Darting Social Research Unit, HMSO in B. Campbell (ed.) *Unofficial Secrets – Child Sexual Abuse: The Cleveland Case*. London: Virago.

Local Authority Social Services Act (1970) London: The Stationery Office.

Lorenz, W. (2004) 'Research as an element in social work's ongoing search for identity' in R. Lovelock, K. Lyons, and J. Powell (eds) *Reflecting on Social Work – Discipline and Profession*. Aldershot: Ashgate.

Lovelock, R. and Powell, J. (2004) 'Habermas/Foucault for social work: Practices of critical reflection' in R. Lovelock, K. Lyons, and J. Powell (eds) *Reflecting on Social Work – Discipline and Profession*. Aldershot: Ashgate.

Lymbery, M. (1998) 'Care management and professional autonomy: the impact of community care legislation on social work with older people' *British Journal of Social Work*, 28, 863–78.

Lyons, K. and Lawrence, S. (2006) (eds) *Social Work in Europe: Educating for Change*. Birmingham: Venture Press.

Lyotard, J (1984) [1979]) 'The Postmodern Condition: A Report on Knowledge' tr. G. Bennington and B. Massumi. Minneapolis: University of Minnesota Press in Alexander, J. (ed.) (1992) 'The postpositivist epistemological dilemma' in S. Seidman and D. Wagner (eds) *Postmodernism and Social Theory*. Cambridge, MA and Oxford UK: Blackwell.

Macarov, D. (1995) *Social Welfare – Structure and Practice*. London: Sage.

Macdonald, K. (1995) *The Sociology of the Professions*. London: Sage.

Mackenzie, A., Lee, D., Dudley-Brown, S. and Chin, T. (1998) 'Case management in Hong Kong: evaluation of a pilot project in community nursing' *Journal of Clinical Nursing*, 7(3), 291–2.

Magill, M. (2006) 'The future of evidence in evidence-based practice' *Journal of Social Work*, 6(2), 101–115 August.

Mandelstam, M. (1999) (2nd edn) *Community Care Practice and the Law*. London: Jessica Kingsley.

Manning, N. (1999) 'Welfare, ideology and social theory' in J. Baldock, N. Manning, S. Miller and S. Vickerstaff (eds) *Social Policy*. Oxford: Oxford University Press.

Marshall, M., Lockwood, A. and Gath, D. (1995) 'Social Services case-management for long-term mental disorders – a randomised controlled trial' *Lancet*, February 18, 345 (8947: 399–401).

Marshall, T. H. (1950) *Citizenship and Social Class*. Cambridge: Cambridge University Press.

Mason, J. (1996) *Qualitative Researching*. London: Sage.

McAuley, W. J. and Safewright, M. P. (1992) *Evaluation of the Case Management for Elderly Virginians Pilot Project*. Blackburg, VA: Virginia Tech Center for Gerontology.

McAuley, W., Teaster, P. and Safewright, M. (1999) 'Incorporating feminist ethics into case management programs' *The Journal of Applied Gerontology*, 18(1), March 2–24.

McDonald, A. (1999) *Understanding Community Care – A Guide for Social Workers*. Basingstoke: Macmillan.

McGregor, D. (1985) *The Human Side of Enterprise*. London: McGraw-Hill.

Meagher, G. and Healey, K. (2003) 'Caring, controlling, contracting and counting: Governments and non profits in community services' *Australian Journal of Public Administration*, 62(3), 40–51, September.

Meagher, G. and Parton, N. (2004) 'Modernising social work and the ethics of care' *Social Work and Society*, 2(1), http://www.socwork.net/2004/1/articles/426/meagher-Parton2004.pdf.

Means, R. and Smith, R. (1998) (2nd edn) *Community Care – Policy and Practice*. Basingstoke: Macmillan.

Midwinter, E. (1996) *The Development of Social Welfare in Britain*. Buckingham: Open University Press.

Miles, S. (2001) *Social Theory in the Real World*. London: Sage.

Miller, S. (1999) 'The development of social policy' in J. Baldock, N. Manning, S. Miller and S. Vickerstaff (eds) *Social Policy*. Oxford: Oxford University Press.

Mills, C. W. (1959) [1976] *The Sociological Imagination*. New York: Oxford University Press.

Mishra, R. (1998) 'Beyond the nation state: Social Policy in an age of globalization' *Social Policy and Administration*, 32(5), pp. 481–500.

Modernising Social Services – Promoting Independence, Improving Protection, Raising Standards (1998) Cm 4169. The Stationery Office.

Moffatt, K. (1999) 'Surveillance and government of the welfare recipient' in A. Chambon, A. Irving and L. Epstein (eds) *Reading Foucault for Social Work*. New York: Columbia University Press.

Munro, E. and Calder, M. (2005) 'Where has child protection gone?' (Reports and Surveys) *The Political Quarterly Publishing Co. Ltd.* Oxford: Blackwell Publishing

Murphy, R. (1990) 'Proletarianization or bureaucratisation: the fall of the professional?' in R. Torstendahl and M. Burrage (eds) *The Formation of Professions – Knowledge, State and Strategy*. London: Sage.

National Health Services and Community Care Act (1990) London: The Stationery Office.

Neate, P. (1996) 'Strapped for Cash' *Community Care*, 1 August 1996, vi–vvii.

Newman, J. and Clarke, J. (1995) 'Going about our business? The managerialization of public services' in J. Clarke, A. Cochrane and E. McLoughlin (eds) *Managing Social Policy*. London: Sage.

—— (1995) 'The managerialization of public services' in J. Clarke, A. Cochrane and E. McLoughlin (eds) *Managing Social Policy*. London: Sage.

Newton, J. et al., (1996) *Care Management: Is it Working?* London: The Sainsbury Centre for Mental Health.

Niemala, P. and Hamalainen, J. (2001) 'The role of social policy in social work' in A. Adams, P. Erath and M. Shardlow (eds) *Key Themes in European Social Work: Theory, Practice, Perspectives*. Dorset: Russell House Publishing.

O'Brien, M. and S. Penna (1998) *Theorising Welfare – Enlightenment and Modern Science*. London: Sage.

O'Neil, O. (2002) Reith Lecture, http://www.bbc.co.uk/radio4/reith2002/.

Oakley, A. (1999) in F. Williams, J. Popay and A. Oakley (eds), *Welfare Research: A Critical Review*. London UCL Press.

Orme, J. (2001) 'Regulation or fragmentation? Directions for social work under new labour' *British Journal of Social Work* 31: 611–24.

Orme, J. and Glastonbury, B. (1993) *Care Management*. Basingstoke: Macmillan.

Parry, N., Rustin, M. and Satyamurti, C. (1979) *Social Work, Welfare and the State*. London: Edward Arnold.

Parton, N. (1994) 'Problematics of government, (post) modernity and social work' *British Journal of Social Work*, 24, 9–32.

—— (1996) (ed.) *Social Theory, Social Change and Social Work*. London: Routledge.

—— (2004) 'Post-theories for practice: Challenging the dogmas' in L. Davies and P. Leonard (eds) (2004) *Social Work in a Corporate Era – Practices of Power and Resistance*. Aldershot: Ashgate.

Parton, N. and O'Bryne (2000) *Constructive Social Work – Towards a New Practice*. Basingstoke: Macmillan.

Payne, M. (1986) *Social Care in the Community*. Basingstoke: Macmillan.

—— (1995) S*ocial Work and Community Care*. Basingstoke: Macmillan.

—— (1996) *What is Professional Social Work*. Birmingham: Venture.

—— (1997) (2nd edn) *Modern Social Work Theory*. Basingstoke: Macmillan.

—— (1999) 'The moral bases of social work' *European Journal of Social Work*, 2(3), 247–58.

—— (2005) (3rd edn) *Modern Social Work Theory*. Hampshire: Palgrave Macmillan.

Pearsall, J. (1998) (ed.) *The New Oxford Dictionary of English*. New York: Oxford University Press.

Penna, S. and O'Brien, M. (1996) 'Postmodernism and social policy: a small step forwards?' *Journal of Social Policy*, 25(1), 39–61.

Petch, A. (2002) 'Work with adult service users' in M. Davies (ed.) (2nd edn) *The Blackwell Companion to Social Work*. Oxford: Blackwell Publishers.

Phillips, J. (1996) 'The future of social work with older people' in N. Parton (ed.) *Social Theory, Social Change and Social Work*. London: Routledge.

Philp, M. (1979) 'Notes on the form of knowledge in social work' *Sociological Review*, 27(1), 83–111.

Pietroni, M. (1995) 'The nature and aims of professional education for social workers: a postmodern perspective' in M. Yellowy and M. Henkel (eds) *Learning and Teaching in Social Work – Towards Reflective Practice*. London: Jessica Kingsley Publishers.

Piven, F. and Cloward, R. (1993 [1971]) (Second Vintage Edition) *Regulating the poor: The Functions of Public Welfare*. New York: Vintage Books/Random House.

Plant, R. (1992) 'Citizenship, rights and welfare' in A. Coote (ed.) (1992) *The Welfare of Citizens – Developing New Social Rights*. London: IPPR/Rivers Oram Press.

Pollitt, C. (1993) (2nd edn) *Managerialism and the Public Services.* Oxford: Blackwell Publishers.

Postle, K. (1999) C*are Managers Responses to Working Under Conditions of Postmodernity.* PhD thesis. Department of Social Work Studies, University of Southampton.

—— (2001) 'The social work side is disappearing. I guess it started with us being called care managers' *Practice*, 13(1), 13–26.

—— (2002) 'Working between the idea and the reality: Ambiguities and tensions in care managers' work' *British Journal of Social Work*, 32, 335–51.

Rachman, R. (1997) 'Hospital social work and community care: the practitioner's view' *Social Work in Health Care*, 25 (1), p. 211–22.

Ravetz, J. (2000) *Technology and Power in Social Welfare: Models, Ideology and Information Technology*, http:/www.soton.ac.uk/~chst/both/ravetz.htm (accessed 10 October 2000).

Reade, E. (1987) *Town and Country Planning.* Buckingham: Open University Press. in J. Clarke (1993) 'The comfort of strangers: Social work in context' in J. Clarke (ed.) *A Crisis in Care? Challenges to Social Work.* London: Sage.

Reid, W. and Epstein, L. (1972) *Task Centered Casework.* New York: Columbia University Press.

Reigate, N. (1994) *The Social Worker as Care Manager in Work With Younger Physically Disabled Adults.* Social Work Monograph. Norwich: University of East Anglia.

Rhodes, R. A. W. (1997) *Understanding Governance – Policy Networks, Governance, Reflexivity and Accountability.* Buckingham: Open University Press.

Ritchie, J. and Spencer, L. (1994) 'Qualitative data analysis for applied policy research' in A. Bryman and R. Burgess (eds) *Analysing Qualitative Data.* London: Routledge.

Ritzer, G. (1993) *The McDonaldization of Society: An Investigation into the Changing Character of Contemporary Social Life* (Revised Edition) Thousand Oaks, CA: Pine Forge Press in Kellner, D. (ed.) (1999) 'Theorizing/resisting McDonaldization' in B. Smart (ed.) *Resisting McDonaldization.* London: Sage.

—— (1996) *The McDonaldization of Society – An Investigation into the Changing Character of Contemporary Social Life.* Thousand Oaks (CA): Pine Forge Press.

—— (1999) 'Assessing the resistance' in B. Smart (1999) (ed.) *Resisting McDonaldization.* London: Sage

—— (2004) *The McDonaldization of Society – Revised New Century Edition.* Thousand Oaks (CA): Pine Forge Press.

Roach, M. (1992) *Rethinking Citizenship. Welfare, Ideology and Change in Modern Society.* Cambridge: Polity Press. in J. Harris and C. McDonald, (2000) 'Post-Fordism, the welfare state and the personal social services: A comparison of Australia and Britain' *British Journal of Social Work*, 30, 51–70.

Rogers, C. (1961) *On Becoming a Person: A Therapist's View of Psychotherapy.* London: Constable.

—— (1951) *Client Centered Therapy: Its Current Practice, Implications and Theory.* London: Constable.

Rosenau, P. (1992) *Post-Modernism and the Social Sciences – Insights, Inroads, and Intrusions*. Princeton, NJ: Princeton University Press.

Rothschild, E. (1973) *Paradise Lost: The Decline of the Auto-Industrial Age*. New York: Vintage Books in P. Brown and H. Lauder (2001) *Capitalism and Social Progress*. Basingstoke: Palgrave.

Russell, B. (2002) 'Watchdog warns of crisis as workers quit public sector' *Guardian*. 3 September 2002.

Saleebey, D. (1990) *The Strengths Perspective in Social Work Practice*. New York: Longman.

Salskov-Iversen, D. (1999) 'Clients, Consumers or Citizens? Cascading Discourses on the Users of Welfare' in M. Dent, M. O'Neill and C. Bagley (eds) *Professions, New Public Management and the European Welfare State*. Staffordshire: Staffordshire University Press.

Sampaio, R. (2006) *The Hermeneutic Conception of Culture*, http://www.bu.edu/ wcp/Papers/Cult/CultSamp.htm (Assessed May 2006).

Sanghera, J. (2007) *Shame*. London: Hodder and Stoughton.

Sardar, Z. 'A believer's guide to scepticism' *New Statesman*.19 March 2007.

Sarup, M. (1993) (2nd edn) *An Introductory Guide to Post-Structuralism and Postmodernism*. London: Harvester Wheatsheaf.

Schon, D. (1983) *The Reflective Practitioner – How Professionals Think in Action*. USA: Basic Books.

Schweppe, C. (2007) 'Resisting the new rationale of social work' in M. Lavallette and I. Ferguson (eds) *International Social Work and the Radical Tradition*. Birmingham: Venture Press.

Seebohm Report (1968) *Report of the Committee on Local Authority and Allied Personal Social Services*, Cmnd 3703, London: The Stationery Office.

Seidman, S. (1992) 'Theory as Narrative with Moral Intent' in S. Seidman and D. Wagner (eds), *Postmodernism and Social Theory*. Cambridge, MA and Oxford UK: Blackwell.

Sheldon, B. (1978a) 'Theory and Practice in Social Work'. *British Journal of Social Work*, 8, pp. 1–32.

Sheldrake, J. (1996) *Management Theory – From Taylorism to Japanization*. London: International Thomson Business Press.

Sheppard, M. (1995) *Care Management and the New Social Work – A Critical Analysis*. London: Whiting and Birch.

—— (2006) *Social Work and Socail Exclusion – The Idea of Practice*. Aldershot: Ashgate.

Sim, S. (2006) *Empires of Belief – Why We Need More Scepticism and Doubt in the Twenty-first Century*. Edinburgh: Edinburgh University Press.

Smale, G. and Tuson, G. (1993) *Empowerment, Assessment, Care Management and the Skilled Worker*. National Institute for Social Work – Practice and Development Exchange. London: The Stationery Office.

Smart, B. (1999) 'Resisting McDonaldization' in B. Smart (ed.) *Resisting McDonaldization*. London: Sage.

—— (2000) (2nd edn) 'Postmodern social theory' in B. Turner (ed.) *The Blackwell Companion to Social Theory*. Oxford: Blackwell.

Smith, D. (1987) 'The limits of positivism in social work research' *British Journal of Social Work*, 17(4), pp. 401–16.

Spicer, J. (1997) in B. Campbell (ed.) *Unofficial Secrets – Child Sexual Abuse: The Cleveland Case*. London: Virago.

Spratt, T. and Houston, S. (1999) 'Developing critical social work in theory and in practice: child protection and communicative reason' *Child and Family Social Work*, 4, 315–24.

Stainton, T. (1998) 'Rights and rhetoric of practice' in A. Symonds and A. Kelly (eds) *The Social Construction of Community Care*. Basingstoke: Macmillan.

Stalker, K, (1994) 'Implementing care management in Scotland: An overview of initial progress' *Care in Place*, 1(2).

Stanley, N. (1991) 'User-practitioner transactions in the new culture of community care' *The British Journal of Social Work*, 29, 417–35.

Stephenson, O. and Parsloe, P. (1978) *Social Service Teams: The Practitioners View*. London: DHSS, in D. Howe (eds) (1986) *Social Workers and Their Practice in Welfare Bureaucracies*. Aldershot: Gower Publishing Company.

Stern Review on the Economics of Climate Change (2006), http://www.hm-treasury. gov.uk/independent_reviews/stern_review_economics_climate_change/stern_ review_report.cfm (accessed 23 March 2007).

Stoker, G. (1989) 'Creating a local government for a post-Fordist society' in Stewart and Stoke (eds) (1989) *The Future of Local Government*. Basingstoke: Macmillan.

Symonds, A. and Kelly, A. (1998) (eds) *The Social Construction of Community Care*. Basingstoke: Macmillan.

Taylor, F. W. (1947) *Scientific Management*. New York: Harper and Row.

Taylor-Gooby, P. (1994) 'Postmodernism and social policy: A great leap backward?' *Journal of Social Policy*, 2, 385–404.

—— (1999) 'The future of social policy' in J. Baldock, N. Manning, S. Miller and S. Vickerstaff (eds) *Social Policy*. Oxford: Oxford University Press.

Tester, K. (1999) 'The moral malaise of McDonaldization: The values of Vegetarianism' in B. Smart (ed.) *Resisting McDonaldization*. London: Sage.

Thane, P. (1982) *The Foundations of the Welfare State*. Harlow, Essex: Longman.

Thatcher, M. (1987) 'Talking to Women's Own magazine, 31 October 1987, http:// briandeer.com/social/thatcher-society.htm (accessed 27 March 2007).

Thomas, M. and Pierson, J. (1995) *Dictionary of Social Work*. London: Collins Educational.

Thompson, D. (1996) (ed.) *The Oxford Compact English Dictionary*. Oxford: Oxford University Press.

Thompson, N. (2000) *Theory and Practice in Social Work*. BASW: Macmillan.

—— (2002) 'Anti-discriminatory practice' in M. Davies (ed.) (2nd edn) *The Blackwell Companion to Social Work*. Oxford: Blackwell Publishers.

Titmuss, R. (1965) 'Goals of today's welfare state' in P. Anderson and R. Blackburn (eds) *Towards Socialism*. London: Fontana.

—— (1971) *The Gift Relationship; From Human Blood to Social Policy*. London: Pantheon Books.

Tompsett, H. (2005) 'A question of principles', *Professional Social Work* (December 2005) British Association of Social Work.

Toren, N. (1972) *Social Work: The Case of a Semi-Profession*. London: Sage.

Toulmins, S. (1985) 'The return of cosmology' in W. Anderson (1995) *The Truth About the Truth – De-confusing and Re-constructing the Postmodern World*. New York: G. P. Putnam.

Twigg, J. (1999) 'Social care' in J. Baldock, N. Manning, S. Miller and S. Vickerstaff (eds) *Social Policy*. Oxford: Oxford University Press.

Ungerson, C. (2003) 'Commodified care work in European labour markets' *European Societies*, 5(4), 377–96.

United Nations Convention on the Rights of the Child (1989), http://www.hrweb. org/legal/child.html (accessed 13 March 2007).

United Nations Universal Declaration of Human Rights (1948), http://www.opsi. gov.uk/acts/acts1998/80042--d.htm (accessed 13 March 2007).

Van Heugten, K. and Daniels, K. (2001) 'Social workers who move into private practice: the impact of the socio-economic context' *British Journal of Social Work*, 31, 739–55.

Voice of the Child in Care, http://www.islington.gov.uk/Directories/page. aspx?dir=local_services&docid=0901336c803d3cdf&title=Directory%20of%20 Local%20Services (accessed 20 March 2007).

Walker, S. (2001) 'Tracing the contours of postmodern social work' *British Journal of Social Work*, 32, 29–39.

Walsh, K. (1995) *Public Services and Market Mechanisms – Competition, Contracting, and the New Public Management*. Basingstoke: Macmillan.

Walton, R. G. (1975) *Women in Social Work*. London: Routledge in N. Parry, M. Rustin and C. Satyamurti (eds) (1979) *Social Work, Welfare and the State*. London: Edward Arnold.

Ward, P. (1999) 'Alpha – the McDonaldization of Religion', *Anvil*, 15 (4 November 1999) 279–86.

Washington, J. and Paylor, I. (1998) 'Europe, social exclusion and the identity of social work' in *European Journal of Social Work*, 1(3), pp. 327–38.

Webb, A. and Wistow, G. (1987) *Social Work, Social Care and Social Planning: The Personal Social Services Since Seebohm*. Harlow, Essex: Longman.

Webb, S., Moriarty, J. and Levin, E. (1998) *Short Report – Research on Community Care: Social Work and Community Care and Community Care Arrangements for Older People with Dementia*. London: National Institute for Social Work Research Unit.

White, M. and Epston, D. (1990) *Narrative Means to Therapeutic Ends*. New York: Norton.

White, V. and Harris, J. (1999) 'Professional Boundaries Re-defined. Three Discourses on the users of welfare' in M. Dent, M. O'Neill and C. Bagley (eds) *Professions, New Public Management and the European Welfare State*. Staffordshire: Staffordshire University Press.

Wilding, P. (1982) *Professional Power and Social Welfare*. London: Routledge and Kegan Paul.

Williams, F. (1992) 'Somewhere over the rainbow: universality and diversity in social policy' in N. Manning and R. Page (eds) *Social Policy Review*, 4. Nottingham: Social Policy Association.

Williams, F., Popay, J. and Oakley, A. (1999) 'Changing paradigms of welfare' in F. Williams, J. Popay and A. Oakley (eds), *Welfare Research: A Critical Review*. London UCL Press.

Williams, J. (2001) '1998 Human Rights Act: Social work's new benchmark' *British Journal of Social Work*, (31).

Wilson, G. (1993) 'Conflicts in case management: the use of staff in community care' *Social Policy and Administration*, 27(2), 109–23.

—— (1998) 'Staff and users in the postmodern organisation – modernity, postmodernity and user marginalisation' in M. Berry and C. Hallett (eds) *Social Exclusion and social work – Issues of Theory, Policy and Practice*. Lyme Regis: Russell House Publishing.

Witkin, S. and Saleebey, C. (2007) *Social Work Dialogues – Transforming the Canon in Inquiry, Practice and Education*. Alexandria, Virginia: Council on Social Work Education Press.

Index